Navigating the Digital Landscape

Navigating the Digital Landscape: Understanding Customer Behaviour in the Online World

EDITED BY

NRIPENDRA SINGH
Pennsylvania Western University, USA

POOJA KANSRA
Lovely Professional University, India

AND

S. L. GUPTA
BIT Noida Campus, India

United Kingdom – North America – Japan – India – Malaysia – China

Emerald Publishing Limited
Emerald Publishing, Floor 5, Northspring, 21-23 Wellington Street, Leeds LS1 4DL

First edition 2024

Reprints and permissions service
Contact: www.copyright.com

British Library Cataloguing in Publication Data
A catalogue record for this book is available from the British Library

ISBN: 978-1-83549-273-4 (Print)
ISBN: 978-1-83549-272-7 (Online)
ISBN: 978-1-83549-274-1 (Epub)

INVESTOR IN PEOPLE

Contents

List of Figures and Tables   *vii*

About the Contributors   *xi*

**Chapter 1   Influence of Fashion Bloggers on Setting Trends and
Purchase Decision of Young Indian Metropolitan Women**   *1*
Sabina Sethi, Bharti Panwar and Nidhi Goyal

**Chapter 2   What Does the Rise of Avatars Mean for Consumers?
A Systematic Literature Review and Future Research Opportunities**   *17*
Atul Dahiya and Diptiman Banerji

**Chapter 3   Does Effective Handling of Negative E-Word of Mouth
on Social Media Influence Customers' Behavioral Intentions in the
Context of Online Travel Agencies**   *39*
Durgesh Agnihotri, Pallavi Chaturvedi and Vikas Tripathi

**Chapter 4   Antecedents of Healthy Lifestyle of Young Consumers:
A Cross-Sectional Study of Sri Lanka**   *65*
*P. G. S. A. Jayarathne, Narayanage Jayantha Dewasiri and K. S. S.
N. Karunarathne*

**Chapter 5   Artificial Intelligence and Augmented Reality: A Business
Fortune to Sustainability in the Digital Age**   *85*
Henry Jonathan, Hesham Magd and Shad Ahmad Khan

**Chapter 6   A Qualitative Inquiry Into Preference of Bahraini
Fashion Designers Towards Fashion Shows Versus Digital Fashion
Shows, and Factors Influencing Their Choice**   *107*
Nidhi Goyal

Chapter 7 Students Perspective Toward Online Teaching in Higher Education During COVID-19: A Cross-Sectional Analysis *119*
Pooja Kansra

Chapter 8 Extending the Technology Acceptance Model as Predictor to Explore Student's Intention to Use an Online Edtech Platform in India *129*
Jitendra Singh Rathore and Neha Goyal

Chapter 9 Metamorphosis of Retail Purchase Through Customer Segmentation in Pandemic Times *149*
Upasana Diwan, D. D. Chaturvedi and S. L. Gupta

Chapter 10 Impact of the Pandemic on Consumer Behavior – A Review *167*
Ulfat Andrabi, Aaliya Ashraf and Priyanka Chhibber

Chapter 11 Consumers in the Pandemic: Contented or Discontented *181*
Kriti Arya and Richa Chauhan

Chapter 12 COVID-19 Impact on Consumer Preferences Toward Convenience Store Versus Hypermarkets *217*
Ajay Singh and Rahul Gupta

List of Figures and Tables

Chapter 1

Fig. 1.1.   Various Sources of Fashion-Related Information and Latest Trends.   9

Fig. 1.2.   Preference of Blogs.   10

Fig. 1.3.   Role of Fashion Blogger in Providing Information About Latest Fashion Trends.   11

Fig. 1.4.   Influence of Bloggers in Purchase of Branded Items.   12

Chapter 2

Fig. 2.1.   Protocol Used for the Present Review: "SPAR-4-SLR."   20

Fig. 2.2.   Year-Wise Distribution of Retrieved Articles.   22

Fig. 2.3.   Geographical Distribution of Retrieved Articles (Provided Courtesy of OpenStreetMap).   24

Fig. 2.4.   Keyword Co-Occurrence of Author Keywords of Retrieved Articles.   27

Chapter 3

Fig. 3.1.   Conceptual Model Represents the Influence of Factors Like Empathy, Responsiveness, Apology, and Paraphrasing on Customer Satisfaction and Repurchase Intention.   43

Fig. 3.2.   Structural Model Results.   53

Chapter 5

Fig. 5.1.   Artificial Intelligence's Global Influence From Applications in Different Fields (Fabian, 2018).   89

Fig. 5.2.   Comparative Analysis of AI and AR
              Toward Competing Size, Revenue, Funding,
              and Investments Predictable Up to 2030.   91

Fig. 5.3.   The Exponential Growth of Augmented
              Reality Usage During the Last Decade
              (Alsop, 2022).   91

Fig. 5.4.   Use Cases of Augmented Reality Applications
              in Different Sectors in the Digital Age
              (Johnson, 2022).   92

Fig. 5.5.   Principal Applications Sectors of AR and VR
              in the Present Scenario (Top 14 Industries That
              Use Virtual Reality Applications to Redefine User
              Experience. https://www.holopundits.com/blog/
              2021/03/top-14-industries-that-use-virtual-reality-
              applications-to-redefine-user-experience.html).   95

Fig. 5.6.   Machine Learning-Enabled Technology
              Applications in Different Sectors and
              Functions Executed in Each Sector.   96

Fig. 5.7.   Range of Applications With AI-Enabled
              Technology in Adoption by Different Global
              Companies.   97

Fig. 5.8.   Artificial Intelligence in Different Sectors
              and Corresponding Applications Areas.   100

Chapter 8
Fig. 8.1.   Proposed Conceptual Framework.   137

Chapter 10
Fig. 10.1.   Conceptual Model of the Impact of COVID-19
              on Various Sectors.   170

Chapter 12
Fig. 12.1.   Occupation of Respondents.   224
Fig. 12.2.   Respondents Rating Toward Fear of Going
              Outside.   225
Fig. 12.3.   Hypermarket versus Convenience Store Visit.   225
Fig. 12.4.   Respondents Choice of Buying Essential
              Commodities.   226

Fig. 12.5.   Factors for Outside Visits for Retail Buying
             During Pandemic.   226
Fig. 12.6.   Choice of Retail Shopping.   227

Chapter 2

Table 2.1.   Journal-Wise Distribution of Retrieved
             Articles.   22
Table 2.2.   Citation-Per-Year of Retrieved Articles.   24
Table 2.3.   Citation-Per-Journal of Retrieved Articles.   25
Table 2.4.   Top Five Most Cited Papers in the Retrieved
             Articles.   27
Table 2.5.   Broad Contexts of Avatar Studies as Seen
             in the Retrieved Articles.   28
Table 2.6.   Citations Per Author of Retrieved Articles.   36

Chapter 3

Table 3.1.   Measurement Model.   49
Table 3.2.   AVE, ASV, MSV, and Cronbach's Alphas.   50
Table 3.3.   AVE: Construct Validity.   52
Table 3.4.   Path Model Results.   53
Table 3.5.   Hypothesis Testing.   54

Chapter 4

Table 4.1.   Results of the Convergent Validity.   76
Table 4.2.   Cronbach's Alpha Values.   76
Table 4.3.   Values for Discriminant Validity.   76
Table 4.4a. Descriptive Statistics.   77
Table 4.4b. One-Sample Test.   77
Table 4.5a. Model Summary.   77
Table 4.5b. Coefficients.   77

Chapter 7

Table 7.1.   Demographic Profile of Students.   122
Table 7.2.   Benefits of Attending Online Classes
             During COVID-19.   123

Table 7.3.   Challenges of Online Classes During
COVID-19.   124

Table 7.4.   Willingness for Attend Online Teaching
in Post COVID-19.   125

Chapter 8

Table 8.1.   Models of Technology Acceptance.   131

Table 8.2.   Researches Based on TAM Model With
Different External Factors.   133

Table 8.3.   Research Gap and Objectives for the Study.   137

Table 8.4.   Conceptual Framework Factors and Constructs.   138

Chapter 9

Table 9.1.   Contingency Table for Convenience Score and
Demographics.   154

Table 9.2.   Contingency Table for Feedback Management
and Memographics.   156

Table 9.3.   Contingency Table for Credit Availability and
Demographics.   157

Table 9.4.   Contingency Table for Billing Facilities and
Demographics.   158

Table 9.5.   Segmentation of Online Consumers Based
on Convenience Factor During Pandemic.   159

Table 9.6.   Segmentation of Online Consumers Based
on Feedback Management Factor During
Pandemic.   160

Table 9.7.   Segmentation of Online Consumers Based on
Credit Availability Factor During Pandemic.   161

Table 9.8.   Segmentation of Online Consumers Based on
Billing Facility Factor During Pandemic.   162

Chapter 11

Table 11.1.   Literature Review (TCCM Framework).   190

Chapter 12

Table 12.1.   Tabulation of Factors Considered for Outside
Buying.   227

About the Contributors

Durgesh Agnihotri holds a PhD in Business Management and works as an Associate Professor in the Department of Management Studies, GL Bajaj Institute of Technology and Management, Greater Noida, India. He has more than 13 years of experience of teaching PG programs. He has published articles in national/international journals of repute. His areas of interest are service marketing, digital marketing, influencer marketing sustainable consumer behavior, and research methodology.

Ulfat Andrabi is a researcher currently pursuing PhD in Human Resource Management at Lovely Professional University in Punjab, India. Her academic journey reflects her passion for exploring the intricacies of workforce dynamics. Ulfat's educational foundation includes an MBA degree obtained from Baba Ghulam Shah Badshah University in Rajouri, Jammu, where she honed her skills in management and leadership. Before that, she completed her bachelor's degree at the University of Kashmir. Throughout her academic career, Ulfat has made notable contributions to the field of Human Resource Management. She stands out as an accomplished scholar with three research papers published in UGC CARE (University Grants Commission - Consortium for Academic and Research Ethics) recognized journals. Her research focus lies in the intersection of work–life balance and organizational commitment, with a specific emphasis on the healthcare sector in the state of Punjab. Furthermore, she has actively participated in five international conferences, where she has shared her insights and engaged in valuable academic discourse.

Kriti Arya is working as an Assistant Professor in K R Mangalam University, Gurugram (Haryana) in School of Management and Commerce. She is pursuing her PhD in commerce from Banasthali Vidyapith, Niwai, Tonk (Rajasthan). She has been awarded JRF and SRF by the UGC. She has completed her master's degree in Commerce from Indira Gandhi National Open University, Delhi, and her graduation (Commerce) from Maharishi Dayanand University (Haryana). She has contributed to research through her research interest including mental health, pandemic, consumer behavior, Indian ethos and human resource management. She believes in doing work with excellence and contributes in research and academics with utmost honesty for the development of the youth, society, and the country.

Aaliya Ashraf is a research scholar at Mittal School of Business, Lovely Professional University. Her research domain is human resource management. Aaliya studied at Lovely Professional University where she earned her Bachelor's in Commerce. Further, she was awarded with MBA (HR & IB) degree from the same University. Aaliya is a gold medalist of her batch in her bachelor's degree. Aaliya has published three papers so far in UGC care journals. Furthermore, she has participated and presented papers in about seven national and international conferences. Aaliya has experience working as a Teaching Assistant at Lovely Professional University. Aaliya's areas of interest include human resource management, organizational behavior, performance management systems, international business, and cross-cultural management.

Diptiman Banerji (PhD) is a Professor of Marketing at the O.P. Jindal Global University's Jindal Global Business School, India. His research work has been published in reputed journals like the Journal of Macromarketing, Journal of Computer Information Systems, Journal of Business and Industrial Marketing, International Journal of Consumer Studies, Asia Pacific Journal of Marketing and Logistics, International Journal of Retail and Distribution Management, Journal of Strategic Marketing, AMS Review, and Health Marketing Quarterly, among others. He was a winner of the Emerald Literati Award 2019 for "Outstanding Paper" for his International Journal of Retail and Distribution Management publication and the "Highly Commended Award" at the 2019 IRSSM Dubai symposium and the 2022 IRSSM India symposium (sponsored by the Journal of Service Management).

D. D. Chaturvedi is presently working as an Associate Professor in Economics, SGGSCC, University of Delhi. He has written over 150 books and 50 research papers in reputed national and international journals. He has many patents to his credit and also the project director of many renowned projects of the Government of India. He has also supervised many PhD students under his expert guidance.

Dr Pallavi Chaturvedi is a PhD in Business Management and working as Faculty member at Amity College of Commerce and Finance, Amity University, Noida, India. She has over 14 years of experience of teaching PG courses. She has published articles in national/international journals of repute. Her areas of interest are consumer behavior, sustainable behavior and research methodology.

Richa Chauhan is working with Jaypee Business School, JIIT Noida as an Assistant Professor (Senior Grade). She achieved her MBA from ICFAI University, Dehradun, and PhD in Management from Banasthali Vidyapith. With more than 12 years as an academician, she contributed to many research endeavors, including emotional intelligence, spirituality, indigenous management, consumer behavior, and human resource management. She strongly believes the role of an academician is not only to nurture young minds to bring in a fundamental change in approach to problem-solving but also to embark upon constant research endeavors for the development of the industry and society at large.

Priyanka Chhibber is a Professor (Associate), COD HRM-I (QD03) in Human Resource Management at Mittal School of Business, (ACBSP USA, accredited) Lovely Professional University, Phagwara, Punjab. Her area of creative research includes poverty, entrepreneurship, intellectual capital, value creation, human resource development, skill gap, mentoring, creativity, and innovation. In addition to her passionate teaching and research experience, she worked with textile manufacturing concerns and served as an HRD officer at SEL Manufacturing Co. Ltd, Chandigarh Road, Ludhiana, India. She has published and presented research papers in various national and international journals like World Review of Entrepreneurship, Management and Sustainable Development, International Journal of Public Sector Performance Management (IJPSPM), Inderscience, and IGI Global to name a few. Her accomplishments include receiving a best research paper award from a renowned university on the topic "Gender Diversity: An approach toward agile women employees" in association with Curtin University, Australia. She also gave a webinar on leading topics like creativity and innovation.

Atul Dahiya is a Doctoral Research Scholar in the Marketing area at Jindal Global Business School, O.P. Jindal Global University, India. His research interests include consumer well-being, consumer behavior, and consumer psychology for social impact.

Narayanage Jayantha Dewasiri is a Professor in Finance attached to the Department of Accountancy and Finance, Sabaragamuwa University of Sri Lanka. Further, he currently serves as the Brand Ambassador at Emerald Publishing, UK, and the Vice President of the Sri Lanka Institute of Marketing. He is a pioneer in applying triangulation research approaches in the management discipline. He serves as the Co-Editors-in-Chief of the South Asian Journal of Marketing published by Emerald Publishing, Managing Editor of the South Asian Journal of Tourism and Hospitality published by the Faculty of Management Studies, Sabaragamuwa University of Sri Lanka.

Upasana Diwan (PhD, UGC NET, MBA) is working as an Associate Professor at Rukmini Devi Institute of Advanced Studies. She has more than 16 years of teaching experience and is a keen researcher in the area of Customer-Based Brand Equity Valuation. Her expertise also covers the areas of accounting, financial management, international finance, security analysis, and trade finance which is supported by many publications and books. Other than this, she is actively involved in training students in the areas of verbal and written communication.

Neha Goyal is a doctoral student at Department of Commerce, WISDOM, Banasthali vidyapith, India. She has 5 years of teaching experience in marketing and her area of research include marketing, consumer behavior, and online marketing. Her recent research area is Edtech platforms.

Nidhi Goyal is an academic practitioner with a decade of experience in higher education in India and Kingdom of Bahrain. She has achieved the status of Fellow (Advance HE) in recognition of attainment against the UK Professional

Standards Framework for teaching and learning support in higher Education. She obtained her PhD and MSc degree in Textile Clothing, from University of Delhi. Her PhD research project was on nano finishing for textiles, in collaboration with Indian Institute of Technology (IIT Delhi) and was awarded with Gold medal for her research. She has made significant contributions to her field, with research published in reputed journals and books, and serves as a reviewer for academic publications. Nidhi aspires for student success and community engagement, and her goal is to empower and inspire individuals by providing holistic education that cultivates not only professional growth but also fosters responsible and compassionate members of society.

Rahul Gupta has an interest in areas like marketing, sales, retail management, and supply chain management. He has done FDPM from IIM Ahmadabad, PhD from Kumaun University, Nainital, and MBA from the U.P.T.U., Lucknow. He worked around 11 Years with some of the leading firms dealing in Industrial Products and instrumental in conducting training programs in Sales, Marketing and Quality Improvement Techniques. He has over 15 years of teaching experience and is currently working with Amity Business School, Amity University, Uttar Pradesh, Sec -125, Noida campus and has been a consultant with a variety of industries and firms.

S. L. Gupta is currently working as the Professor and Director of BITS Noida. He brings with him a rich experience of 27 years in academia. His Professional Qualifications includes, an Executive Programme in Retail Management from IIM-Kolkata and a PGDBM (Marketing) from CMD Modinagar, India, and MCom from University of Rajasthan, Jaipur, India. His fields of specialization are sales and distribution management, marketing research, marketing of service, retail management, research methodology. He has to his credit many publications in national and international journals. He has published eight books, which are internationally recognized and recommended in many universities and colleges, and research papers on his area of specialization.

P. G. S. A. Jayarathne holds the position of Professor in Marketing at SLIIT Business School, Sri Lanka, and is permanently affiliated with the Department of Marketing Management at the University of Sri Jayewardenepura. She also serves as a Senior Editor at Emerald Publishing's South Asian Journal of Marketing and is a Board of Study member at the Sri Lanka Institute of Marketing. With numerous publications in prestigious journals such as International Journal of Operations and Production Management and Production Planning and Control, she brings extensive expertise to her roles.

Henry Jonathan has a PhD in Environmental Sciences with specialization in health, safety, and environment field and experienced in research guidance and supervision of dissertation projects to masters and bachelor's students. He holds membership with professional bodies like IOSH, OSHA. In addition, he holds many certificate courses and accreditations in HSE from leading institutions and a lead auditor in EMS ISO 14001:2015. He has worked with international organizations like the World Bank, WWF in various capacities and projects in Asia region. He is a reviewer for many international journals and has reviewed and published research papers on various topics. He has published many editorial book chapters, newsletter articles, and chapters with leading international publishers. He has working knowledge in preparing academic policies and reports related to administration and execution of functionalities.

Pooja Kansra is presently working as a Professor and Head of Economics at Mittal School of Business, Lovely Professional University, Phagwara, Punjab (India). She has a teaching experience of 14 years. Her areas of research include health economics, labor economics, gender economics, insurance and informal sector, and digitalization. She is an avid researcher and presented papers in various national and international conferences. She is the recipient of several best paper awards from reputed institutions such MAIMS, IBS, NIT Srinagar, Delhi University and Lovely Professional University. She has to her credit various research papers published in Scopus Indexed Journals including Journal of Consumer Behavior (Wiley, ABDC A category), Economic and Political Weekly (EPW), Journal of Health Management (Sage Publications), Global Business Review (Sage Publications), International Journal of Diabetes in Developing Countries (Springer Publications), Health and Population: Perspectives and Issues (MOHFW), etc.

K.S.S.N. Karunarathne is a Temporary Assistant Lecturer attached to the Department of Accountancy and Finance, Faculty of Management Studies, Sabaragamuwa University of Sri Lanka.

Shad Ahmad Khan, PhD, is serving as the Program Chair of Business Administration and Assistant Professor in College of Business, University of Buraimi in Sultanate of Oman. He has a Doctorate in Electronic Marketing from Faculty of Management Studies and Research, Aligarh Muslim University. He is an active researcher who has a professional strength in the area of Business Management and Marketing. He has vast experience of organizing international events like conferences and seminars. His area of interest is data sciences, green practices, entrepreneurship, administration sciences, and marketing.

Hesham Magd, PhD, has more than 25 years of combined experience in traditional and nontraditional higher education teaching, training, consultancy, community development, academic administration, curricula design, organizational change and development, distinguished research and scholarly writing, resulting in Honors, awards and recognition for academic excellence and outstanding achievement. Hesham is currently heavily involved in international accreditation and reshaping the aviation education in Oman and offer strategic direction on the direction of the sector. In his previous appointments throughout the world in British, European, and American-oriented Curriculum (Middle East, USA, and UK), he has been the driving force behind strategic institutional development during the time of profound change in the Higher Education in the Middle East. Hesham has broad knowledge of the UK, US, Middle East University Systems, and Quality and accreditation systems (AACSB, AABI, OAAA, NCAAA).

Bharti Panwar is results-driven and detail-oriented educator and fabric and apparel science postgraduate with a strong passion for textiles and the fashion industry. She has completed MSc in Fabric and Apparel Science, from Lady Irwin College, University of Delhi, specializing in fabric development, garment construction, and textile testing. She is experienced in conducting research, analyzing data, and implementing innovative solutions, and proficient in utilizing technology and software for fabric design and production. She has completed BEd from Chaudhary Charan Singh University and pursuing a career in academics.

Jitendra Singh Rathore is an Assistant Professor at Department of Commerce and Management – WISDOM, Banasthali Vidyapith, India. He has over 18 years of experience in both industry and academics and teaches marketing management, sales and distribution management, international marketing to undergraduate and postgraduate students. Prior to joining academics, he worked in Banking, Financial Services and Insurance (BFSI) sector with organizations such as Bajaj Allianz, Kotak Securities, and SBI cards in various capacities for around 5 years. His areas of research interest include e-commerce, sharing economy, channel and distribution management, shopping behavior of consumer in digital age, etc.

Sabina Sethi, PhD, is an esteemed academician with a combined teaching and research experience spanning over 27 years. In addition to her doctoral qualification, she holds a Postgraduate Diploma in Sales and Marketing Management from the All India Management Association (A.I.M.A.). Presently, she is serving as a Professor at Lady Irwin College, University of Delhi. Dr Sabina Sethi's expertise lies in the realm of Textile Science and Clothing. She has led pivotal research in a collaborative project with N.I.T.R.A., backed by the Ministry of Textiles. Her innovative work resulted in the development of a prototype utilizing ultrasonic energy for textile processing. Dr Sethi's scholarly contributions are well-documented with several publications in peer-reviewed journals. She has numerous edited, authored, and co-authored books to her credit. Her expertise extends to curriculum development for esteemed institutions like Delhi University and the National Institute of Open Learning (NIOS) and many others. She also serves on the Board of Studies of several esteemed universities. Her wide-ranging academic interests encompass marketing research, fashion retailing and merchandising, life cycle assessment, sustainable extraction, fiber characterization and application from natural sources, apparel and textile design, and traditional textiles.

Ajay Singh is a Professor in Marketing Area at ABES Business School, Ghaziabad. He holds PhD in Management from Jaypee Institute of Information Technology (Deemed University), NOIDA, UGC NET in Management, MBA (Marketing & Finance), B Tech (Electronics). He has a total experience of around 17 Years in Academics and Industry. As an Avid Researcher his areas of interest includes retail management, services marketing, consumer behavior, online marketing, and marketing research. He has Published quality research papers in Scopus, ABDC, UGC Care-1 Listed, international and national refereed journals.

He has also presented and published research papers in international and national conferences.

Vikas Tripathi is a Professor and Head of the Department of Management studies at GL Bajaj Institute of Technology and Management, Greater Noida, India. He has published scores of research papers in national/international journals/ conferences. His areas of interest are research methodology, international business, and operations management. He has 20 plus years of teaching experience with specialization in marketing and operations management.

Chapter 1

Influence of Fashion Bloggers on Setting Trends and Purchase Decision of Young Indian Metropolitan Women

Sabina Sethi[a], Bharti Panwar[a] and Nidhi Goyal[b]

[a]Lady Irwin College, India
[b]Royal University for Women, Bahrain

Abstract

Blogs are websites that contain posts about a wide range of topics, often written by fashion enthusiasts referred to as bloggers. With the increasing prevalence and popularity of digital media and social media, fashion bloggers help to attract business and influence and engage various stakeholders, especially customers. The present exploratory study provided valuable insights regarding fashion consumption, preference, and buying behavior of young women consumers of metropolitan cities of India like Delhi, Hyderabad, Bangalore, Pune, and Mumbai. The study was conducted under the domain of exploratory study. Snowball and Purposive random sampling techniques were employed to identify and reach respondents of both categories – women consumers and bloggers. A conscious attempt was made to include women from different demographics such as age, marital status, income, area of residence, employment status, etc. Primary data were collected with the help of questionnaires. The findings of the research revealed bloggers through their blogs are the new trendsetters and influence fashion adoption, especially by the young social media savvy consumers. Their blogs impact public perceptions of fashion and sometimes are precursors of new fashion trends. The findings of the study interestingly brought forth the fact that millennial women buying decision is significantly influenced by fashion blogs for the purchase of clothing and accessories. The findings also clearly indicated that blogs significantly influenced respondents' attitude toward the purchase of branded merchandise. Fashion bloggers besides providing information and inspiration to the blog readers, also at times assist and/or give consultation to their followers.

Navigating the Digital Landscape, 1–16
Copyright © 2024 Sabina Sethi, Bharti Panwar and Nidhi Goyal
Published under exclusive licence by Emerald Publishing Limited
doi:10.1108/978-1-83549-272-720241001

Keywords: Purchase behavior; digital marketing; fashion bloggers; social media; retail; merchandise

Introduction

According to the famous designer and singer Pharrell Williams, fashion is not something that exists in the dresses only, but it also influences the individual's personality, their perspective of the world, their destination and contributes to shaping one's social and cultural background (Leitch, 2023). Fashion is one of the most visible and therefore prominent facets of our day-to-day life. Fashion communicates, that is why it is said clothes have a *'Silent language'*. Clothing exhibits the characteristics of the wearer, their personality, lifestyle, attitude, values, and status in the society and reflects individuality of a person. Clothes also add a dimension to a person's self-image and self-identity.

Since the 20th century, a revolution has been happening in the world of fashion due to the influence of electronic and print media in the fashion industry. Earlier, people got fashion information from television, radio, telephone, books, magazines, newspaper, etc. However, in the last 10 years, a new media, *social media*, is influencing the fashion purchases of the young women. Fashion trends are now being shared with the help of different social media platforms like Facebook, Twitter, YouTube and Instagram. These platforms are being employed to showcase new trends and styles to audience. These social media platforms offer them a wardrobe of looks and fashions that will ultimately aid them in accomplishing their goals. A social media influencer (SMI) can be defined as a digital celebrity who is seen as an opinion leader in the digital market, who is involved in engaging and communicating to a mass audience that is unknown to the influencer (Abidin, 2016; Uzunoğlu & Misci Kip, 2014).

The latest entrant in the fashion space on these platforms is *'Fashion Blog'* and *'Fashion Blogger'*, which is gaining popularity among the fashion-conscious young women. Fashion blogs are online journals that provide information about the fashion industry, clothing and personal style. Presently, 'Fashion Bloggers' or 'Fashion Influencers' are playing a vital role in the fashion consumption of the young women. They are one of the most effective ways to persuade the purchase decision/s among the young women of different backgrounds, occupation, status etc. One must follow the most recent fashion trends in order to stay current with the rapidly changing fashion industry, and for this reason, customers follow fashion bloggers. Fashion bloggers have the ability to influence the opinions or buying decisions of a brand's target audience largely due to their social media following and they help fill the gap between the company and their consumers. Bloggers share their experience and give recommendation/s; they are an effective way of *'Internet marketing'* of products directly to the target customers. Bloggers generally share videos and posts about the style tips, fashion care tips and outfit ideas with their followers. They create awareness about latest styles and popularize selective trends (Lim et al., 2017).

Regardless of their age, caste, community, color, or religion, the majority of young ladies want to look unique every day. By dressing in distinctive fashion trends, people want to appear stylish and attractive every day of their life. To stay informed, young women follow fashion bloggers on social media. Young ladies who care about fashion typically seek for relevant content on social media before purchasing any fashion item. The first action, therefore, by young fashion consumer is to explore a good fashion blog or a fashion blogger. Consumers are influenced by the content of the blog and this ultimately guides their purchase action. Demographic factors such as age, income, education, nature of employment, marital status, city of residence, cultural background, etc., also influences their buying behavior and purchase actions.

Digital or Online Marketing

The process of promoting and selling goods and services online, also known as digital marketing or online marketing, involves the use of internet marketing tools including social media marketing, search engine marketing, and email marketing. It is a type of marketing that promotes products and services using the internet and digital technology that is based online, including desktop computers, mobile phones, and other digital media and platforms. This includes email, social media, and web-based advertising as marketing channels, as well as text and multimedia messaging. The way brands and businesses utilize technology to sell themselves has changed as a result of its evolution in the 1990s and 2000s. Digital media has become more integrated into marketing strategies as people now use digital devices instead of going to physical stores, and therefore digital marketing campaigns are becoming more popular. Effective blogging is an essential part of an overall digital marketing strategy. Brands have a good reason to include online marketing in their marketing plans.

The fashion and lifestyle products, social media has proved to be effective tool for communication as it enables a large number of people to become engaged in a variety of fashion events. In the fashion industry, a digital environment helps keep track of what's famous and what's valued. People are more engaged in the purchasing process because of the proliferation of various fashion trends in the digital world, and many people are inspired by a wide variety of domestic and international fashion brands. As a result, the fashion industry is now focusing on the digital channels, which integrate technology with the latest fashion trends. With the use of digital technology, co-creation and brand co-creation between fashion bloggers and consumers have become a new way to create value.

Fashion Blog, Bloggers and Their Influence on Consumer

Fashion blogs are a relatively new and yet, a powerful marketing tool. Blogs allow readers to be up to date on the current content, deals, and tips. Free and unpaid blogs of bloggers benefit companies as it increases their marketing value without spending a single penny. Blogs offer a way to connect with a sizable audience that is geographically dispersed, which in turn raises awareness and promotes sales. Fashion blogging can influence fashion marketing at an unimaginable level. Blogs are asynchronous online venues that provide users with a scope of online interactions and are a useful tool in computer-mediated communication. Blogs are unique online environments that combine news and information with self-expression.

Blogging Is Beneficial in a Number of Ways to Various Stakeholders and Individuals

- With a relatively low operational cost, blogging creates an opportunity to establish and expand one's own business. It is a great career option for educated women who have turned into 'real time fashion journalists'. Blogging empowers young women to create their own individualistic and independent media content, in which they can post photographs of themselves posing in different outfits.
- Blogging has emerged as international subculture that would provide quality content on the latest brands, current society trends, beauty, fashion and lifestyle products, e-commerce, street style and personal style.
- Fashion blogging can bring revolutionary change in the highly competitive fashion industry as well as fashion conscious youngsters. The existing business can make more profit via blogging by getting more exposure on right channels (Jones, 2017).

The influence of fashion bloggers on setting trends and purchase decisions of young Indian metropolitan women is a topic that has received increasing attention from researchers in recent years. Several studies have examined the impact of social media, including, fashion bloggers on purchase intention and brand loyalty of Indian women (Banerjee & Dey, 2020; Bhatt & Tandon, 2020; Mishra & Sharma, 2019; Singh, 2018; Singh & Jain, 2019). Overall, the literature suggested that fashion bloggers have a significant influence on setting trends and purchase decisions of young Indian metropolitan women. Their influence can be seen through the impact on purchase intention, brand loyalty, purchase behavior, and overall consumer behavior.

When it comes to making choices in fashion buzz, fashion bloggers are of great help! Presently, the most commonly used platforms for influencers marketing are:

Instagram	Using Instagram fashion influencers or fashion bloggers as a marketing channel can be a very efficient and cost-effective way to promote a product or service. When a product or service is recommended by an influencer they trust, audiences are much more likely to purchase it.

(Continued)

YouTube Videos	YouTubers post a variety of videos about fashion and beauty tips, which are widely circulated around the world. Audiences can watch and do their own make-up when viewing these videos, they are encouraged to try out these tips and techniques.
Facebook	Influencer marketing on Facebook works on the same concepts as influencer marketing on any other online platform. It begins with a brand finding a Facebook user with a medium-to-large (and highly engaged) following, who is similar to the brand's target demographic. The company then contacts the influential Facebook user to see if they'd be interested in sharing more about the brand's goods on their page.
Blogs	Fashion Blogs are regular entries of commentary, descriptions of events, or other material such as graphics or video, they are typically maintained by a person or company. Since 2011, fashion blogs have increased in popularity, with subjects including the industry as a whole, personal style, and reviews of clothing pieces and collections.
Twitter, LinkedIn, Pinterest and Other Miscellaneous Applications	There are various applications in short called 'apps' that are currently being used by bloggers to connect with their target audience such as Twitter, LinkedIn, Pinterest, etc. These apps are widely used today to influence how people perceive and capture fashion. These photo apps are aimed at a younger demographic. Their ease and instantaneous qualities are the reason for their success.

Successful fashion bloggers reach and influence millions of followers in real time. While keeping in mind what consumers desire, bloggers create a platform for companies to understand what people want next.

- *Fashion Bloggers Act as a Trendsetter*
  Followers are inspired by the *brand-new trends* shown by fashion bloggers. By displaying an uncommon sense of style, bloggers have the ability to start new

trends. They create awareness about latest styles and popularize selective trends. Fashion bloggers try to create new ideas and trigger the purchase of these items by young women.

- *Fashion Bloggers as Self-confidence Booster*
  Fashion-oriented followers consider bloggers as their guiding light who help them in making the right buying choices that ultimately these clothes/fashion items give their self-confidence a big boost! These fashion bloggers are regarded as role models or fashion idols by their followers. The content of fashion blogs generally is motivational, inspiring and about self-confidence.

- *Fashion Bloggers As 'Authentic' Content Creator*
  Fashion bloggers differentiate themselves from professional mainstream fashion platforms by creating authentic and personal content that they produce and share with their audiences (Bruns, 2005). Representing oneself online as a fashion celebrity takes place within a commercial context of branding and advertising practices. Bloggers are 'authentic' people. They're average people, just like you and me. They aren't size zero models, and they dress in a 'normal manner'. They will show their readers what they are wearing and the brands they prefer.

The six main types of impacts of fashion bloggers on young women's pre-purchasing decisions on social media platforms are: opinion leader endorsement, celebrity endorsement, electronic word of mouth (eWOM), online group engagement, support of conversation, and opinion democratization.

(1) *Opinion Leader Support*
   Opinion leaders are able to influence and change the perception and behavior of their audience. Opinion leader endorsement holds utmost significance as it leaves a powerful impact on consumers' purchasing decisions. They have detailed knowledge about issues they are writing/commenting on. They are not only subject matter experts who share their experience with their target audience but they also influence consumers to get involved with the current fashion trends. They can be considered contemporary opinion leaders, people who are considered knowledgeable and trustworthy by others, 'creating a "two-step" flow' interpersonal influence within trusted social networks.

(2) *Celebrity Support*
   Celebrity support or endorsement is the act of well-known persons utilizing their fame and notoriety to support businesses, their goods, or services that directly affect their fans or followers. As a result, celebrity endorsers have the potential to sway audiences and influence their buying decisions.

(3) *Electronic Word of Mouth (eWOM)*

eWOM is an interaction among digital users which proliferates information on multiple online platforms. The network of blogs is performing an important role in creating trends, sharing news and opinion, and spreading information via word-of-mouth.

(4) *Online Consumer Engagement*

Consumers share their views, thoughts, and experiences with companies by engaging in the interaction on Web 2.0 channels, for example, social media. Web 2.0 is the term used to describe a variety of web sites and applications that allow anyone to create and share online information or material they have created. A key element of the technology is that it allows people to create, share, collaborate and communicate. This bidirectional interaction has the potential to impact and enhance buying behavior and customer purchase decisions.

(5) *Dialogic Co-creation Value*

Consumers and merchants engage in dialogic co-creation of value in which consumers evaluate the experience of the items as a contextual value and retailers work to satisfy that value by supplying goods or developing technology in response to the consumers' evaluations.

(6) *Democratization of Opinion*

Ordinary consumers' opinions can be heard on the internet due to democratization of opinion, which allows them to share and communicate their experiences with goods, which helps marketers create brand strategies and affects consumers' buying decisions.

Earlier social media channels such as TV and magazines transformed the choices of young women, but with the advancement of technology, new generation is shifting toward the extensive use of the internet which is impacting the choices made by young women. The present generation is more conscious about their appearance and likes to stay updated about fashion, for which they rely on social media, magazines and fashion bloggers. Fashion bloggers create new dressing ideas, trigger fashion purchases and influence clothing choices of young women. Blogs were the most popular medium being utilized by the influencers to stay connected within their digital social circle (Tanwar et al., 2021). Thus, the study was conceptualized and undertaken to understand the influence of fashion blogger in driving the fashion choices of young women. The study also aimed to comprehend the buying behavior of young women from metropolitan cities of India like Delhi, Hyderabad, Bangalore, Pune, and Mumbai and how it is affected by both internal and external influencers (internal influencers include family, friends, age, culture and external influencer include fashion bloggers). An attempt was also made to understand various strategies used or planned by the bloggers to influence the fashion purchases of women during COVID-19.

Objectives of the Study

General Objective: To understand the influence of fashion bloggers on the fashion consumption of young women (age: 18–35 years).

Specific Objectives:

- To analyze how fashion blogs influence women consumer's purchase actions and in turn impact their purchasing decisions.
- To identify the strategies being planned by fashion bloggers to influence the purchase of the young women during COVID-19.
- To study the impact of demographic and other lifestyle variables on the fashion consumption of young women.

Methodology

The study was carried out under the domain of Exploratory Study as there was no predefined problem.

Sample Selection

Respondent sample included 90 women consumers and 9 fashion bloggers. Snowball and purposive random sampling techniques were employed to identify and reach respondents of both categories – women consumers and bloggers for the study. A conscious attempt was made to include women from different demographics such as age, marital status, income, area (states), employment status, etc. Different demographics were chosen as they reflect different persuasive and buying behavior. Respondents from metropolitan cities from India (Delhi, Bangalore, Mumbai, Pune, Hyderabad) were purposively chosen for carrying out the research. Further, education was a prerequisite as only educated women would have access and knowledge of the internet, they are more likely to be aware of social media and mostly likely users/followers of popular social media platforms including fashion blogs. A sample size of 90 women consumers was taken under the various age groups, viz., 18–24 years, 25–29 years and 30–35 years.

Data Collection and Analysis

Primary data were collected with the help of simple questionnaires. The questionnaire for 'bloggers', contained questions that focused on the strategies employed by them to influence their followers and the second questionnaire developed for 'young women consumers', focused on their clothing preferences and the influence of fashion blogs on their purchase behavior. The questionnaire was administered online to the selected samples of consumer and bloggers on the various social media platform such as Instagram, Facebook, and Email.

Secondary data were collected through extensive review of literature from various published articles, research papers, newspaper and magazine articles, social media posts and various studies done globally related to fashion bloggers and consumers.

The collected data were tabulated and analyzed, the findings were collated, studied, analyzed and presented in a systematic manner. Findings were discussed, co-relations drawn wherever applicable, and conclusion were drawn on the basis of the data collected and compiled.

Results and Discussion

Influence of Fashion Blogs on Purchase Decision of Young Women Consumers

The study highlights the changing preferences of the young fashion consumers in terms of their media usage. Till a few years ago, fashion magazines, fashion shows and their coverage in print and T.V., etc., were the main sources of fashion-related information and celebrities were the role models. However, the study indicated that blogs were the primary source of information for young women consumers with 48% of women respondents following fashion blogger and vloggers on different social media. YouTube videos were the second most popular source providing information about latest fashion trends (36%) and only 8% of respondents now read fashion magazines to find about latest fashions (Fig. 1.1). A study on preferences of millennials for social media advertising in Delhi NCR also corroborates this trend (Arora et al., 2018).

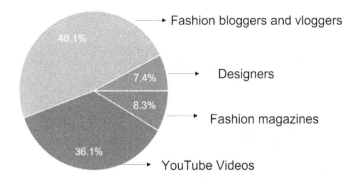

Fig. 1.1.   Various Sources of Fashion-Related Information and Latest Trends.

Preference of Young Women Consumers in Reference to Content of Blogs

Fashion bloggers generally pen down their views about the latest clothing trends, matching accessories, apparel industry, celebrity fashion choices on various print media as well as online media websites. In order to know the preferable content viewed on blogs, respondents were asked to choose the most appropriate option (Fig. 1.2).

Most of the young women (49%) showed preference for blogs focusing on clothing and accessories. The representation also highlights that 24% of women respondents followed personal and lifestyle blogs. Consumers were also getting influenced by the personal lifestyle of blogger, as they shared a variety of content centered on and inspired by their personal lives – especially family, home, travel, fitness, etc. Interestingly, as compared to clothing, accessories and personal blogs, beauty blogs and product reviews were less preferred by the young women consumers.

Role of Fashion Bloggers in Providing Information About Latest Fashion Trends and on Consumer Purchase Action

Nowadays fashion bloggers are actively guiding women about latest trends. They provide short and crisp summary of the fashion shows and other events being held, they help save consumers' time and effort as women don't have to spend hours now, to watch videos of fashion events. Bloggers are facilitating them by providing authentic information. Fig. 1.3 clearly indicates that majority of the women respondents (52%) believed that fashion bloggers help them in acquiring information about the latest fashion trends and around 24% respondents strongly agreed with this view.

The fashion bloggers have the power to create fresh trends when they display an unconventional dressing style. A blogger may create a modest outfit using western brands and traditional dress elements which would feature long trousers or skirt, long-sleeved loose blouse, high heels, statement handbag and traditional

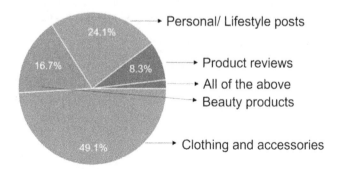

Fig. 1.2.   Preference of Blogs.

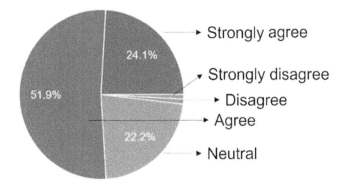

24.1%

51.9%

22.2%

- → Strongly agree
- ↘ Strongly disagree
- → Disagree
- → Agree
- → Neutral

Fig. 1.3.   Role of Fashion Blogger in Providing Information About Latest Fashion Trends.

headscarf. They create awareness about latest styles and popularize selective trends.

Fashion bloggers try to create new ideas and trigger the purchase of these items by young women. Branded items of clothing and accessories are not only a means of looking stylish and classy but also a way to show off your wealth and status in society. Different sources help in creating awareness of the branded items, and fashion bloggers are one of them. They provide relevant information regarding branded items and further guide their followers to verified sites, where they can get more information about the brands.

Bloggers also sometimes collaborate with brands and therefore are able to give special discounts to their audiences, which attracts more women to the blog and also enhances their purchase of branded items. Fashion bloggers also share their collaboration efforts with the brand across social mediums. They document their unique styles around the collaborated pieces on their blogs, again, increasing conversation and awareness about products and the designers who create them. While only 11% women respondent did not agree with the statement probably because of their mind set, attitude onwards money, spending/saving and other psychological factors or it might simply be that these branded items were beyond their budget (Fig. 1.4).

Important Features of Blog in Purchase Decision

Blogs consist of pictures, texts, videos and references. Fashion bloggers engage in research for any product advertised on their web pages. For a clear emphasis, they upload suitable and explanatory video, photographs, text and images in blogs related to fashion clothing and accessories. Pictorial and video representation help in better understanding and provide context to the blog. For fashion and lifestyle

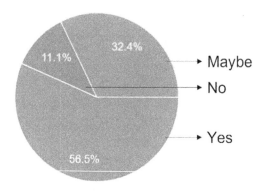

Fig. 1.4.   Influence of Bloggers in Purchase of Branded Items.

products, visual appeal has the maximum impact and was popularly used in traditional media. The same is true even for social media platforms as indicated by the response of the consumers. Respondents preferred viewing videos, followed by pictorial representations as it gave them more information in less time and helped them make rationale decision. Only 6% of female participants considered text to be an important factor in their purchase decision, maybe it gave them relevant and useful information about the specific product.

In all age groups from 18 to 35 years, fashion bloggers had a significant influence on the fashion choices made the young metropolitan Indian women. 78% of the respondents felt that fashion bloggers influenced their fashion purchase decisions and only 22% women responded that they were not influenced by fashion bloggers.

Strategies Planned by Fashion Bloggers to Influence Purchase

The findings of the study revealed that Instagram was the most preferred social media platform by the fashion bloggers to influence their target audience. After Instagram, YouTube and Facebook were acceptable in terms of use. While Tumbler and Twitter were least preferred platforms for promoting fashion by the bloggers.

It has been pointed out that fashion and beauty are the most prominent industries that are predominantly making use of influencer marketing where the influencers promote brands by embedding their products in their content in a creative manner (Bailey, 2016; Gurrieri & Cherrier, 2013).

Majority of fashion bloggers (44%) post their content on their preferred platform *every other day* to boost their social media engagement and influence buying decisions among young women and around 33% bloggers publish their content on daily basis. Whereas 11% of bloggers post weekly and similarly 11% respondents posted monthly.

In light of the COVID-19 pandemic, many fashion bloggers have had to adapt their strategies to continue to engage with their audience and influence their purchasing decisions. Some of these as highlighted by the study are:

- As the pandemic has caused a shift toward a more comfortable and casual fashion style, fashion bloggers have adapted their content to focus on comfortable and affordable fashion. They are showcasing outfits that are easy to wear at home or for running errands, while still being fashionable. Bloggers are also featuring affordable clothing brands to cater to the financial constraints of their audience.
- Emphasis on visual content: Fashion bloggers gave more emphasis to video content as they are more interactive and helped in better understanding and engagement with the audience during the pandemic. Bloggers uploaded high quality images with the text and links to sites. Review of secondary data by researcher also corroborated that there has been an increment in the quality of the advertorial and brand campaign content created by the SMIs.
- Social media engagement: Social media engagement has been a crucial strategy for fashion bloggers during COVID-19. They have been engaging with their followers through various social media platforms, such as Instagram, Twitter, and TikTok, by responding to comments, hosting Q&A sessions, and sharing their daily routines. This strategy has helped them build a more personal connection with their followers and has increased their influence on their purchase decisions. This content is creatively written in the form of a review or opinion woven with the display of their everyday lives online.
- Influencer collaborations and partnerships: Fashion bloggers are increasingly collaborating with brands to create sponsored content that promotes products to their followers. During the pandemic, fashion bloggers have had to be more selective in their collaborations, focusing on brands that align with their personal brand and values and offer products that are relevant to the consumers. Bloggers and brands are increasingly working together to create content that resonates with their followers.
- Literature review also confirmed the increasing influence of user-generated content (UGC). Several studies have revealed that consumers' final purchase decision is progressively being made based on UGC such as customer reviews and feedback rather than on traditional advertising media (Venkataraman & Raman, 2016).
- Digital events: With the cancellation of physical fashion events, fashion bloggers have turned to digital events to showcase their products and promote their brands. They are attending and promoting virtual fashion shows to their followers. They are providing their followers with behind-the-scenes content, exclusive interviews with designers, and curated fashion collections from these shows.

The findings of a study by Leung et al. (2022) show that influencer originality, follower size, and sponsor salience are the important factors that enhance effectiveness of influencer marketing.

Impact of Demographic and Other Lifestyle Variables on the Fashion Consumption of Young Metropolitan Indian Women

Demography and other lifestyle variables play an important role in the fashion consumption of young women. Demographic segmentation divides consumers into groups based on variables such as age, gender, income, occupation, marital status, race or ethnicity, religion, and social class. An attempt was made to study if variables like demographics impacted the purchase decision of young metropolitan women. Are women from different demographic backgrounds influenced differently by bloggers content?

- Geographical area plays an important role in the fashion choices of young women. Different geographical areas have different culture, values and even fashion choices. Analysis of consumer responses revealed that majority of respondent were from Delhi (33%), 20% from Hyderabad, 16% from Mumbai, 15% from Bangalore and 13% from Pune. These cities have a sizeable number of educated working women, with access to modern facilities, internet, exposure to fashion, relatively more freedom of choice, etc., and this has a direct impact on their fashion preferences.
- Earlier media channels such as television, newspaper, radio, and magazines influenced the choices of young women, but with the advancement of technology and arrival of internet in our lives, there is a shift toward online content and social media platforms specially in case of the young generation. The access to internet has impacted the fashion choices of young women. Women are actively using social media platform to stay updated about the fashion. The most preferred social media were Instagram and Facebook, while 39% young women preferred Instagram 32% were on Facebook.
- Socialization is a crucial process that mainly involves family and friends. Family size and structure also play a significant role in influencing the fashion choice of young women. 80% respondents said that family and friends play an important role in their fashion choices.
- Young fashion-conscious women follow fashion bloggers as well as social media channels. They search and research content on social media before buying any clothing or fashion product. While exploring a good fashion blog or a fashion blogger, women are influenced by their content. Their final purchase behavior action is also driven by demographic factors such as age, income, locale, culture, family life cycle stage, profession, etc. Fashion bloggers also felt that demographics play an important role in the fashion consumption of young women consumer. Fashion bloggers also categorize clothes according to age, color, price and occasions which helps women consumer make informed choices that will suit them and will enhance their self-image.

Conclusion

Fashion plays an important role and impacts the lifestyle and fashion choices of young women. Today, social media is a popular media among consumers to keep up to date with the new fashion trends. Young women are influenced by fashion bloggers as well as social media channels. Fashion bloggers have evolved over the years and have become prominent part of the fashion industry and have a powerful impact on the fashion choices of young women. Fashion bloggers generally pen down their views about the latest clothing trends, matching accessories, apparel industry, beauty tips, celebrity fashion choices, and street fashion trends on various print media as well as online media websites. Brands have also started collaborating with bloggers to promote their products. The present study analyzed the influence of fashion bloggers on the fashion consumption of young metropolitan women and also various strategies used/planned by the bloggers to influence the fashion purchases of women. The result of research indicates that young women from metropolitan cities of India followed fashion bloggers on different social media and they were also influenced by the bloggers. Also, demography and other lifestyle variables play an important role in the fashion consumption of young metropolitan women.

Limitations of the Study

Despite the interesting theoretical and practical implication of this study, it is still subject to some limitations. First, the data used were collected using convenience snowball sampling, a non-probability sampling technique. The use of this sampling method may be considered inappropriate by some; however, employing a probability sampling method was impractical in our framework. Second, the study was conducted only with young women in the age group of 18–35 years and that too who were residents of metropolitan cities of India.

Scope for Further Work

Similarly, new studies can be conducted for comparison of outcomes in other contexts, such as with different age groups, genders, and non-metropolitan residents of Tier II and Tier II Indian cities, as well as in other developing countries. Finally, it would be interesting to conduct a qualitative study to assess the Influence of Fashion Bloggers on Setting Trends and Purchase Decision of consumers' purchase intention in future research. Qualitative researches generate more in-depth information and descriptive data which can provide valuable insights into the reasons for particular behavior, and therefore, different outcomes might be seen.

References

Abidin, C. (2016). Visibility labour: Engaging with influencers' fashion brands and #OOTD advertorial campaigns on Instagram. *Media International Australia*, *161*(1), 86–100. https://doi.org/10.1177/1329878x16665177

Arora, T., Agarwal, B., & Kumar, A. (2018). A study of Millennials's preferences for social media advertising in Delhi NCR. *Indian Journal of Marketing*, *48*(10), 34–51. https://doi.org/10.17010/ijom/2018/v48/i10/132334

Bailey, S. (2016). *Performance anxiety in media culture: The trauma of appearance and the drama of disappearance.* Springer.

Banerjee, P., & Dey, S. (2020). An empirical study on the role of fashion bloggers on consumers' purchase decision: A study on Indian Millennials. *Journal of Contemporary Management Research*, *14*(1), 39–47.

Bhatt, R., & Tandon, U. (2020). Impact of social media on consumer behavior: An empirical study of Indian Millennials. *Journal of Retailing and Consumer Services*, *52*.

Bruns, A. (2005). *Gatewatching: Collaborative online news production.* Peter Lang.

Gurrieri, L., & Cherrier, H. (2013). Queering beauty: Fatshionistas in the fatosphere. *Qualitative Market Research: An International Journal*, *16*(3), 276–295.

Jones, L. (2017). Style for life: A fashion blog analysis. http://thesis.honors.olemiss. edu/912/1/Thesis%20PDF.pdf

Leitch, L. (2023, February 15). *'Fashion Is a Way' – How Pharrell Williams's philosophy could make him and Louis Vuitton a great fit (plus great fits).* [Article] Vogue. https://www.vogue.com/article/fashion-is-a-way-how-pharrell-williamss-philosophy-could-make-him-and-louis-vuitton-a-great-fit-plus-great-fits

Leung, F. F., Gu, F. F., Li, Y., Zhang, J. Z., & Palmatier, R. W. (2022). Influencer marketing effectiveness. *Journal of Marketing*, *86*(6), 93–115. https://doi.org/10.1177/00222429221102889

Lim, X. J., Radzol, A. R., Cheah, J., & Wong, M. W. (2017). The impact of social media influencers on purchase intention and the mediation effect of customer attitude. *Asian Journal of Business Research*, *7*(2).

Mishra, A., & Sharma, V. (2019). The role of fashion bloggers on young Indian consumers' purchase decision. *Journal of Consumer Marketing*, *36*(5), 585–596.

Singh, R. (2018). The impact of fashion bloggers on purchase intention and brand loyalty of Indian women. *Journal of Marketing Communications*, *24*(2), 117–134.

Singh, R., & Jain, K. (2019). The influence of fashion bloggers on purchase behaviour of Indian youth. *Journal of Indian Business Research*, *11*(3), 279–296.

Tanwar, A., Chaudhry, H., & Srivastav, M. (2021). Influencer marketing as a tool of digital consumer engagement: A systematic literature review. *Indian Journal of Marketing*, *51*(10), 27. https://doi.org/10.17010/ijom/2021/v51/i10/166439

Uzunoğlu, E., & Misci Kip, S. (2014). Brand communication through digital influencers: Leveraging blogger engagement. *International Journal of Information Management*, *34*(5), 592–602. https://doi.org/10.1016/j.ijinfomgt. Accessed on 21 March 2023 on Brand communication through digital influencers: Leveraging blogger engagement – ScienceDirect.

Venkataraman, N., & Raman, S. (2016). Impact of user-generated content on purchase intention for fashion products: A study on women consumers in Bangalore. *Indian Journal of Marketing*, *46*(7), 23–35. https://doi.org/10.17010/ijom/2016/v46/i7/97125

Chapter 2

What Does the Rise of Avatars Mean for Consumers? A Systematic Literature Review and Future Research Opportunities

Atul Dahiya and Diptiman Banerji

Jindal Global Business School, India

Abstract

As avatars are increasingly becoming popular, both scholars and businesses are acknowledging the vast potential that avatars hold for the future. Despite this growing interest in avatars, no review articles have attempted to provide a comprehensive overview of avatar literature and its implications for consumers. The present review addresses this gap using the combination of descriptive analysis (for corpus performance), bibliometric analysis (for corpus performance and emerging themes), and thematic analysis (for emerging themes and implications as well as future research opportunities). We conducted a review of 47 Scopus-indexed articles from 34 journals between year 2006 and 2023. By examining the corpus performance of avatar literature, the emerging themes, and future research opportunities, this review offers scholars a comprehensive overview of the subject matter.

Keywords: Avatars; consumers; systematic literature review; descriptive analysis; bibliometric analysis; thematic analysis

Introduction

Avatars are being increasingly used, driven by the growth of digital technology. It is anticipated that the market for avatars will achieve a valuation of USD 527.58 billion by the year 2030 (Emergen Research, 2022). Avatars are anthropomorphic digital entities capable of interacting (Crolic et al., 2022), controlled by humans or AI/software. Avatars provide a unique opportunity for consumers as well as marketers. Avatars are being used in virtual reality experiences for entertainment

Navigating the Digital Landscape, 17–37
Copyright © 2024 Atul Dahiya and Diptiman Banerji
Published under exclusive licence by Emerald Publishing Limited
doi:10.1108/978-1-83549-272-720241002

and education (Kato et al., 2022), providing new ways for consumers to engage with content. It is also being used in online customer service, allowing consumers to interact with virtual representatives for assistance (Jones et al., 2022). Avatars have the ability to alter how customers browse for products and engage with them, making the process more convenient and personalized (Liu et al., 2021).

Avatars have become an increasingly important aspect of the digital world and are being used in various consumer contexts. From being used as company representatives and personal shopping assistants to being employed as conversation partners and recommendation agents, avatars are transforming the way businesses interact with their customers (Jin & Sung, 2010). As such, it is crucial to study the effects of avatar use in consumer contexts to gain a better understanding of how avatars impact consumer behavior and attitudes. This knowledge can inform and improve marketing strategies, leading to more effective customer engagement and satisfaction (Jones et al., 2022).

The previous review research for avatar literature like Miao et al.'s (2022) article has its limitations. It majorly focusses on the definitions of avatars, avatar effectiveness, and largely on avatar marketing. On the other hand, the present review provides a comprehensive picture of avatar literature in consumer contexts. To do so, present review uses the combination of *descriptive analysis* for corpus performance, *bibliometric analysis* for corpus performance and emerging themes, and *thematic analysis* for emerging themes as well as the future research opportunities. Therefore, scholars can gain a comprehensive and state-of-the-art overview of avatar literature by consulting this indispensable review.

Avatars in consumer contexts have garnered huge interest from both research scholars and industries; despite this, the literature remains fragmented. It therefore calls for the consolidation of literature using systematic literature review. Our review is structured similarly to the high-caliber review papers that are published in prestigious journals; firstly, we create the following broad research questions (RQs):

RQ1. What is the corpus-based performance of avatar literature?
RQ2. What are the emerging themes and implications in avatar literature?
RQ3. What are the future research opportunities for avatar literature in consumer contexts?

The subsequent parts of this chapter are structured in the following manner: Section 2 expounds on the theoretical synthesis; Section 3 delineates the methodology; Section 4 presents the results and findings; Section 5 highlights potential future research opportunities; Section 6 acknowledges the limitations; Appendix 1 provides supplementary information; and the References section concludes the chapter.

Theoretical Synthesis

Avatars have been defined in several ways depending on the context. In general, it refers to a virtual representation (Tawira & Ivanov, 2022) or online representation

(Mennecke & Peters, 2013) of an individual in a virtual environment or online world. It can be used to interact with other avatars or objects within the environment and often takes on characteristics that are similar to its user's personality (Gonzales-Chávez & Vila-Lopez, 2021; Kozinets, 2012; Persky et al., 2019). The avatar can also be customized with different skins or features, such as clothing or accessories, to represent its user's identity (Joseph, 2021; Mennecke & Peters, 2013; Phillips Melancon, 2011). Avatars can be created by capturing images from multiple angles with the help of 3D scanners or generated by users themselves using images or graphics that they choose (Shin & Saeidi, 2023). Avatars are used for various purposes, including as a tool for expressing one's identity (Koles & Nagy, 2012), representing a business or salesperson in an e-commerce platform (Mull et al., 2015), delivering product information (Holzwarth et al., 2006), marketing communication (Elsharnouby et al., 2022), supporting co-creation activities (Matzler et al., 2011), also representing physical products or services within a virtual realm (Wuest et al., 2015).

Studying avatars in consumer contexts is important for the following reasons. The use of avatars is increasing in virtual environments, where they are being employed as representatives of businesses, personal assistants for shopping purposes, conversational partners, and agents for providing recommendations to users (Jin & Sung, 2010). Understanding how different personalities of avatars can influence consumer behavior and attitudes is crucial for effective marketing strategies (Mennecke & Peters, 2013). The use of avatars enabled businesses to interact with customers in new and exciting ways, satisfying their demands and creating a highly interpersonal shopping experience (Dwivedi et al., 2022). Studying the effects of avatar use in various contexts can potentially be used to mitigate biases and prejudices in society (Kozinets, 2012), as well as provide insights on how websites can successfully capture consumers' attention for a longer time (Aguirre-Rodriguez et al., 2015).

Moreover, avatars can improve the user interfaces, potentially increasing customer satisfaction and provide a way for users to interact with other people in virtual environments and navigate through 3D spaces more easily (Lau & Ki, 2021; Lee & Chung, 2008). Avatars can also be used to deliver e-health interventions in virtual environments and provide a unique way of presenting health information and advice (Jin & Sung, 2010).

In the fashion retail industry, avatars are becoming popular as a way to engage customers and increase online sales (Holzwarth et al., 2006). By understanding how different features of avatars affect consumer behavior, retailers can better design VR apps that meet customer needs and motivate positive behaviors (Ainsworth et al., 2008; Elsharnouby et al., 2022).

Furthermore, studying avatars can enhance our comprehension of the virtual world phenomenon and offer valuable perspectives on consumer behavior (Yoo et al., 2015). Avatars can help to understand how consumers interact with the game and their purchase intention (Gammoh et al., 2018), as well as how users perceive chatbots and their attitudes toward this technology (De Cicco et al., 2020). Understanding how people react toward human-like avatar-based ads will help advertisers better understand their target audience's preferences (Gammoh et al., 2018).

Methodology

The SPAR-4-SLR framework (Scientific Procedures and Rationales for Systematic Literature Reviews), as illustrated in Fig. 2.1, is a well-structured and rigorous approach of conducting a systematic literature review (Paul et al., 2021). The first step in this framework, referred to as "Assembling," involved identifying the review domain as "Avatar" and "Consumer." Our research questions include RQ1 (Corpus Performance); RQ2 (Emerging Themes and Implications); and

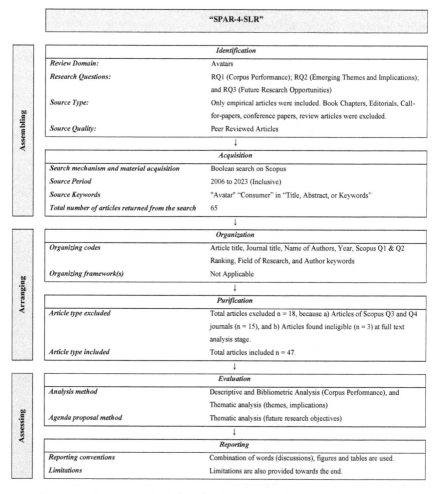

Fig. 2.1.   Protocol Used for the Present Review: "SPAR-4-SLR."

RQ3 (Future Research Agenda). Our source type is "Journals" and document type is "Articles" using source quality of "Scopus." To acquire the articles, we used our keywords "Avatar" "Consumer" in Scopus database search bar where we did not narrow down our search using any search period. Our search was restricted to articles written in the English language. Additionally, we limited our search to articles published in the fields of "Business, Management and Accounting," as well as "Psychology." Toward the end of this stage, we retrieved a total of $n = 65$ articles which were then arranged using organizing codes and comma-separated-values files (CSV files).

In the SPAR-4-SLR framework, "arranging" is the second stage, where we used "Author Name, Year, Article Name, Journal Name, Country, Author Keywords, and Number of Citations" as organizing codes. We downloaded and used CSV file from Scopus which eliminates the need of organizing frameworks. We then purified the data based on inclusion and exclusion criteria. We excluded articles which were (a) Scopus Q3 and Q4 ranked articles ($n = 15$); and (b) Articles failed at full text analysis because of irrelevancy ($n = 3$). Toward the end of this stage, we retrieved a total of $n = 47$ articles which were then assessed for evaluation and reporting.

The third stage in SPAR-4-SLR is *assessing*, where we evaluated the retrieved articles on the basis of descriptive analysis (year-wise distribution, journal-wise distribution, and geographical distribution), bibliometric analysis (using VOS-viewer, CSV file, and MS Excel for keywords co-occurrence, citations-per-year (CPY), citations-per-journal (CPJ), the most cited articles, and the citation-per-author (CPA)), and thematic analysis (for emerging themes, implications, and future research objectives). To report our findings, we use words for narration, tables, and figures for evidence. We also provide limitations to our study toward the end of the present article.

Results and Findings

Corpus Performance

Corpus Performance Based on Descriptive Analysis

We use descriptive analysis for providing evidence on corpus performance, where we first show the year-wise distribution of retrieved articles. Fig. 2.2 shows that the avatar literature in consumer contexts is steadily rising over years (from one article in 2006 to 11 articles in 2022) and the upward trendline shows the expected growth of the literature in future as well.

Table 2.1 provides the list of Scopus Q1 and Q2 ranking journals who have published avatar literature over the years. Journal-wise distribution shows a list of 34 journals in total, out of which 24 are Scopus Q1-ranked journals and 10 Scopus Q2-ranked journals. *"Computers in Human Behavior," "Journal of Business Research,"* and *"Journal of Research in Interactive Marketing"* are the Scopus Q1 journals, and *"Psychology and Marketing"* is the Scopus Q2 journal publishing most avatar literature in the present corpus.

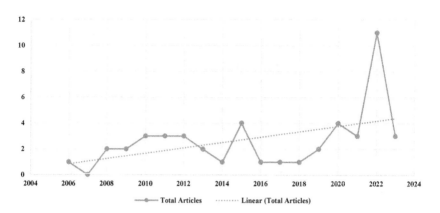

Fig. 2.2.   Year-Wise Distribution of Retrieved Articles.

Table 2.1. Journal-Wise Distribution of Retrieved Articles.

Source Title	Scopus Q-Ranking	Total Articles Per Source Title
Computers in Human Behavior	Q1	4
Journal of Business Research	Q1	3
Journal of Research in Interactive Marketing	Q1	3
Asia Pacific Journal of Marketing and Logistics	Q1	2
Cyberpsychology, Behavior, and Social Networking	Q1	2
International Journal of Retail and Distribution Management	Q1	2
Journal of Fashion Marketing and Management	Q1	2
Business Horizons	Q1	1
Fashion and Textiles	Q1	1
Industrial Management and Data Systems	Q1	1
International Journal of Consumer Studies	Q1	1
International Journal of Electronic Commerce	Q1	1

Table 2.1. *(Continued)*

Source Title	Scopus Q-Ranking	Total Articles Per Source Title
Journal of Brand Management	Q1	1
Journal of Consumer Culture	Q1	1
Journal of Interactive Marketing	Q1	1
Journal of Marketing	Q1	1
Journal of Marketing Management	Q1	1
Journal of Product and Brand Management	Q1	1
Journal of Retailing and Consumer Services	Q1	1
Journal of Services Marketing	Q1	1
Journal of the Association for Consumer Research	Q1	1
Problems and Perspectives in Management	Q1	1
Production Planning and Control	Q1	1
Technovation	Q1	1
Psychology and Marketing	Q2	3
Frontiers in Psychology	Q2	1
Innovative Marketing	Q2	1
Journal of Hospitality and Tourism Insights	Q2	1
Journal of Theoretical and Applied Electronic Commerce Research	Q2	1
Marketing Intelligence and Planning	Q2	1
Marketing Letters	Q2	1
Journal of Research in Marketing and Entrepreneurship	Q2	1
Journal of Social Marketing	Q2	1
Psychological Reports	Q2	1

The geographical distribution (see Fig. 2.3) of avatar literature indicates that the United States of America have the highest number of articles ($n = 19$) followed by China ($n = 6$) and the United Kingdom ($n = 5$). We used CSV file data from Scopus to create a geographical distribution map in excel.

Fig. 2.3.   Geographical Distribution of Retrieved Articles (Provided
Courtesy of OpenStreetMap).

Corpus Performance Based on Bibliometric Analysis

To provide citations-based corpus performance we used bibliometric analysis,
where we used CSV file data from Scopus as the basis to provide evidence. We
first elaborate on CPY data of retrieved avatar articles (see Table 2.2). Our
findings suggest that the year 2006 received most citations with 434 citations for
one article, followed by year 2009 with 274 citations for two articles, and then
year 2010 with 127 citations for three articles. One interesting observation here is
that CPY data make it evident that the avatar literature is not receiving greater
attention that it deserves despite the growth it is expected to achieve in coming
years.

Table 2.2. Citation-Per-Year of Retrieved Articles.

Year	Total Articles	Citation Per Year
2023	3	1
2022	11	25
2021	3	21
2020	4	53
2019	2	8
2018	1	7
2017	1	34
2016	1	11

Table 2.2. *(Continued)*

Year	Total Articles	Citation Per Year
2015	4	90
2014	1	6
2013	2	24
2012	3	28
2011	3	105
2010	3	127
2009	2	274
2008	2	95
2006	1	434

Citation-per-journal as shown in Table 2.3 informs us the number of citations the journals publishing avatar literature have received. Table 2.3 shows that *Journal of Marketing* is the most cited journal for avatar literature with 434 citations, followed by *Computers in Human Behavior* with 231 citations, and then *Technovation* with 202 citations. These are also the most cited Scopus Q1 journals. On the other hand, *Psychology and Marketing* is the most cited Scopus Q2 journal with 91 citations.

Table 2.3. Citation-Per-Journal of Retrieved Articles.

Source Title	Citations
Journal of Marketing	434
Computers in Human Behavior	231
Technovation	202
Psychology and Marketing	91
Journal of Interactive Marketing	72
International Journal of Retail and Distribution Management	42
Journal of Services Marketing	34
Journal of Brand Management	33
Production Planning and Control	32
Journal of Fashion Marketing and Management	23
Cyberpsychology, Behavior, and Social Networking	17
Journal of Research in Interactive Marketing	15

(Continued)

Table 2.3. *(Continued)*

Source Title	Citations
Journal of Business Research	12
Journal of Theoretical and Applied Electronic Commerce Research	12
Journal of the Association for Consumer Research	11
Psychological Reports	9
Asia Pacific Journal of Marketing and Logistics	8
Marketing Intelligence and Planning	8
Marketing Letters	8
Business Horizons	7
International Journal of Electronic Commerce	7
Journal of Hospitality and Tourism Insights	6
Journal of Product and Brand Management	6
Fashion and Textiles	5
Journal of Consumer Culture	5
Innovative Marketing	3
Journal of Marketing Management	3
International Journal of Consumer Studies	2
Problems and Perspectives in Management	2
Industrial Management and Data Systems	1
Journal of Research in Marketing and Entrepreneurship	1
Journal of Retailing and Consumer Services	1
Frontiers in Psychology	0
Journal of Social Marketing	0

Table 2.4 lists the top five articles that received the most citations in the retrieved avatar corpus. The most cited articles come from *Journal of Marketing* in the year 2006, this article is a work of Holzwarth et al. (2006) in Germany. Kohler et al.' (2009) study, published in Austria in *Technovation*, emerged as the second-most-cited article in our literature review. Whereas, the third-most-cited article was published in *Computers in Human Behavior* in 2011 by Kohler et al. (2011) in Austria. These citation-based findings show consistency from the start, for example, the most cited article comes from the most cited journal and the most cited year which informs the consistency of the present literature review.

Table 2.4. Top Five Most Cited Papers in the Retrieved Articles.

Authors	Year	Citations	Source Title	Country
Holzwarth et al. (2006)	2006	434	*Journal of Marketing*	Germany
Kohler et al. (2009)	2009	202	*Technovation*	Austria
Kohler et al. (2011)	2011	95	*Computers in Human Behavior*	Austria
Lee and Chung (2008)	2008	92	*Computers in Human Behavior*	South Korea
Bélisle and Bodur (2010)	2010	79	*Psychology and Marketing*	Canada

Emerging Themes and Implications

Emerging Themes and Implications Based on Bibliometric Analysis

We begin the discussion of emerging themes and implications by providing evidence using bibliometric analysis. We used VOSviewer to get a keyword co-occurrence diagram which elaborates on the major contexts wherein avatar literature has focused (see Fig. 2.4). To arrive at keyword co-occurrence diagram, we use the Scopus CSV file and the author keywords provided in it. In our VOSviewer analysis we used full-counting and kept our threshold of minimum occurrences of keywords at 2. This gave us 16 keywords which met the threshold,

Fig. 2.4. Keyword Co-Occurrence of Author Keywords of Retrieved Articles.

out of which 15 keywords formed the part of largest connected keywords. Keyword co-occurrence gives us the broad picture of contexts in which avatars has been studied.

Fig. 2.4 shows that there are five major contexts in which avatars has been studied in our retrieved articles. Following this diagram, Table 2.5 makes an elaborated discussion on each of these contexts. Each cluster represents a broad context, for example, cluster 1 (red) broadly discusses avatars and their uses for social presence and enjoyment, cluster 2 (blue) talks about avatars in virtual reality and e-commerce, cluster 3 (yellow) looks at the avatars for branding and consumer behavior, cluster 4 (green) elaborates on avatars in innovation and co-creation, and cluster 5 (purple) discusses avatars in marketing and augmented reality (AR). Table 2.6 (see Appendix 1) shows the complete list of citations per author.

Table 2.5. Broad Contexts of Avatar Studies as Seen in the Retrieved Articles.

Clusters	Colors	Keywords	Broad Contexts
Cluster 1	Red	Avatar, Social Presence, Enjoyment, Chatbot	Avatars in Social Presence and Enjoyment.
Cluster 2	Blue	Virtual Reality, E-commerce, Personalization	Avatars in Virtual Reality and E-Commerce.
Cluster 3	Yellow	Consumer Behavior, Branding, Virtual Worlds	Avatars in Branding and Consumer Behavior.
Cluster 4	Green	Second Life, Co-creation, Innovation	Avatars in Innovation and Co-Creation.
Cluster 5	Purple	Marketing, Augmented Reality	Avatars in Marketing and Augmented Reality.

Emerging Themes and Implications Based on Thematic Analysis

- Theme 1: Avatars in Social Presence and Enjoyment.

Avatars are an important aspect in creating social presence in online environments (De Cicco et al., 2020). They are digital representations of a person or character and help to provide visual cues and facilitate relationship-building through appearance, behavior, and interactions (Jin & Sung, 2010; Joseph, 2021; Whalen et al., 2019).

In addition to increasing social presence, avatars are also linked to enjoyment when used in virtual environments such as chatbots (Bélisle & Bodur, 2010; Butt et al., 2021; Wu et al., 2022). A chatbot's interaction with a user becomes more immersive with the use of an avatar, which in turn fosters trust between them

(Butt et al., 2021; Jin & Sung, 2010). Additionally, incorporating avatars in chatbot interactions has been shown to enhance perceived enjoyment among millennials (Foster et al., 2022; Jin, 2012).

Avatars also provide a more immersive experience for users in virtual environments, which contributes to enjoyment (Jin, 2010; Jin & Sung, 2010; Lee & Chung, 2008; Mull et al., 2015). By allowing people to interact with each other and navigate 3D spaces, they add a fun element to the user interface that would otherwise be missing (Butt et al., 2021; Foster et al., 2022; Keng & Liu, 2013; Mull et al., 2015). Additionally, customization options such as clothing or facial features allow users to express themselves through their avatars, creating unique characters that represent their own personalities within the virtual environment (Elsharnouby et al., 2022; Holzwarth et al., 2006). To summarize, avatars have a significant impact on establishing a sense of social presence and enhancing enjoyment in virtual settings.

- Theme 2: Avatars in Marketing and Augmented Reality.

Avatars have become a valuable tool for businesses looking to improve their customer experience and increase their bottom line (Lau & Ki, 2021; Saad & Choura, 2022). In marketing, avatars offer numerous benefits such as providing a more interactive and engaging experience for customers. This increased engagement can lead to increased customer loyalty, which is crucial in today's highly competitive market (Lau & Ki, 2021). Avatars also offer manufacturers the ability to customize their products to meet consumer preferences, allowing them to better target specific market segments and improve profitability (Jin, 2009). Additionally, avatars allow retailers greater control over pricing strategies by tailoring prices based on individual consumer's willingness to pay (Lau & Ki, 2021; Tawira & Ivanov, 2022; Wu et al., 2022). The utilization of avatars in digital marketing may result in more successful advertising initiatives (Saad & Choura, 2022). Avatars also provide personalized customer service by quickly and accurately responding to questions or requests from users, which helps to build trust with potential customers (Persky et al., 2019).

The implications of avatars in AR are significant. Avatars can provide a more immersive and interactive experience for consumers, influencing brand interactions within AR and leading to more effective digital marketing campaigns (Lau & Ki, 2021; Tawira & Ivanov, 2022). Furthermore, avatars have the potential to provide valuable insights into consumer buying behavior, providing marketers with both quantitative and qualitative market research data that would otherwise be difficult or impossible to obtain through traditional methods (Jin, 2009). In conclusion, avatars have become a valuable tool for businesses looking to improve their customer experience and increase their bottom line. With the potential to influence brand interactions within AR, provide personalized customer service, and gather valuable market research data, avatars have the capacity to transform the way businesses engage with their customers.

- Theme 3: Avatars in Virtual Reality and E-Commerce.

Avatars in virtual reality provide a more immersive and engaging experience for users (Yoo et al., 2015). They serve as digital representations of individuals and offer a sense of presence and connection in the digital world. In the realm of e-commerce, avatars play a crucial role in providing a more personalized shopping experience for customers (Aguirre-Rodriguez et al., 2015; Yoo et al., 2015). Additionally, avatars allow retailers to customize experiences based on individual customer needs and provide tailored shopping recommendations (Ainsworth et al., 2008; Phillips Melancon, 2011).

Avatars in e-commerce offer an advantage of presenting audio or text descriptions of products to customers through prerecorded text-to-speech (TTS) voice sound clips (Jin, 2009). This enhances the overall customer experience and helps them make informed purchase decisions (Aguirre-Rodriguez et al., 2015; Ainsworth et al., 2008; Ballantyne & Nilsson, 2017). Furthermore, adoption of virtual try-on (VTO) apps can also help reduce traffic in brick-and-mortar stores during times when physical distancing is necessary, such as during pandemics or other health crises (Tawira & Ivanov, 2022). In conclusion, the usage of avatars in virtual reality and e-commerce is important in customizing the shopping experience for consumers. They allow companies to tailor marketing activities and products specifically toward individual customers based on their preferences or body type (Mennecke & Peters, 2013), creating an immersive online shopping environment that is tailored just for them (Gonzales-Chávez & Vila-Lopez, 2021).

- Theme 4: Avatars in Innovation and Co-Creation.

Avatars play an active role in the innovation process, from idea generation to product launch (Kohler et al., 2009, 2011; Matzler et al., 2011). They provide a unique opportunity for manufacturers and consumers to collaborate on innovation projects, allowing them to create products more quickly and efficiently than traditional methods (Kohler et al., 2009). Integrating users of virtual worlds into the new interactive product development processes can provide companies with valuable insights from their consumer base that may be challenging or unfeasible to obtain in the physical world, resulting in an interactive and effective approach to product development (Kohler et al., 2011).

In the virtual world of Second Life, avatars provide users with a unique way to express their identity or personality through their appearance, clothing style, and accessories (Koles & Nagy, 2012). Avatars can help to create a more immersive experience for users when interacting with really new products (RNPs), leading to positive attitudes toward the product and increased comprehension. Visual cues from avatars also allow potential adopters to reduce uncertainty about RNPs by seeking information through various communication channels (Seyed Esfahani & Reynolds, 2021).

There are numerous implications of using avatars for co-creation and innovation (Kohler et al., 2011; Matzler et al., 2011). Avatars allow participants to express their ideas and opinions in an immersive environment, which could lead to innovative solutions not achievable through traditional methods (Matzler et al., 2011). The use of avatars also allows companies to gain valuable insights into consumer behavior within virtual worlds, which can be used when designing future products and services (Kohler et al., 2009; Seyed Esfahani & Reynolds, 2021).

• Theme 5: Avatars in Branding and Consumer Behavior.

Avatars provide a way for individuals to create and customize their representation within virtual environments, which can influence their interactions with other users and brands (Dwivedi et al., 2022). For instance, operating elderly avatars can positively affect participants' attitudes toward prosocial behaviors, such as donating money to nonprofit organizations (Yoo et al., 2015). Furthermore, avatars' usage can provide marketers with insight into consumer behavior and motivations within virtual worlds, allowing them to customize their advertising, promotions, and product offerings to better fit the preferences of these individuals (Dwivedi et al., 2022; Mennecke & Peters, 2013).

The implications of avatars for virtual worlds and branding are significant (Dwivedi et al., 2022). Marketers must be aware of user motivations when using avatars and how they influence consumer behavior in virtual environments (Dwivedi et al., 2022). By understanding factors such as openness to experience or social comparisons, marketers can tailor their advertising campaigns accordingly and create successful marketing strategies that will resonate with consumers (Mennecke & Peters, 2013; Moriuchi, 2023). Avatars also provide an opportunity for social connection and self-expression, which can contribute to creating immersive and engaging virtual worlds for users (Moriuchi, 2023). Further, the use of avatars in virtual environments can provide valuable insights for marketers looking to better understand consumer behavior and create more effective branding strategies.

Future Research Directions

Avatar literature in consumer contexts is an emerging field of study that investigates how avatars influence consumer behavior and attitudes. In this regard, there are numerous potential research opportunities worth exploring which can enhance the overall user experience of avatars in consumer contexts.

First, subsequent research could explore how customizing avatars affects consumer behavior and attitudes. This research can explore how customization influences avatar identification and how social norms affect preferences for avatar customization. Furthermore, the effects of avatar customization on decision-making processes of consumers as well as their brand loyalty could be explored.

Second, future research may explore how avatar representation affects consumer attitudes and behavior. Research in this area could investigate how realistic versus stylized avatars impact consumer engagement, trust, and brand perception. Additionally, the influence of avatar diversity and inclusivity on consumer attitudes and behavior could be studied.

Third, subsequent research can examine the effects of avatar interactivity on consumer behavior and attitudes. Research in this area could investigate how interactive avatars influence consumer engagement, learning, and product evaluations. Moreover, the effects of avatar interactivity on consumer trust, perceived value, and purchase intentions could be examined.

Fourth, another potential area of research is the study of avatar-mediated communication in consumer contexts. This could involve examining how consumers use avatars to communicate with others in virtual environments, and how this impacts their social behavior. Researchers could also investigate how avatar-mediated communication differs from face-to-face communication, and how this impacts consumer behavior.

Fifth, future research could explore how factors such as personality, self-construal, and regulatory focus influence consumer attitudes and behavior toward avatars. This research could help marketers understand the types of consumers are more inclined to engage with avatar-based marketing campaigns and tailor their strategies accordingly.

Sixth, as avatar literature continues to evolve and become more immersive, there is a need to develop and test new avatar-based marketing strategies that go beyond traditional advertising formats. For example, marketers could explore the potential of using avatar-based product demonstrations, VTOs, or interactive storytelling experiences to engage consumers and create memorable brand experiences. This research could help marketers stay at the forefront of avatar-based marketing innovation and develop more effective ways to reach and engage consumers.

Seventh, researchers can explore how different cultures interpret and use avatars in unique ways. For example, some cultures may be more receptive to using avatars for social interactions while others may view them primarily as gaming tools.

Eighth, future research could explore how avatars are used for self-expression, impression management, and other identity-related goals; as online environments become more ubiquitous, avatars may play an important role in how people construct and manage their online identities.

Lastly, a final potential research direction is the investigation of avatar-based interventions in consumer contexts. This could include studying the effectiveness of avatars as tools for behavior change, such as promoting healthy eating or increasing physical activity. Additionally, researchers could explore how avatars can be used to improve consumer education and decision-making, such as through interactive product demonstrations or virtual shopping experiences.

Limitations

This review has its own limitations, just like any other articles. Despite being a thorough review of the avatar literature, the limitations offer prospective scholars direction on how to shape the corpus's future. Following are the limitations to our review:

First, the present review is limited to Scopus database. Although prior research like Donthu et al. (2021) and Paul et al. (2021) have supported the usage of Scopus, using more than one database can provide broader coverage and more generalizability of the results.

Second, the present review uses only Scopus Q1 and Q2 journal articles. The future research can include Q3- and Q4-ranked journals to avoid missing out some findings.

Third and lastly, this review focuses on the corpus performance, emerging themes, and future research opportunities of avatar literature in consumer contexts. We did not extensively explore the theories or methods that support avatar literature, subsequent research can delve into theories and methods.

References

Aguirre-Rodriguez, A., Bóveda-Lambie, A. M., & Miniard, P. W. (2015). The impact of consumer avatars in Internet retailing on self-congruity with brands. *Marketing Letters*, *26*, 631–641.

Ainsworth, A. B., Bonifield, C., & Tomas, A. (2008). Where avatars come from: Exploring consumers' motivations in virtual worlds. *Innovative Marketing*, *4*(4).

de Amorim, I. P., Guerreiro, J., Eloy, S., & Loureiro, S. M. C. (2022). How augmented reality media richness influences consumer behaviour. *International Journal of Consumer Studies*, *46*(6), 2351–2366.

Azer, J., Anker, T., Taheri, B., & Tinsley, R. (2023). Consumer-driven racial stigmatization: The moderating role of race in online consumer-to-consumer reviews. *Journal of Business Research*, *157*, 113567.

Ballantyne, D., & Nilsson, E. (2017). All that is solid melts into air: The servicescape in digital service space. *Journal of Services Marketing*, *31*(3), 226–235.

Bélisle, J.-F., & Bodur, H. O. (2010). Avatars as information: Perception of consumers based on their avatars in virtual worlds. *Psychology and Marketing*, *27*(8), 741–765.

Butt, A. H,, Ahmad, H., Goraya, M. A., Akram, M. S., & Shafique, M. N. (2021). Let's play: Me and my AI-powered avatar as one team. *Psychology and Marketing*, *38*(6), 1014–1025.

Crolic, C., Thomaz, F., Hadi, R., & Stephen, A. T. (2022). Blame the bot: Anthropomorphism and anger in customer–chatbot interactions. *Journal of Marketing*, *86*(1), 132–148.

De Cicco, R., Silva, S. C., & Alparone, F. R. (2020). Millennials' attitude toward chatbots: An experimental study in a social relationship perspective. *International Journal of Retail & Distribution Management*, *48*(11), 1213–1233.

Donthu, N., Kumar, S., Pandey, N., & Lim, W. M. (2021). Research constituents, intellectual structure, and collaboration patterns in Journal of International Marketing: An analytical retrospective. *Journal of International Marketing*, *29*(2), 1–25.

Dwivedi, Y. K., Hughes, L., Wang, Y., Alalwan, A. A., Ahn, S. J., Balakrishnan, J., Barta, S., Belk, R., Buhalis, D., & Dutot, V. (2022). Metaverse marketing: How the metaverse will shape the future of consumer research and practice. *Psychology and Marketing*, *40*, 750–776.

Elsharnouby, M. H., Jayawardhena, C., Liu, H., & Elbedweihy, A. M. (2022). Strengthening consumer–brand relationships through avatars. *Journal of Research in Interactive Marketing*, 1–21. ahead-of-print.

Emergen Research, E. R. (2022, January). *Digital human avatar market forecast | Digital human industry trend by 2030.* https://www.emergenresearch.com/amp/industry-report/digital-human-avatar-market

Foster, J. K., McLelland, M. A., & Wallace, L. K. (2022). Brand avatars: Impact of social interaction on consumer–brand relationships. *Journal of Research in Interactive Marketing, 16*(2), 237–258.

Gammoh, B. S., Jiménez, F. R., & Wergin, R. (2018). Consumer attitudes toward human-like avatars in advertisements: The effect of category knowledge and imagery. *International Journal of Electronic Commerce, 22*(3), 325–348.

Gonzales-Chávez, M. A., & Vila-Lopez, N. (2021). Designing the best avatar to reach millennials: Gender differences in a restaurant choice. *Industrial Management & Data Systems, 121*(6), 1216–1236.

Holzwarth, M., Janiszewski, C., & Neumann, M. M. (2006). The influence of avatars on online consumer shopping behavior. *Journal of Marketing, 70*(4), 19–36.

Jin, S.-A. A. (2009). The roles of modality richness and involvement in shopping behavior in 3D virtual stores. *Journal of Interactive Marketing, 23*(3), 234–246.

Jin, S.-A. A. (2010). The roles of regulatory focus and medical recommendation avatars' trustworthiness in virtual environment–based e-health. *Cyberpsychology, Behavior, and Social Networking, 13*(4), 461–466.

Jin, S.-A. A. (2012). Self-discrepancy and regulatory fit in avatar-based exergames. *Psychological Reports, 111*(3), 697–710.

Jin, S.-A. A., & Sung, Y. (2010). The roles of spokes-avatars' personalities in brand communication in 3D virtual environments. *Journal of Brand Management, 17*, 317–327.

Jones, C. L. E., Hancock, T., Kazandjian, B., & Voorhees, C. M. (2022). Engaging the Avatar: The effects of authenticity signals during chat-based service recoveries. *Journal of Business Research, 144*, 703–716.

Joseph, D. (2021). Battle pass capitalism. *Journal of Consumer Culture, 21*(1), 68–83.

Kato, R., Kikuchi, Y., Yem, V., & Ikei, Y. (2022). Reality avatar for customer conversation in the metaverse. *International Conference on Human-Computer Interaction*, 131–145.

Keng, C.-J., & Liu, C.-C. (2013). Can avatar and self-referencing really increase the effects of online 2-D and 3-D advertising? *Computers in Human Behavior, 29*(3), 791–802.

Kohler, T., Fueller, J., Stieger, D., & Matzler, K. (2011). Avatar-based innovation: Consequences of the virtual co-creation experience. *Computers in Human Behavior, 27*(1), 160–168.

Kohler, T., Matzler, K., & Füller, J. (2009). Avatar-based innovation: Using virtual worlds for real-world innovation. *Technovation, 29*(6–7), 395–407.

Koles, B., & Nagy, P. (2012). Virtual customers behind avatars: The relationship between virtual identity and virtual consumption in second life. *Journal of Theoretical and Applied Electronic Commerce Research, 7*(2), 87–105.

Kozinets, R. V. (2012). Me/my research/avatar. *Journal of Business Research, 65*(4), 478.

Lau, O., & Ki, C.-W. (2021). Can consumers' gamified, personalized, and engaging experiences with VR fashion apps increase in-app purchase intention by fulfilling needs? *Fashion and Textiles, 8*, 1–22.

Lee, K. C., & Chung, N. (2008). Empirical analysis of consumer reaction to the virtual reality shopping mall. *Computers in Human Behavior, 24*(1), 88–104.

Li, J., Huang, J., & Li, Y. (2023). Examining the effects of authenticity fit and association fit: A digital human avatar endorsement model. *Journal of Retailing and Consumer Services, 71*, 103230.

Lima, V. M., Pessôa, L. A., & Belk, R. W. (2022). The Promethean biohacker: On consumer biohacking as a labour of love. *Journal of Marketing Management*, *38*(5–6), 483–514.

Liu, Y., Liu, Y., Xu, S., Cheng, K., Masuko, S., & Tanaka, J. (2021). *An interactive AR-based virtual try-on system using personalized avatars: Augmented walking and social fitme.*

Matzler, K., Füller, J., Kohler, T., & Stieger, D. (2011). Avatar-based innovation: How avatars experience co-creation projects in second life. *Problems and Perspectives in Management*, *9*(2), 21–32.

Mennecke, B. E., & Peters, A. (2013). From avatars to mavatars: The role of marketing avatars and embodied representations in consumer profiling. *Business Horizons*, *56*(3), 387–397.

Miao, F., Kozlenkova, I. V., Wang, H., Xie, T., & Palmatier, R. W. (2022). An emerging theory of avatar marketing. *Journal of Marketing*, *86*(1), 67–90. https://doi.org/10.1177/0022242921996646

Moriuchi, E. (2023). Bridging social marketing and technology in the disability field: An empirical study on the role of cybernetic avatar and social inclusion. *Journal of Social Marketing*. ahead-of-print.

Mull, I., Wyss, J., Moon, E., & Lee, S.-E. (2015). An exploratory study of using 3D avatars as online salespeople: The effect of avatar type on credibility, homophily, attractiveness and intention to interact. *Journal of Fashion Marketing and Management*, *19*, 154–168.

Paul, J., Lim, W. M., O'Cass, A., Hao, A. W., & Bresciani, S. (2021). Scientific procedures and rationales for systematic literature reviews (SPAR-4-SLR). *International Journal of Consumer Studies*, *45*(4), O1–O16.

Persky, S., Kistler, W. D., Klein, W. M., & Ferrer, R. A. (2019). Internet versus virtual reality settings for genomics information provision. *Cyberpsychology, Behavior, and Social Networking*, *22*(1), 7–14.

Phillips Melancon, J. (2011). Consumer profiles in reality vs fantasy-based virtual worlds: Implications for brand entry. *Journal of Research in Interactive Marketing*, *5*(4), 298–312.

Ramanathan, J., & Purani, K. (2014). Brand extension evaluation: Real world and virtual world. *The Journal of Product and Brand Management*, *23*(7), 504–515.

Saad, S. B., & Choura, F. (2022). Effectiveness of virtual reality technologies in digital entrepreneurship: A comparative study of two types of virtual agents. *Journal of Research in Marketing and Entrepreneurship*, *24*, 195–220.

Seyed Esfahani, M., & Reynolds, N. (2021). Impact of consumer innovativeness on really new product adoption. *Marketing Intelligence & Planning*, *39*(4), 589–612.

Shin, E., & Saeidi, E. (2023). Whole body shapes and fit problems among overweight and obese men in the United States. *Journal of Fashion Marketing and Management: An International Journal*, *27*(1), 100–117.

Tawira, L., & Ivanov, A. (2022). Leveraging personalization and customization affordances of virtual try-on apps for a new model in apparel m-shopping. *Asia Pacific Journal of Marketing and Logistics*, *35*, 451–471.

Venkatesh, A. (2016). Social media, digital self, and privacy: A socio-analytical perspective of the consumer as the digital avatar. *Journal of the Association for Consumer Research*, *1*(3), 378–391.

Wang, J., & Fan, X. (2020). Co-production strategy, retail competition, and market segmentation. *Asia Pacific Journal of Marketing and Logistics, 32*(2), 607–630.

Whalen, E. A., Belarmino, A., & Taylor, S., Jr (2019). Share and share alike? Examining the maturation of the sharing economy through a craft beer exchange. *Journal of Hospitality and Tourism Insights, 2*, 309–325.

Wu, J., Joo, B. R., Sina, A. S., Song, S., & Whang, C. H. (2022). Personalizing 3D virtual fashion stores: An action research approach to modularity development. *International Journal of Retail & Distribution Management, 50*(3), 342–360.

Wu, X., & Santana, S. (2022). Impact of intrinsic and extrinsic gaming elements on online purchase intention. *Frontiers in Psychology, 13*.

Wuest, T., Hribernik, K., & Thoben, K.-D. (2015). Accessing servitisation potential of PLM data by applying the product avatar concept. *Production Planning & Control, 26*(14–15), 1198–1218.

Yoo, S.-C., Peña, J. F., & Drumwright, M. E. (2015). Virtual shopping and unconscious persuasion: The priming effects of avatar age and consumers' age discrimination on purchasing and prosocial behaviors. *Computers in Human Behavior, 48*, 62–71.

Appendix 1

Table 2.6. Citations Per Author of Retrieved Articles.

Authors	Citations
Aguirre-Rodriguez et al. (2015)	8
Ainsworth et al. (2008)	3
Azer et al. (2023)	0
Ballantyne and Nilsson (2017)	34
Bélisle and Bodur (2010)	79
Butt et al. (2021)	11
de Amorim et al. (2022)	2
De Cicco et al. (2020)	39
Dwivedi et al. (2022)	1
Elsharnouby et al. (2022)	0
Foster et al. (2022)	7
Gammoh et al. (2018)	7
Gonzales-Chávez and Vila-Lopez (2021)	1
Holzwarth et al. (2006)	434
Jin and Sung (2010)	33
Jin (2009)	72
Jin (2010)	15
Jin (2012)	9

Table 2.6. *(Continued)*

Authors	Citations
Jones et al. (2022)	5
Joseph (2021)	5
Keng and Liu (2013)	17
Kohler et al. (2009)	202
Kohler et al. (2011)	95
Koles and Nagy (2012)	12
Kozinets (2012)	7
Lau and Ki (2021)	5
Lee and Chung (2008)	92
Li et al. (2023)	1
Lima et al. (2022)	3
Matzler et al. (2011)	2
Mennecke and Peters (2013)	7
Moriuchi (2023)	0
Mull et al. (2015)	23
Persky et al. (2019)	2
Phillips Melancon (2011)	8
Ramanathan and Purani (2014)	6
Saad and Choura (2022)	1
Seyed Esfahani and Reynolds (2021)	8
Shin and Saeidi (2023)	0
Tawira and Ivanov (2022)	3
Venkatesh (2016)	11
Wang and Fan (2020)	5
Whalen et al. (2019)	6
Wu and Santana (2022)	0
Wu et al. (2022)	3
Wuest et al. (2015)	32
Yoo et al. (2015)	27

Chapter 3

Does Effective Handling of Negative E-Word of Mouth on Social Media Influence Customers' Behavioral Intentions in the Context of Online Travel Agencies

Durgesh Agnihotri[a]*, Pallavi Chaturvedi*[a] *and Vikas Tripathi*[a]

[a]GL Bajaj Institute of Technology and Management, India
[b]Amity College of Commerce and Finance, Amity University, India

Abstract

In the present study, we examined how effectively online travel agencies (OTAs) handle negative e-word-of-mouth on social media platforms like Facebook, Twitter, and Instagram. We collected data from 497 participants using survey method. To test the hypotheses formulated from the existing literature, structural equation modeling was adopted in this study. The results from structural equation modeling indicate effective handling of the negative e-word of mouth (e-WOM) on social media websites significantly affects customer satisfaction and repurchase intention. The current research work provides insight into social media recovery efforts and service fairness when handling negative e-WOM. The study recommends that customers can distinguish the differences between general efforts and adaptive complaint-handling efforts, and dissimilarities may influence satisfaction, repurchase intentions, etc. Although empathy, apology, responsiveness, and paraphrasing are considered pioneer strategies in complaint handling, customers' negative e-WOM, and firms' recovery management, but the current study is among a few to categorize OTAs' handling of negative e-WOM and complaint handling efforts in the social media environment.

Keywords: Complaint handling; service justice; social media; service failures; e-word of mouth; adaptive strategies

Navigating the Digital Landscape, 39–64
Copyright © 2024 Durgesh Agnihotri, Pallavi Chaturvedi and Vikas Tripathi
Published under exclusive licence by Emerald Publishing Limited
doi:10.1108/978-1-83549-272-720241003

Introduction

The second stage advancement of the internet through web 2.0 has characterized and transformed the internet from static to dynamic. Web 2.0 developed user-generated content (UGC), which has provided several corporations an edge to develop content to interact with the customers in effectively (Aljarah et al., 2022; Sugathan et al., 2018). Web 2.0 has also created prospects to have a dynamic existence on social media platforms for almost all the major service industries like hospitality, tourism, banking, and retail to have a huge customer base on virtual platforms (Jacobs & Liebrecht, 2022). Especially, the hotel industry has taken tremendous advantage of internet transformation and becomes one of the fastest-rising domains and a substantial contributor to the progression of the hospitality business (Ghorbanzadeh et al., 2022). The tourism and hospitality industry endures to magnify and expand, becoming one of the fastest developing and prevalent economic segments globally in the 21st century (Cheng et al., 2019). The industry has grown with the help of several key transformations that happened over a due course of time. Out of which, online booking of accommodation and travel has played a vital role in strengthening the industry (Cheng et al., 2019). Furthermore, travel shopping via online travel agencies (OTAs) has become a key part of the hospitality sector (Zhang et al., 2019). Subsequently, OTAs have provided the advantage of a booking engine and complete solutions for accommodation along with instant payment and booking confirmation. In simple words, the multifunctionality of OTAs has brought all tourism-related activities under one roof (Inversini & Masiero, 2014). Therefore, it has become extremely easy for customers to plan their travel and accommodate anywhere in the world. However, it does not assure the progress of the hospitality sector as regular innovative efforts are imperative to fulfill customers' ever-rising demands (Jeong & Lee, 2017; Tamwatin et al., 2015). Therefore, service-providing firms (OTAs) try to put in their best efforts to deliver services effectively, but fail a few times to fulfill consumers' expectations due to service heterogeneity and unpredictability in service delivery (Desai & De Souza, 2015; Kotler et al., 2016; Park et al., 2020), which further causes service failure (Koc, 2017).

Preceding studies have explained that service failures significantly affect customers' orientation toward the service providers (Cheng et al., 2019). A few studies observed that failure of service is a big reason behind customers' anger, anxiety, distrust, and disappointment along with financial losses (Fan & Niu, 2016; Soares et al., 2017). Considering the gravity of service failure, several service organizations have realized the gravity of failure on the lucrativeness and success of their businesses. To overcome the negative effect, organizations put in the best of their efforts to ensure corrective measures to handle service failure effectively by developing an effective structure to manage customers' concerns, issues, and complaints (Matikiti et al., 2019). However, firms and customers have altered their ways of complaining and responding respectively due to the unparalleled ease of use of modern electronics methods like social media (Lin et al., 2018). Especially, Facebook, Instagram, and Twitter have emerged as a combination of emerging interface between customers and organizations through UGC (Schaefers & Schamari, 2015; Sugathan et al., 2018). According to Pinto and Mansfield (2011), consumers can easily express their concerns, negative feelings and emotions with the concerned service providers through social media, which has also enabled an extensive user base to raise their voices.

Preceding studies have stated that social media has opened new ways to communicate between OTAs and tourists and has created tremendous opportunities for customers to write freely about their experiences (Cooper et al., 2019). Social media platforms provide a powerful tool for service providers to connect with their customers, build relationships, resolve issues, and influence their purchasing decisions (Agnihotri, Chaturvedi, et al., 2023). A few studies have suggested that, businesses need to put in their best efforts into understanding how social media affects consumer behavior as social media has become an integral part of individual's daily lives. Consumers use social media platforms to research products, read reviews, connect with brands, share experiences, raise complaints, and make purchasing decisions (Chen et al., 2019; Matikiti et al., 2019). Additionally, businesses also need to stay current with social media trends and adapt their marketing strategies due to the increasing importance of social media in the digital age. However, public accessibility of social media has created opportunities at one end but created huge challenges for organizations to respond appropriately to those visible direct and indirect complaints (Einwiller & Steilen, 2015). Besides, the number of experiences, testimonials, comments, and reviews have increased enormously since social media is evolved as a platform to share experiences, a feeling toward service encounters or failure (Jain et al., 2018). Therefore, firms have started using the omnipresence of the social media as a center of extreme attention for handling customers' negative emotions and expressions (Chen et al., 2019). A few preceding studies have defined these negative expressions and reviews as negative e-WOM (Jin & Phua, 2014; Sugathan et al., 2018). Further, negative e-WOM is described as a type of customer complaint behavior (Sashi et al., 2019). Therefore, it becomes imperative for service-providing firms to utilize social media platforms diligently to handle negative e-WOM to influence the future purchase intention of customers. Besides, service providers may lose out on existing and potential customers to competitors who have a strong social media presence and have a clear understanding of social media marketing strategies if they don't adapt to the increasing importance of social media (Agnihotri, Chaturvedi, et al., 2023; Jeong & Lee, 2017). Therefore, it becomes appropriate to investigate how effective handling of negative e-WOM on social media transform customer satisfaction their repurchase intention, especially in the South Asian region like India since a huge number of UGC is shared on Facebook, Instagram, and Twitter pages of leading OTAs (Make my trip, Yatra.com, goibibo.com, hotels.com, and cleartrip.com).

Henceforth, this study puts in efforts to investigate how effective handling of negative e-WOM transform customer satisfaction and their repurchase intent.

Theoretical Framework

Negative E-WOM

Lau and Ng (2001) argued that antagonistic impact of service failures is enlarged when consumers share their unacceptable experiences on several social media platforms. Even one post through e-word of mouth (e-WOM) can reach out many and influence them through UGC, particularly when the post is about negative experiences. Further, Sparks and Browning (2010) defined negative e-WOM as a symbol of dissatisfaction that is publicized with the drive of emitting feelings and information with virtually present others. Zeelenberg and Pieters (2004) stated that social media provides a platform where customers release their negative emotions through e-WOM. Abney et al. (2017) figured out four reasons for negative e-WOM: selflessness (to avert others from suffering the same issue), apprehension reduction, retaliation, and guidance seeking. Hennig et al. (2004) stated that e-WOM has grown vastly over social media and any negative comments can have serious repercussions on the value and credibility of the brand. Several individuals raised their first issue on the social media, instead of giving a review on the service provider's official web page or app (Sahin et al., 2017). Social media has amalgamated into individual's personal space and transformed the way of communication between the service providers and consumers (Jain et al., 2018). The effortlessness of sharing complaints by other users significantly upsurges the prospective reachability of every complaint, especially in the tourism industry, where customers rely on online reviews and e-WOM (Yoon, 2015). In fact, these complaints and reviews are of utmost importance for service providers, as these complaints could have turned into vital information for determining mistakes and unique opportunities to overcome service failure (Sahin et al., 2017).

Equity Theory and Service Justice

Equity theory is a broadly used notion in the framework of customers "complaint handling and service recovery" (Lin & Lin, 2011; Singh & Crisafulli, 2016), which has further strengthened justice theory (Adams, 1965). Equity theory states that customers who receive honest treatment tend to feel satisfied, which further results in positive predisposition toward service-providing firms (Adams, 1965). Cakici et al. (2019) has redefined the equity theory as it explains customers' realization of the value, they receive between how much they spend and how much they get from the service providers. Therefore, several service firms have come up with astonishing efforts to ensure customer satisfaction, but fail to satisfy due to unique characteristics of diversity, inseparability, and elusiveness in service delivery (Sahin et al., 2017). However, a few service firms set up an organized system for identifying service failures and handling complaints to enhance customer satisfaction and retention but fail to implement with consistency. Since, it is imperative for service firms to transform customers' unpleasant experiences into pleasant experiences through effective complaint-handling procedures (Mattila, 2001); the current study integrates justice theory as a vital part for handling customers' complaints linked to the efforts of OTAs for retaining existing customers. Justice focuses on the perception of customers that service providers are providing fair and consistent treatment (Harris et al., 2013; Jeong & Lee, 2017). Moreover, the central idea is that customers anticipate receiving fair treatment, and if they observe that they do not get fair treatment or their complaints are not handled in an appropriate manner, adverse responses may take place that will tarnish firm's reputation and future behavioral intentions (Cheng et al., 2019). In addition, the justice theory can be assessed based on three distinctive dimensions, that is, outcome, process, and communication (Agnihotri, Chaturvedi, et al., 2023; Kim et al., 2018), which is further renamed as PJ (procedural justice), IJ (interactional justice), and DJ (distributive justice). Besides, PJ associates with the assumption that the procedures followed in delivering outcomes are genuine (Singh & Crisafulli, 2016). According to Prasongsukarn and Patterson (2012), IJ relates to the interaction between employees and customers during complaint handling. According to Schoefer and Ennew (2005), IJ conveys the customer's experience during complaint resolution. Further, DJ discusses to the insight of impartiality in the dispersal of resources among individuals (Narteh, 2016).

There is a role for justice theory in both the physical and virtual worlds, particularly in relation to complaint handling online. In spite of the poor human interface in the complaint handling procedure, service justice dimensions are available in the social media context (Holloway & Beatty, 2003). In addition, Abney et al. (2017) has advised to utilize empathy, apology, and paraphrasing as integral component of IJ during complaint-handling procedures. Since this study highlights on negative e-WOM and complaints of social media users, this study attempts to comprehend how complaint-handling efforts, which emphasize IJ components such as empathy, apology, and paraphrasing, can influence consumer outcomes via social media. Therefore, IJ components empathy, apology, and paraphrasing are incorporated in conceptual framework (see Fig. 3.1). Moreover, unrestricted and ubiquitous nature of social media platforms allows swift and personalized procedures to handle complaints and negative e-WOM (Hennig-Thurau & Thurau, 2003). In addition, vigorously created messages to customers'

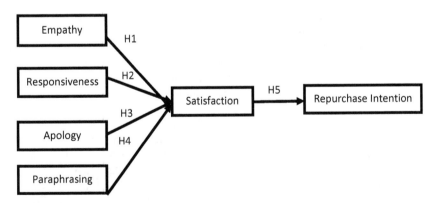

Fig. 3.1.   Conceptual Model Represents the Influence of Factors Like Empathy, Responsiveness, Apology, and Paraphrasing on Customer Satisfaction and Repurchase Intention.

comments or tweets have improved complaint handling on social media by reducing response time, which in turn has increased the collaboration between customers and service-providing firm. Therefore, responsiveness as a component of PJ is also incorporated in the conceptual framework.

Empathy

Zeithaml et al. (1988) have defined empathy as a progression of having personalized and affiliated consideration for customers. Furthermore, preceding studies have specified that empathy is an amalgamation of rational and emotional compass (Jones & Shandiz, 2015). The employees' capability to analyze the customer's state from their perspective is considered as rational viewpoint of empathy (Daniels et al., 2014). Subsequently Bahadur et al. (2018) correlated empathy with employees' ability to understand customer perspectives and emotional states during complaint handling. Preceding studies have suggested that social media provides ease of developing association and resonance between service organizations and customers (Markovic et al., 2018; Peters et al., 2013). Further, Itani and Inyang (2015) highlighted that firms' actions, including complaint-handling procedures, have more clarity and transparency on social media platforms. Further, any healthy interaction on these platforms might makes customers feel delighted about the way they their complaints are handled along with the resolutions (Karande et al., 2007). Further, the methods of dealing with customers at the time of complaint handling is fairly significant as customers' future behavioral intentions depend upon the interaction they have during the complaint-handling procedure (Blodgett et al., 1997; Itani & Inyang, 2015). Preceding studies have suggested that an empathetic reply to any negative comment on social media leads to positive behavioral outcomes that further positively affects the customers' way of look at the organization (Radu et al., 2019; Umasuthan et al., 2017). In addition, Agnihotri and Krush (2015) have specified that the employees' empathetic responses upsurge positivity in dissatisfied customers and help in retaining existing customers. Past research studies have addressed the affiliation between employee empathy and customer satisfaction in physical settings. On contrary, the role of Facebook, Instagram, and Twitter in providing personalized virtual experiences during customer and service provider interaction is still untapped and might have a deciding role in persuading customers' intents (Sugathan et al., 2018). However, considering the importance of social media, several travel agencies tried to console customers through customized empathetic responses on Facebook and Instagram in order to upsurge the positive predisposition of annoyed customers during COVID pandemic (Xu et al., 2022). So, based on existing literature, it is imperious to examine the effect of empathetic responses by OTAs against negative reviews on customer satisfaction. Hence, it is posited:

H1: An empathetic response to negative online reviews/tweets/posts has a significant impact on customer satisfaction in the context of OTAs.

Responsiveness

Customers' grievances are significantly affected by how fast service providers respond to their complaints as a means of obtaining effective resolution (Adil et al., 2022; Dickinger & Bauernfeind, 2009). Furthermore, Weber and Sparks (2004) have suggested that effective responsiveness increases customer affiliation toward service-providing firm and lead them to reconsume the services. In addition, technology enthusiasts who have a strong affinity for new technologies may be heavily influenced by response time when it comes to satisfaction and repurchase intentions (Mattila & Mount, 2003; Tang et al., 2018). Therefore, customers look for a quick response from the service-providing firm after raising the complaint on Facebook, Twitter, or Instagram. Besides, the justice theory has mentioned the importance of responsiveness where the complainer evaluates the sincerity of the organization to handle complaints through prompt and personalized responses (Abney et al., 2017). Subsequently Siu et al. (2013) stated that the organization is considered responsible and reliable, if it gives quick and prompt responses to both failure and its perseverance. A few researchers have advocated that delayed and sluggish responses might be the root of customer disappointment and will indicate the casual approach of the organization toward customers (Blodgett et al., 1993). A few researchers revealed that many customers search and compare OTAs for purchase and they explore reviews on social media about those OTAs before purchasing (Abney et al., 2017; Inversini & Masiero, 2014). Moreover, a few studies have highlighted the increase in the use of social media platforms for responding instantly and publicly against the negative comments of customers (Mason et al., 2021). Kumar and Kaur (2020) stated that instant responsiveness on social media has increased enormously postpandemic. Hence, it becomes imperative to understand how promptly OTAs are responding against the negative e-WOM in postpandemic era because any prompt response by OTAs against negative reviews might transform customer satisfaction and may influx new customers as well. Therefore, it is hypothesized as:

H2: A prompt response to negative online reviews/tweets or comments has a significant impact on customer satisfaction

Apology

However, tourism reservation has increased immensely through OTAs due to lucrative offers provided by OTAs and so customers' reliability on these OTAs for effective service delivery (Inversini & Masiero, 2014). Whereas, in case of service failure or dissatisfaction, customers blame OTAs for not fulfilling their commitments and start spreading negative e-WOM on different platforms (Chennattuserry et al., 2022) to outburst their anger (Sahin et al., 2017). Hence, it is necessary for OTAs to handle customers' complaints effectively and instantly because any negative spread over social media platforms may tarnish an OTA's reputation and trustworthiness (Zeelenberg & Pieters, 2004). Subsequently, the preceding study by Jeong and Lee (2017) emphasized on handling customers' complaints through customized and adaptive strategies such as apology and empathy. A formal apology demonstrates accountability, expresses regret, indicates concern, and requests forgiveness (Radu et al., 2019). Additionally, prior studies found that customers feel less liable toward service providers who apologized (Jeong & Lee, 2017; Sugathan et al., 2018). Moreover, any apologetic response on social media may benefit the service firm to strengthen its image among other virtually present potential customers (Radu et al., 2019). It is also more promising for complainants when service failures are fully accepted than when the provider refuses to acknowledge complaints (i.e., an excuse) (Weiner, 2000). Hence, it is posited:

> *H3:* An apologetic response to negative online comments/reviews significantly influences customer satisfaction.

Paraphrasing

The development of Web 2.0 allows customers and firms to share information and enable interactions between them on social media (Rashid et al., 2019). The interface between firms and customers on social media is noticeable to other nonparticipant social media users. Therefore, the importance of effectively articulated comments and responses cannot be ignored (Roschk et al., 2013) as any discussion between firm and customer is evident to others. Further, a few studies have highlighted that service providers' way of writing in response to any complaint or negative comment develops a better understanding with customers (Hussein & Hassan, 2017; Malthouse et al., 2013). Thus, better paraphrased and articulated responses against the direct or indirect complaints in form of negative tweet or comment can show to both the complainer and prospective customers that the organization considers such issues very seriously (Hennig-Thurau et al., 2010), and the reviews, comments, and tweets are recited meticulously. However, the responses during the complaint handling on social media platforms classically develop from predefined content copies, which are based on frequently asked questions, but an adaptive paraphrased comment by the firm might influence customers' behavioral intentions (Sugathan et al., 2018). A few recent studies have highlighted that better paraphrased information on social media increase UGC, which may further help the service-providing firm connect and affiliate with the several virtually present potential customers (Agnihotri, Kulshreshtha, et al., 2023; Yang et al., 2019). Moreover, paraphrased responses create better understanding, decrease the resolution time, and increase the credibility of the firm, which might enrich customer experience during complaint handling (Maecker et al., 2016). Hence, it becomes important to examine the impact of better-paraphrased responses against negative reviews and e-WOM on satisfaction of customer in the social media environment. Hence, it can be assumed that:

> *H4:* Paraphrased responses against negative online reviews/comments are positively correlated to customer satisfaction.

Customer Satisfaction and Repurchase Intention

Customer satisfaction measures the equivalent evaluation between pre- and postpurchase expectations (Chiu & Cho, 2021). Previously, Mao and Lyu (2017) described it as transforming expectations and desires into delights. Further, Siu et al. (2013) defined customers' positive intent and loyalty based on their satisfaction level. Han et al. (2020) defined that the continuing customer association of the firm is explained by customer satisfaction. A study (Agnihotri et al., 2022a) in the context of hospitality sector has suggested that if customers have delightful service experience with the firm as per their requirements and expectations, they become more content and are convinced to avail services from the same OTAs in the upcoming time. The service organizations have self-confessed the importance of retaining the existing customers as it is comparatively costlier to get new customers than retaining the old ones (Agnihotri et al., 2022b; Chaturvedi et al., 2022a). Similarly, repurchase intention is a positive predisposition toward a service-providing firm for availing the similar service in future (Hellier et al., 2003; Li, 2015). Such intentions are only possible, if customers had some meaningful previous experiences with the service provider (Haverila & Haverila, 2018). To be precise, repurchase intent can be measured as a result of customer enriched customer experience (Chiu & Cho, 2021; Han et al., 2020; Mao & Lyu, 2017). Earlier studies have also emphasized on the arbitrating role of customer satisfaction in influencing customers' future intentions (Garbarino & Johnson, 1999). Li (2015) highlighted that repurchase intentions depends on several factors such as past purchase experience, service resolution, and service value received by individuals. It is further assumed that customers who got a positive resolution from the service provider are more inclined toward repeating purchases from the same service provider (Bijmolt et al., 2014). Subsequently, satisfaction with positive disconfirmation leads to multiple behavioral results, which include intent to repurchase (Barnes et al., 2016) and to spread positive e-WOM (Molinari et al., 2008; Velazquez et al., 2015). A few recent studies have found that marketers often try to engage with those customers who got satisfied with their complaint handling efforts in order to increase their trust and advocacy toward the firm, which may further lead to repurchase (Han et al., 2020; Hewett et al., 2016; Majeed et al., 2022). Hence the estimated hypotheses will be:

> *H5:* Customer satisfaction significantly influences customers repurchases intention.

Research Methodology

Sample and Respondent Profile

In the current research work, the formulated hypotheses are empirically tested through a survey analysis. The respondents aimed for this study contained avid vacationers in India who had come across service failure experience followed by service recovery efforts by OTAs (Make my trip, Yatra.com, goibibo.com, hotels.com, and cleartrip.com) in the social media environment.

The sample was selected due to their ability to provide insights on complaint handling efforts as they have experienced such efforts from the service firm. Consequently, the study has used retrospective sampling technique as it gives flexibility to formulate hypotheses about the affiliation between output and experience (Jager et al., 2017). Therefore, participants were first requested to recall a complaint-handling experience with OTAs in the social media environment and respond to the questions on the basis of their previous experience. The retrospective sampling method was used by applying a convenience sampling technique because data were not available about the respondent to define particular customer (Sekaran & Bougie, 2013). In addition, convenience sampling is used due to its effectiveness to implement (Matikiti et al., 2019).

The data were collected in two stages. First, data were collected from the users on Facebook through UGC where dissatisfied customers were raising issues on Facebook after service failure. Facebook messenger to share the questionnaire with these active users. The questionnaire was sent along with a personal message to each targeted user. Second, data collection was done through the shopping mall intercept method. This method includes approaching respondents randomly in a shopping mall and briefing them about the purpose of the study and collecting responses after getting confirmation to participate (Bruwer, 1996). The flexibility and resourcefulness of this method makes it more suitable for the study (Bruwer, 1996). Therefore, 326 shoppers from shopping malls were finalized for the study who were regular and active on Facebook and shared issues or grievances on the social media pages of OTAs. The data were collected during the autumn and winter season (September 2021–December 2021). In total, 625 questionnaires were distributed among participants (physically and digitally). After excluding incomplete questionnaire, 497 responses were analyzed. Based on the previous studies, a sample consisting more than 300 responses is suitable to perform factor analysis (Hair et al., 2015). Hence, the sample size of 497 seems suitable for further analysis.

Measures

The development of appropriate measurements has been facilitated by an inclusive theoretical framework. Total seven constructs were analyzed in this study: empathy, responsiveness, paraphrasing, apology, customer satisfaction, and repurchase intention. Research constructs were measured using previously validated multiitem scales. However, these were rephrased based on the context of the current study. Four items scale was used to measure apology (Radu et al., 2019). Furthermore, the three items scale was used to measure responsiveness (Hocutt et al., 2006). Further, three items scale was used to measure empathy (Homburg & Stock, 2005). Similarly, three items scale was used to measure customer satisfaction (Westbrook & Oliver, 1981). Also, three items scale was used to measure repurchase intention (Maxham & Netemeyer, 2003). Finally, three items scale was used to measure paraphrasing.

Further, an exploratory factor analysis (EFA), a reliability assessment, and a confirmatory factor analysis (CFA) were also conducted. Using a seven-point Likert scale, the participants were asked to rate 19 items on a scale consisting responses that ranged from "strongly disagreed" to "strongly agreed." (Abney et al., 2017). In addition, conceptualized framework was examined by conducting the structural equation modeling.

Data Analysis

Measurement Model

Few scales were developed based on preceding studies, specialists' opinions, and focus interviews with avid social media users. A pretest was conducted using a shopping mall intercept method to assess the reliability and validity of the adapted scale items along with developed scale items. A total of 214 participants were selected for pretest. The outcome of this test showed that all scales are reliable ($\alpha > 0.70$; Yong & Pearce, 2013). Using SPSS 22, maximum likelihood with rotation was used for EFA. Further, the outcome of this analysis showed strong correlation between items and their respective construct (>0.70). There were seven factors for the study: apology, empathy, paraphrasing, responsiveness, customer satisfaction, and repurchase intention from 19 items (one item dropped due to cross-loading). Further, we have used CFA to measure the reliability and validity of all the scales. We have found that conceptualized model is a good fit through CFA results. Table 3.1 represents the outcome of measurement model and all the analyzed values fall within the standard criteria (Hair et al., 2013; Hu & Bentler, 1999). The values are as follows, CMIN/DF is 2.280, GFI is 0.914, NFI is 0.909, CFI is 0.947, TLI is 0.940, and RMSEA is 0.051. As per prior studies (Chaturvedi et al., 2020; Fornell & Larcker, 1981; Schumacker & Lomax, 2010), we calculated AVE to examine the discriminant validity. The values of AVE calculated for each construct (refer to Tables 3.2 and 3.3) are above 0.5, which provides sufficient evidence for discriminant validity. Overall, the results specify good model fit through convergent validity, values of AVE, and significant loading (Hair et al., 2015). Tables 3.1, 3.2, and 3.3 show the results of the CFA and reliability analysis.

Table 3.1. Measurement Model.

Fit Indices	Recommended Value	Studies	Calculated Value
χ^2/df	<3	Marsh et al. (2004)	2.280
GFI	>0.90	Hair et al. (2015)	0.914
TLI	>0.90	Awang (2012)	0.940
CFI	>0.90	Awang (2012)	0.947
NFI	>0.90	Arifin and Yusoff (2016)	0.909
RMSEA	<0.08	Brown and Cudeck (1993)	0.051

Table 3.2. AVE, ASV, MSV, and Cronbach's Alphas.

Items	Factors	Standard Factors Loading	Cronbach's Alpha/AVE
Apology			
Service provider gave acknowledgment that mistake has been made	Radu et al. (2019)	0.826	α = 0.776, AVE = 0.552
Service provider expressed acceptance of responsibility		0.735	
Service provider showed expression of remorse		0.699	
Service provider offered a recovery		0.705	
Responsiveness			
Service provider quickly acknowledged the service failure	Hocutt et al. (2006)	0.837	α = 0.845 AVE = 0.664
Service provider's response was quick after service failure		0.763	
Service provider remained responsive throughout the process of complaint resolution		0.809	
Empathy			
Service provider exhibited consideration for my state	Homburg and Stock (2005)	0.851	α = 0.853 AVE = 0.660
Put themselves into my situation		0.777	
Put in efforts to understand me		0.807	
(Developed)			
Solutions were explained and articulated in an easy way		0.888	α = 0.884 AVE = 0.773
The language used was simple		0.846	
The language was easy to understand		0.808	

Table 3.2. *(Continued)*

	Customer Satisfaction		
I am happy with the service received throughout the process of complaint resolution	Westbrook and Oliver (1981)	0.805	α = 0.882 AVE = 0.713
The service offered addressed my needs appropriately		0.837	
I am pleased with the solution provided for the issue I faced		0.889	

	Repurchase Intention		
I will keep on buying services from the particular service firm only	Maxham and Netemeyer (2003)	0.891	α = 0.829, AVE = 0.621
Next time when I need services there is a high possibility that I will select the same service provider		0.776	
I am willing to make more purchases in future with this service provider		0.683	

Hypotheses Testing and Results of the Structural Model

The structural equation modeling tool is used in this study as it overcomes the gaps of bivariate analysis by analyzing cause-and-effect relationships between independent and dependent variables (Hair et al., 2015). Please refer to Fig. 3.2 for an illustration of this relationship. In the structural model, empathy, responsiveness, apology, and paraphrasing are independent and satisfaction is a dependent variable. Also, we have used the commonly referred fit indices to examine the model fit for the conceptualized model (Agnihotri et al., 2023a). The values of all the fit indices (Chi-square = 374.370; degree of freedom = 147; χ^2/df is 2.547) falls within the acceptable criteria as per the suggestions of preceding studies. Similarly, the values of CFI, GFI, NFI, and TLI are 0.949, 0.922, 0.919, 0.940, respectively (Refer Table 3.3), which fulfill the required criteria of values >0.90 (Hair et al., 2015). Further, the value of RMSEA indicates good fit as it falls within the suggested value (0.056 < 0.08).

Table 3.3. AVE: Construct Validity.

	CR	AVE	MSV	ASV	S	A	R	P	E	FR	RP
Satisfaction (S)	0.882	0.713	0.036	0.021	0.844						
Apology (A)	0.831	0.552	0.224	0.105	0.160	0.743					
Responsiveness (R)	0.845	0.646	0.144	0.060	-0.014	0.379	0.804				
Paraphrasing (P)	0.885	0.719	0.224	0.070	0.062	0.473	0.264	0.848			
Empathy (E)	0.853	0.660	0.063	0.039	0.189	0.231	0.233	0.167	0.812		
RP	0.829	0.621	0.027	0.006	0.164	0.001	0.049	-0.052	-0.012	-0.035	0.788

Fig. 3.2.   Structural Model Results.

To assess the framed hypotheses, path coefficients were calculated (see Table 3.4). A standardized coefficient analysis revealed that the path between each construct fits the (Hair et al., 2015) standard values ($p < 0.005$ for all instances). Based on the results, empathy moderately affects customer satisfaction, as empathy and customer satisfaction have a positive relationship (*H1: β* = 0.176, $t = 2.876$, $p = 0.004 < 0.005$). Radu et al. (2019) reinforce this output by stating that empathy shown by the service provider during compliant handling increases customer satisfaction. Further, the outcomes of the current study are similar to the previous study of Sugathan et al. (2018) as empathy is considered as an important element for productive communications between customer and firm that generally lead to philanthropic spur and pro-social behavior. Furthermore, responsiveness also has a significant association with the customer satisfaction (*H2: β* = 0.169, $t = 3.039$, $p = 0.002 < 0.005$). The findings are aligned with the findings of Lacey (2007) and Chalmers (2016). Henceforth, responsiveness proved a moderate driver toward an increase in customer satisfaction. In addition, an apology for a negative online review positively influences customer satisfaction as an apology increases customer satisfaction (*H3: β* = 0.499, $t = 6.132, p = 0.00 <$ 0.005). The results are in line with the findings of the study by Radu et al. (2019).

Table 3.4. Path Model Results.

Fit Indices	Recommended Value	Studies	Calculated Value
χ^2/df	<3	Marsh et al. (2004)	2.547
GFI	>0.90	Hair et al. (2015)	0.922
TLI	>0.90	Awang (2012)	0.940
CFI	>0.90	Awang (2012)	0.949
NFI	>0.90	Arifin and Yusoff (2016)	0.919
RMSEA	<0.08	Brown and Cudeck (1993)	0.056

Table 3.5. Hypothesis Testing.

Conceptualized Path	Standardized Estimates	Critical Ratio	P Value	Hypotheses Supported
H1 Empathy-CS	0.176	**2.876**	0.004	Supported
H2 Responsiveness-CS	0.169	**3.039**	0.002	Supported
H3 Apology-CS	0.499	**6.132**	0.000	Supported
H4 Paraphrasing-CS	0.175	**3.123**	0.002	Supported
H5 CS-Repurchase Intention	0.154	**3.637**	0.000	Supported

CS* = Customer Satisfaction.

Subsequently, paraphrasing and customer satisfaction are positively associated. The previous study reinforces the current output by explaining that customers' trust and satisfaction could be increased by the way complaints are handled through customized responses instead of prewritten scripts (Sugathan et al., 2018). Hence, output appears appropriate with past studies in the social media context (*H4:* β = 0.175, t = 3.123, p = 0.002 < 0.005). Furthermore, the findings demonstrate that customer satisfaction is substantially affiliated with customers repurchase intention (*H5:* β = 0.154, t = 3.637, p = 0.000 < 0.005). The results of current study are aligned with the previous studies, which have significantly contributed in the context of complaint and negative e-WOM handling (Bijmolt et al., 2014; Chaturvedi et al., 2022b). These findings entail new dimensions of research regarding consumer–OTAs' interface in social media on handling complaint and negative e-WOM effectively along with examining the effect of these developed adaptive strategies (empathy, responsiveness, apology, paraphrasing) on customer attributes (see Table 3.5).

Managerial Implications

Customer satisfaction is always considered as a keen domain of interest for service providers for decades (Kim et al., 2018). Therefore, service providers give their best efforts to increase the satisfaction of customers, which may have an impact on their repurchase intention, advocacy, and customer loyalty. In addition, these loyalty behaviors include intensification in repetition purchases, a diminution of insensitivity toward price, a reduction in costs, an upsurge in positive WOM communications, and tolerance of in-service failure (Agnihotri et al., 2022b; Naeem, 2020; Prasad et al., 2017). However, service failures are inevitable, where human engrossment is more and service manufacturing and ingestion are concurrent (Sugathan et al., 2018). Henceforth, service firms must absorb to respond and resolve service failures to increase customer satisfaction. It is only possible if organizations implement adequate complaint-handling strategies to reach higher levels of customer satisfaction. The market is highly volatile and dynamic in the contemporary environment and it has become a huge challenge for organizations to retain existing customers especially due to the development of social media. More than 80% of Fortune five hundred companies are having an online presence and deal with customers on the same platform to solve customers' queries (Abney et al., 2017). Gellman (2014) advocated that the complaint behavior on social media has reproduced a unique industry, encompassing organizations steadfast to crisis management. Social media has created a scenario where customers can interact with service providers at ease without any hesitation.

The study has put in genuine efforts to investigate the ways an organization can efficiently interact with their customers using different prominent social media platforms like Facebook, Instagram, and Twitter in the context of complaint handling. As one of the examples of one of the leading OTAs in India, one participant recalled an incident with one of the leading OTAs, where the participant canceled the flight tickets due to some urgency but there was no sign of a refund from the OTA. Hence, the respondent complained and it stated, "I have been waiting to hear from you forever despite providing details through DM," but there was no response from the OTA. It might be more time-consuming and expensive for the firm to respond in a customized and adaptive way, but consumers distinguish and appraise the efforts made by the organizations, which did not happen in the above case. There are several incidents shared by participants during the survey and several shreds of evidence on the official social media pages of OTAs, where there is no response or a flat response without empathy and apology. Hence, the managers/OTAs must understand the customers' issues and complaints with responsiveness, empathy, or unconditioned apology. Therefore, the current study suggests that OTAs must put in their best efforts by being apologetic, empathetic, enduring, and responsive to minimize customers' annoyance after a service failure and to ensure better customer retention (Gao et al., 2022; Wang et al., 2014). Furthermore, the organization must focus on empowering its employees too as employees' motivation has a significant impact on their performance (Ravazzani & Hazée, 2022). Responsibility and authority motivate employees to make decisions quickly and it further ensures swift procedures as per the customer's needs. Subsequently, the organizations must develop training practices and endeavor to strategize schedules to reply modestly to any negative emotion toward service failure. The organizations must provide training on language skills where employees can be proficient in different regional languages as many of the customers might not be comfortable in the English language. Primarily, OTAs must establish effective communication with customers through social media during the complaint-handling process and encourage them to raise the concerns and issues faced by them. This will enable them to know their customers in a better way to resolve their issues and complaints. Most importantly, the study recommends that customers can distinguish the dissimilarities between general efforts and adaptive efforts of handling customers' issues, and dissimilarities in handling negative e-WOM can influence satisfaction, repurchase intentions, etc. As a result of this study, firms can be better equipped to handle complaints when they encounter social media service failures and negative e-WOM, which contributes to establishing new domains for understanding how firms interact with customers.

Conclusion

Effective complaint handling on social media can significantly influence customer repurchase intention for OTAs. Social media has become a powerful tool for customers to voice their complaints and opinions about products and services, including those provided by OTAs. Therefore, a well-handled complaint on social media can have a positive impact on customer loyalty and repurchase intention.

The findings of the study have identified that different dimensions of complaint handling like empathy, responsiveness, paraphrasing, and apology significantly influence customer satisfaction. The study has put in genuine efforts to investigate the ways a service-providing firm can efficiently interact with their customers using prominent social media platforms like Facebook and Instagram in the context of complaint handling. The findings of the study support the belief that customers understand a constructive variance in personalized responses against other less modified responses may benefit organizations to decide the right allocation of social media resources. The findings further suggest that OTAs can transform the customers' negative experience to positive based on their personalized and customized interaction with them by using quick, empathetic, apologetic, and paraphrased responses.

The findings of the current study have shown that customers who receive a prompt and apologetic response to their complaint on social media are more likely to repurchase from the firm in the future. In contrast, customers who experience poor complaint handling or receive no response to their complaint on social media are more likely to switch to a competitor or post negative reviews about the service firm, which can tarnish the firm's credibility and discourage potential customers.

Therefore, it is essential for OTAs to have effective complaint handling procedures in place and to monitor and respond promptly, humbly in a customized manner to complaints on social media platforms. This can help build customer trust and loyalty, improve the service firm's brand value, and ultimately upsurge repurchase intention.

Future Research Directions and Limitations

The current study has a few limitations. First, the respondents were requested to reply based on their previous negative experience with the service-providing firm. Some respondents were unable to recollect the exact issues and recovery process as these happened long time back. The current study is aligned with empathy, apology, paraphrasing, and responsiveness on service firm employees to handle complaints on social media. However, future research can explore the use of artificial intelligence (AI) in customer service by investigating the impact of AI-driven complaint handling on customer satisfaction and repurchase intention. The vitality of the social media environment leads to another feasible prospect by investigating the influence of other Facebook users in the service recovery effort as collective feelings and inputs from noncustomers may affect complaint-handling efforts. Therefore, communication between Facebook users could affect the perceived severity of the service failure among themselves. Future research should explore enhancing customer experience in a better way by involving customers during complaint-handling procedures. In addition, it would be interesting to examine the impact of cultural differences on customers "expectations and responses on social media." Future studies may emphasize the impact of effective complaint handling on firm's reputation and brand value. Finally, the use of social media influencers as part of complaint handling would be interesting since they have a significant impact on customer perceptions and behaviors.

References

Abney, A., Pelletier, M., Ford, T., & Horky, A. (2017). #IHateYourBrand: Adaptive service recovery strategies on Twitter. *Journal of Services Marketing, 31*(3), 281–294.

Adams, J. (1965). Inequity in social exchange. *Advances in Experimental Social Psychology, 2*(1), 267–299.

Adil, M., Sadiq, M., Jebarajakirthy, C., Maseeh, H. I., Sangroya, D., & Bharti, K. (2022). Online service failure: Antecedents, moderators and consequences. *Journal of Service Theory and Practice, 32*(6), 797–842.

Agnihotri, D., Chaturvedi, P., Kulshreshtha, K., & Tripathi, V. (2023). Investigating the impact of authenticity of social media influencers on followers' purchase behavior: Mediating analysis of parasocial interaction on Instagram. *Asia Pacific Journal of Marketing and Logistics.* (ahead-of-print). https://doi.org/10.1108/APJML-07-2022-0598

Agnihotri, R., & Krush, M. T. (2015). Salesperson empathy, ethical behaviors, and sales performance: The moderating role of trust in one's manager. *Journal of Personal Selling and Sales Management, 35*(2), 164–174. https://doi.org/10.1080/08853134.2015.1010541

Agnihotri, D., Kulshreshtha, K., & Tripathi, V. (2022). Emergence of social media as new normal during COVID-19 pandemic: A study on innovative complaint handling procedures in the context of banking industry. *International Journal of Innovation Science, 14*(3/4), 405–427.

Agnihotri, D., Kulshreshtha, K., Tripathi, V., & Chaturvedi, P. (2023a). Does green self-identity influence the revisit intention of dissatisfied customers in green restaurants? *Management of Environmental Quality, 34*(2), 535–564. https://doi.org/10.1108/MEQ-03-2022-0076

Agnihotri, D., Kulshreshtha, K., Tripathi, V., & Chaturvedi, P. (2022b). "Actions speak louder than words": An impact of service recovery antecedents on customer delight in quick-service restaurants. *Asia-Pacific Journal of Business Administration, 14*(4), 421–444.

Aljarah, A., Sawaftah, D., Ibrahim, B., & Lahuerta-Otero, E. (2022). The differential impact of user- and firm-generated content on online brand advocacy: Customer engagement and brand familiarity matter. *European Journal of Innovation Management.* https://doi.org/10.1108/ejim-05-2022-0259

Arifin, W. N., & Yusoff, M. S. B. (2016). Confirmatory factor analysis of the Universiti Sains Malaysia emotional quotient inventory among medical students in Malaysia. *Sage Open, 6*(2), 1–9.

Awang, Z. (2012). *Structural equation modeling using AMOS graphics.* Penerbit University Teknologi MARA.

Bahadur, W., Aziz, S., & Zulfiqar, S. (2018). Effect of employee empathy on customer satisfaction and loyalty during employee–customer interactions: The mediating role of customer affective commitment and perceived service quality. *Cogent Business and Management, 5*(1), 1–21.

Barnes, D., Collier, J., Howe, V., & Douglas, K. (2016). Multiple paths to customer delight: The impact of effort, expertise and tangibles on joy and surprise. *Journal of Services Marketing, 30*(3), 277–289.

Bijmolt, T., Huizingh, E., & Krawczyk, A. (2014). Effects of complaint behavior and service recovery satisfaction on consumer intentions to repurchase on the internet. *Internet Research, 24*(5), 608–628.

Blodgett, J. G., Granboi, D. H., & Walters, R. G. (1993). The effects of perceived justice on negative word-of-mouth and patronage intentions. *Journal of Retailing, 69*(4), 399–428.

Blodgett, J. G., Hill, D. J., & Tax, S. S. (1997). The effects of distributive, procedural, and interactional justice on post complaint behavior. *Journal of Retailing, 73*(2), 85–210.

Brown, M., & Cudeck, R. (1993). *EQS structural equations program manual.* Multivariate Software Inc.

Bruwer, J. (1996). Marketing a higher educational institution through target market research on its freshmen applicant and enrollee pools. *South African Journal of Higher Education, 10*(2), 120–129.

Cakici, A. C., Akgunduz, Y., & Yildirim, O. (2019). The impact of perceived price justice and satisfaction on loyalty: The mediating effect of revisit intention. *Tourism Review, 74*(3), 443–462.

Chalmers, S. (2016). Ethical fairness in financial services complaint handling. *International Journal of Bank Marketing, 34*(4), 570–586.

Chaturvedi, P., Kulshreshtha, K., & Tripathi, V. (2020). Investigating the determinants of behavioral intentions of generation Z for recycled clothing: An evidence from a developing economy. *Young Consumers, 21*(4), 403–417.

Chaturvedi, P., Kulshreshtha, K., Tripathi, V., & Agnihotri, D. (2022a). Investigating the impact of restaurants' sustainable practices on consumers' satisfaction and revisit intentions: A study on leading green restaurants. *Asia-Pacific Journal of Business Administration.* https://doi.org/10.1108/APJBA-09-2021-0456

Chaturvedi, P., Kulshreshtha, K., Tripathi, V., & Agnihotri, D. (2022b). Exploring consumers' motives for electric vehicle adoption: Bridging the attitude–behavior gap. *Benchmarking: An International Journal.* (ahead-of-print). https://doi.org/10.1108/BIJ-10-2021-0618

Chen, T., Guo, W., Gao, X., & Liang, Z. (2021). AI-based self-service technology in public service delivery: User experience and influencing factors. *Government Information Quarterly, 38*(4), 101520.

Cheng, B., Gan, C., Imrie, B., & Mansori, S. (2019). Service recovery, customer satisfaction and customer loyalty: Evidence from Malaysia's hotel industry. *International Journal of Quality and Service Sciences, 11*(2), 187–203.

Chennattuserry, J. C., Varghese, B., Elangovan, N., & Sandhya, H. (2022). Pandemic recovery strategies: A disaster management tourism framework. In M. E. Korstanje, H. Seraphin, & S. W. Maingi (Eds.), *Tourism through troubled times (Tourism security-safety and post conflict destinations)* (pp. 133–149). Emerald Publishing Limited.

Chiu, W., & Cho, H. (2021). E-commerce brand: The effect of perceived brand leadership on consumers' satisfaction and repurchase intention on e-commerce websites. *Asia Pacific Journal of Marketing and Logistics, 33*(6), 1339–1362.

Cooper, T., Stavros, C., & Dobele, A. (2019). Domains of influence: Exploring negative sentiment in social media. *The Journal of Product and Brand Management, 28*(5), 684–699.

Daniels, K., Glover, J., & Mellor, N. (2014). An experience sampling study of expressing affect, daily affective well-being, relationship quality, and perceived performance. *Journal of Occupational and Organizational Psychology, 87*(4), 781–805.

Desai, P. H., & De Souza, M. F. (2015). Severity and controllability of service failures as perceived by passengers in airline industry. *Turkish Economic Review, 2*(3), 186–195.

Dickinger, A., & Bauernfeind, U. (2009). An analysis of corporate e-mail communication as part of airlines' service recovery strategy. *Journal of Travel & Tourism Marketing, 26*(2), 156–168.

Einwiller, S., & Steilen, S. (2015). Handling complaints on social network sites – An analysis of complaints and complaint responses on Facebook and Twitter pages of large US companies. *Public Relations Review, 41*(2), 195–204.

Fan, Y., & Niu, R. (2016). To tweet or not to tweet? Exploring the effectiveness of service recovery strategies using social media. *International Journal of Operations & Production Management, 36*(9), 1014–1036.

Fornell, C., & Larcker, D. F. (1981). Structural equation models with unobservable variables and measurement error: Algebra and statistics. *Journal of Marketing Research, 18*(3), 382–388.

Gao, J., Yao, L., Xiao, X., & Li, P. (2022). Recover from failure: Examining the impact of service recovery stages on relationship marketing strategies. *Frontiers in Psychology, 13*.

Garbarino, E., & Johnson, M. (1999). The different roles of satisfaction, trust, and commitment in customer relationships. *Journal of Marketing, 63*(2), 70–87.

Gellman, R. (2014). Fair information practices: A basic history. *SSRN Electronic Journal* [Preprint]. https://doi.org/10.2139/ssrn.2415020

Ghorbanzadeh, D., Zakieva, R. R., Kuznetsova, M., Ismael, A. M., & Ahmed, A. A. A. (2022). Generating destination brand awareness and image through the firm's social media. *Kybernetes*. https://doi.org/10.1108/K-09-2021-0931

Hair, J. F., Ringle, C. M., & Sarstedt, M. (2013). Partial least squares structural equation modeling: Rigorous applications, better results and higher acceptance. *Long Range Planning, 46*(1–2), 1–12.

Hair, F. H., William, C. B., Barry, J. B., & Anderson, R. E. (2015). *Multivariate data analysis*. Pearson India.

Harris, K. L., Thomas, L., & Williams, J. A. (2013). Justice for consumers complaining online or offline: Exploring procedural, distributive and interactional justice and the issue of anonymity. *Journal of Consumer Satisfaction, Dissatisfaction and Complaining Behavior, 1*(1), 2619–2639.

Haverila, M., & Haverila, K. (2018). Examination of customer-centric measures among different types of customers in the context of major Canadian ski resort. *Asia Pacific Journal of Marketing and Logistics, 30*(2), 438–459.

Hellier, P., Geursen, G., Carr, R. A., & Rickard, J. A. (2003). Customer repurchase intention: A general structural equation model. *European Journal of Marketing, 37*(11/12), 1762–1800.

Hennig-Thurau, T., Malthouse, E., Friege, C., Gensler, S., Lobschat, L., Rangaswamy, A., & Skiera, B. (2010). The impact of new media on customer relationships. *Journal of Service Research, 13*(3), 311–330.

Hennig-Thurau, T., & Thurau, C. (2003). Customer orientation of service employees—Toward a conceptual framework of a key relationship marketing construct. *Journal of Relationship Marketing, 2*(1–2), 23–41.

Hewett, K., Rand, W., Rust, R. T., & Heerde, H. J. (2016). Brand buzz in the echoverse. *Journal of Marketing, 80*(3), 1–24.

Hocutt, M. A., Bowers, M. R., & Todd Donavan, D. (2006). The art of service recovery: Fact or fiction? *Journal of Services Marketing, 20*(3), 199–207.

Holloway, B. B., & Beatty, S. E. (2003). Service failure in online retailing a recovery opportunity. *Journal of Service Research, 6*(1), 92–105.

Homburg, C., & Stock, R. (2005). Exploring the conditions under which salesperson work satisfaction can lead to customer satisfaction. *Psychology and Marketing, 2*(5), 393–420.

Hu, L. T., & Bentler, P. M. (1999). Cutoff criteria for fit indexes in covariance structure analysis: Conventional criteria versus new alternatives. *Structural Equation Modeling: A Multidisciplinary Journal, 6*(1), 1–55.

Hussein, R., & Hassan, S. (2017). Customer engagement on social media: How to enhance continuation of use. *Online Information Review, 41*(7), 1006–1028.

Inversini, A., & Masiero, L. (2014). Selling rooms online: The use of social media and online travel agencies. *International Journal of Contemporary Hospitality Management, 26*(2), 272–292.

Itani, O. S., & Inyang, A. E. (2015). The effects of empathy and listening of salespeople on relationship quality in the retail banking industry. *International Journal of Bank Marketing, 33*(6), 692–716. https://doi.org/10.1108/ijbm-06-2014-0076

Jacobs, S., & Liebrecht, C. (2022). Responding to online complaints in webcare by public organizations: The impact on continuance intention and reputation. *Journal of Communication Management, 27*(1), 1–20. https://doi.org/10.1108/JCOM-11-2021-0132

Jager, J., Putnick, D. L., & Bornstein, M. H. (2017). More than just convenient: The scientific merits of homogeneous convenience samples. *Monographs of the Society for Research in Child Development, 82*(2), 13–30.

Jain, N., Kamboj, S., Kumar, V., & Rahman, Z. (2018). Examining consumer-brand relationships on social media platforms. *Marketing Intelligence & Planning, 36*(1), 63–78.

Jeong, M., & Lee, S. A. (2017). Do customers care about types of hotel service recovery efforts? An example of consumer-generated review sites. *Journal of Hospitality and Tourism Technology, 8*(1), 5–18.

Jin, S., & Phua, J. (2014). Following celebrities' tweets about brands: The impact of Twitter-based electronic word-of-mouth on consumers' source credibility perception, buying intention, and social identification with celebrities. *Journal of Advertising, 43*(2), 181–195.

Jones, J., & Shandiz, M. (2015). Service quality expectations: Exploring the importance of SERVQUAL dimensions from different nonprofit constituent groups. *Journal of Nonprofit and Public Sector Marketing, 27*(1), 48–69.

Karande, K., Magnini, V., & Tam, L. (2007). Recovery voice and satisfaction after service failure. *Journal of Service Research, 10*(2), 187–203.

Kim, M., Shin, D., & Koo, D. (2018). The influence of perceived service fairness on brand trust, brand experience and brand citizenship behavior. *International Journal of Contemporary Hospitality Management, 30*(7), 2603–2621.

Koc, E. (2017). Book review. *Tourism Management, 61*, 261–262.

Kotler, P., Kartajaya, H., & Setiawan, I. (2016). *Marketing 4.0: Moving from traditional to digital.* John Wiley & Sons.

Kumar, A., & Kaur, A. (2020). Complaint management-review and additional insights. *International Journal of Scientific & Technology Research, 9*(02), 1501–1509.

Lacey, R. (2007). Relationship drivers of customer commitment. *The Journal of Marketing Theory and Practice, 15*(4), 315–333.

Lau, G. T., & Ng, S. (2001). Individual and situational factors influencing negative word of mouth behavior. *Revue Canadienne des Sciences de 1 'Administration, 18*(3), 163–178.

Li, C. (2015). Switching barriers and customer retention: Why customers dissatisfied with online service recovery remain loyal. *Journal of Service Theory and Practice, 25*(4), 370–393.

Lin, J. S. C., & Lin, C. Y. (2011). What makes service employees and customers smile antecedents and consequences of the employees' affective delivery in the service encounter. *Journal of Service Management, 22*(2), 183–201.

Lin, S., Yang, S., Ma, M., & Huang, J. (2018). Value co-creation on social media: Examining the relationship between brand engagement and display advertising effectiveness for Chinese hotels. *International Journal of Contemporary Hospitality Management, 30*(4), 2153–2174.

Maecker, O., Barrot, C., & Becker, J. U. (2016). The effect of social media interactions on customer relationship management. *Business Research, 9*, 133–155.

Majeed, M., Asare, C., Fatawu, A., & Abubakari, A. (2022). An analysis of the effects of customer satisfaction and engagement on social media on repurchase intention in the hospitality industry. *Cogent Business & Management, 9*(1), 2028331.

Malthouse, E. C., Haenlein, M., Skiera, B., Wege, E., & Zhang, M. (2013). Managing customer relationships in the social media era: Introducing the social CRM house. *Journal of Interactive Marketing, 27*(4), 270–280.

Mao, Z., & Lyu, J. (2017). Why travelers use Airbnb again? An integrative approach to understanding travelers' repurchase intention. *International Journal of Contemporary Hospitality Management, 29*(9), 2464–2482.

Marsh, H. W., Hau, K. T., & Wen, Z. (2004). In search of golden rules: Comment on hypothesis-testing approaches to setting cut-off values for fit indexes and dangers in overgeneralizing Hu and Bentler's (1999) findings. *Structural Equation Modeling, 11*(3), 320–341.

Mason, A. N., Narcum, J., & Mason, K. (2021). Social media marketing gains importance after Covid-19. *Cogent Business & Management, 8*(1), 1870797.

Markovic, S., Iglesias, O., Singh, J. J., & Sierra, V. (2018). How does the perceived ethicality of corporate services brands influence loyalty and positive word-of-mouth? Analyzing the roles of empathy, affective commitment, and perceived quality. *Journal of Business Ethics, 148*, 721–740.

Matikiti, R., Roberts-Lombard, M., & Mpinganjira, M. (2019). Customer attributions of service failure and its impact on commitment in the airline industry: An emerging market perspective. *Journal of Travel and Tourism Marketing, 36*(4), 403–414.

Mattila, A. (2001). The effectiveness of service recovery in a multi-industry setting. *Journal of Service Marketing, 15*(7), 583–596.

Mattila, A., & Mount, D. (2003). The impact of selected customer characteristics and response time on e-complaint satisfaction and return intent. *International Journal of Hospitality Management, 22*(2), 135–145.

Maxham, J. G., III, & Netemeyer, R. G. (2003). Firms reap what they sow: The effects of shared values and perceived organizational justice on customers' evaluations of complaint handling. *Journal of Marketing, 67*(1), 46–62.

Molinari, L. K., Abratt, R., & Dion, P. (2008). Satisfaction, quality and value and effects on repurchase and positive word-of-mouth behavioral intentions in a B2B service context. *Journal of Services Marketing, 22*(5), 363–373.

Naeem, M. (2020). Developing the antecedents of social influence for Internet banking adoption through social networking platforms: Evidence from conventional and Islamic banks. *Asia Pacific Journal of Marketing and Logistics, 33*(1), 185–204. https://doi.org/10.1108/APJML-07-2019-0467

Narteh, B. (2016). Service fairness and customer behavioral intention: Evidence from the Ghanaian banking industry. *African Journal of Economic and Management Studies, 7*(1), 90–108.

Park, S., Lee, J. S., & Nicolau, J. L. (2020). Understanding the dynamics of the quality of airline service attributes: Satisfiers and dissatisfiers. *Tourism Management, 81*, 104163.

Peters, K., Chen, Y., Kaplan, A. M., Ognibeni, B., & Pauwels, K. (2013). Social media metrics—A framework and guidelines for managing social media. *Journal of Interactive Marketing, 27*(4), 81–98.

Prasad, S., Gupta, I., & Totala, N. (2017). Social media usage, electronic word of mouth and purchase decision involvement. *Asia-Pacific Journal of Business Administration, 9*(2), 134–145.

Pinto, M. B., & Mansfield, P. (2011). Facebook as a complaint mechanism: An investigation of millennial. *Journal of Behavioral Studies in Business, 4*(1), 1–12.

Prasongsukarn, K., & Patterson, P. G. (2012). An extended service recovery model: The moderating impact of temporal sequence of events. *Journal of Services Marketing, 26*(7), 510–520.

Radu, A., Arli, D., Surachartkumtonkun, J., Weaven, S., & Wright, O. (2019). Empathy and apology: The effectiveness of recovery strategies. *Marketing Intelligence & Planning, 37*(4), 358–371.

Rashid, Y., Waseem, A., Akbar, A., & Azam, F. (2019). Value co-creation and social media: A systematic literature review using citation and thematic analysis. *European Business Review, 31*(5), 761–784.

Ravazzani, S., & Hazée, S. (2022). Value co-creation through social media: A multistakeholder, communication perspective. *Journal of Service Management, 33*(4/5), 589–600.

Roschk, H., Muller, J., & Gelbrich, K. (2013). Age matters: How developmental stages of adulthood affect customer reaction to complaint handling efforts. *Journal of Retailing and Consumer Services, 20*(2), 154–164.

Sahin, I., Gulmez, M., & Kitapci, O. (2017). E-complaint tracking and online problem-solving strategies in hospitality management: Plumbing the depths of reviews and responses on TripAdvisor. *Journal of Hospitality and Tourism Technology, 8*(3), 372–394.

Sashi, C., Brynildsen, G., & Bilgihan, A. (2019). Social media, customer engagement and advocacy: An empirical investigation using Twitter data for quick service restaurants. *International Journal of Contemporary Hospitality Management, 31*(3), 1247–1272.

Schaefers, T., & Schamari, J. (2015). Service recovery via social media. *Journal of Service Research, 19*(2), 192–208.

Schoefer, K., & Ennew, C. (2005). The impact of perceived justice on consumers' emotional responses to service complaint experiences. *Journal of Services Marketing, 19*(5), 261–270.

Schumacker, R. E., & Lomax, R. G. (2010). *A beginner's guide to structural equation modeling* (3rd ed.). Psychology Press, Routledge/Taylor and Francis Group.

Sekaran, U., & Bougie, R. (2013). *Research methods for business* (6th ed.). John Wiley and Sons.

Singh, J., & Crisafulli, B. (2016). Managing online service recovery: Procedures, justice and customer satisfaction. *Journal of Service Theory and Practice, 26*(6), 764–787.

Siu, N. Y.-M., Zhang, T. J.-F., & Yau, C.-Y. J. (2013). The roles of justice and customer satisfaction in customer retention: A lesson from service recovery. *Journal of Business Ethics, 114*(1), 675–686.

Soares, R., Zhang, T., Proença, J., & Kandampully, J. (2017). Why are generation Y consumers the most likely to complain and repurchase? *Journal of Service Management, 28*(3), 520–540.

Sparks, B. A., & Browning, V. (2010). Complaining in cyberspace: The motives and forms of hotel guests' complaints online. *Journal of Hospitality Marketing & Management, 19*(7), 797–818.

Sugathan, P., Rossmann, A., & Ranjan, K. (2018). Toward a conceptualization of perceived complaint handling quality in social media and traditional service channels. *European Journal of Marketing, 52*(5/6), 973–1006.

Tamwatin, U., Trimetsoontorn, J., & Fongsuwan, W. (2015). The effect of tangible and intangible service quality on customer satisfaction and customer loyalty: A SEM approach towards a five-star hotel in Thailand. *Journal of Global Business Advancement, 8*(4), 399–419.

Tang, X., Chang, E., Huang, X., & Zhang, M. (2018). Timing and compensation strategies in service recovery. *Journal of Services Marketing, 32*(6), 755–766.

Umasuthan, H., Park, O., & Ryu, J. (2017). Influence of empathy on hotel guests' emotional service experience. *Journal of Services Marketing, 31*(6), 618–635.

Velazquez, B., Blasco, M., & Gil Saura, I. (2015). ICT adoption in hotels and electronic word-of-mouth. *Academia Revista Latinoamericana de Administracion, 28*(2), 227–250.

Wang, K.-Y., Hsu, L.-C., & Chih, W.-H. (2014). Retaining customers after service failure recoveries: A contingency model. *Managing Service Quality, 24*(4), 318–338.

Weber, K., & Sparks, B. (2004). Consumer attributions and behavioral responses to service failures in strategic airline alliance settings. *Journal of Air Transport Management, 10*(5), 361–367.

Weiner, B. (2000). Intrapersonal and interpersonal theories of motivation from an attributional perspective. *Educational Psychology Review, 12*(1), 1–14.

Westbrook, R. A., & Oliver, R. L. (1981). *Developing better measures of consumer satisfaction: Some preliminary results.* Association for Consumer Research.

Xu, X., Liu, Z., Gong, S., & Wu, Y. (2022). The relationship between empathy and attachment in children and adolescents: Three-level meta-analyses. *International Journal of Environmental Research and Public Health, 19*(3), 1391.

Yang, M., Ren, Y., & Adomavicius, G. (2019). Understanding user-generated content and customer engagement on Facebook business pages. *Information Systems Research, 30*(3), 839–855.

Yong, A., & Pearce, S. (2013). A beginner's guide to factor analysis: Focusing on exploratory factor analysis. *Tutorials in Quantitative Methods for Psychology, 9*(2), 79–94.

Yoon, C. (2015). Research on distributed sensor device resource object collaboration service providing system based on service delivery platform. *Journal of the Institute of Electronics and Information Engineers, 52*(6), 144–150.

Zeelenberg, M., & Pieters, R. (2004). Beyond valence in customer dissatisfaction: A review and new findings on behavioral responses to regret and disappointment in failed services. *Journal of Business Research, 57*(4), 445–455.

Zeithaml, V. A. (1988). Consumer perceptions of price, quality, and value: A means-end model and synthesis of evidence. *Journal of Marketing, 52*(3), 2–22.

Zhang, Z., Li, H., Meng, F., & Li, Y. (2019). The effect of management response similarity on online hotel booking: Field evidence from Expedia. *International Journal of Contemporary Hospitality Management, 31*(7), 2739–2758.

Chapter 4

Antecedents of Healthy Lifestyle of Young Consumers: A Cross-Sectional Study of Sri Lanka

P. G. S. A. Jayarathne[a,b], Narayanage Jayantha Dewasiri[c] and K. S. S. N. Karunarathne[c]

[a]SLIIT Business School, Sri Lanka
[b]University of Sri Jayewardenepura, Sri Lanka
[c]Sabaragamuwa University of Sri Lanka, Sri Lanka

Abstract

Owing to the significance of a healthy lifestyle, we investigate the antecedents of the healthy lifestyle of young consumers in Sri Lanka. 658 structured questionnaires were collected from young consumers in Sri Lanka as part of the survey procedure. The judgmental sampling method is used to choose the respondents. The analysis makes use of both descriptive and inferential statistics. The findings disclose a high degree of healthy lifestyle among young consumers in Sri Lanka. Further findings revealed that health consciousness, collective esteem, and neighborhood environment are the antecedents for a healthy lifestyle. As young consumers are more concerned about a healthy lifestyle, managers in certain industries such as food and beverages, hotels, and restaurants should adopt their products and services in line with a healthy lifestyle.

Keywords: Collective esteem; healthy lifestyle; health consciousness; young consumers; Sri Lanka

Introduction

The idea of lifestyle is really important. There are a number of factors which could impact on its significance including the individual's lifestyle, buying habits, and what, where, and how frequently they buy things. These are crucial elements

Navigating the Digital Landscape, 65–84
Published under exclusive licence by Emerald Publishing Limited
doi:10.1108/978-1-83549-272-720241004

that help firms comprehend their clients. However, considering the significance of lifestyle and the setting of Asia, it is clear that people's way of life is constantly evolving.

Watson and Zibadi (2018) highlighted that "A healthy lifestyle consists of eating a healthy diet, doing regular physical activity (PA), and avoiding toxic habits such as smoking." As an illustration, the nation will have a population that is more productive and healthier, which in turn helps the nation grow. Certain sicknesses, namely, diabetes, obesity, etc., may also be controlled. A new customer segment may emerge in terms of healthy consumption (Jayasuriya, 2016). Owing to the significance of a healthy lifestyle, scholars' attention increased during 2010–2015 (Gadais et al., 2018). Jayasuriya (2016) and Rathnasiri (2021) highlighted the significance of a healthy lifestyle, while other studies have looked into ways to alter one's lifestyle in order to comply with the demands of a higher quality of health, for instance, Jacob et al. (2016) and Gadais et al. (2018).

Among Asian countries, Sri Lanka is in high demand for adopting healthy lifestyles, especially among young adults due to several reasons. Young adults range in age from 20 to 40 (Dewasiri et al., 2021; Rana et al., 2022). They matter to the entire globe, as UN Secretary-General Ban Ki-Moon correctly noted during his visit to Sri Lanka in September 2016 at the Role of Youth Development Conference as "Many of the goals focus on priority areas for young people: quality education, empowering women and girls, and ensuring decent work for all." He also refers to Sri Lanka as a substantial backer to promote the youth agenda world-wide. Thus, the future emphasizes that the lifestyle of young women and men should build up as an investment at the national level, as they represent the highest portion of the country's population (De Soysa & Lewin, 2018).

Compared to other age groups, young individuals need to lead healthier lifestyles. A person's young adult years are crucial for laying the psychological and physical foundations that will guide their behavior for the rest of their lives (Marques et al., 2019). Young people struggle to adopt habits that could reduce their chance of acquiring chronic diseases as adults, including healthy food, physical activity, and even giving up smoking (Taymoori et al., 2012). Unhealthy diets and physical inactivity are the main causes of obesity and overweight, which are major risk factors for many noncommunicable diseases in Sri Lanka (Al-Jawaldeh & Abbass, 2022).

A healthy lifestyle would be caused by some factors. Physical, sociocultural, political, and economic factors influence a healthy lifestyle (Gadais et al., 2018). Among them, physical and sociocultural factors are prominent. Thus, this study focuses on the same. Mainly, in western countries, health consciousness would be one of the reasons people strive toward a healthy lifestyle (Chen, 2011). A healthy lifestyle may also be influenced by the physical neighborhood environment of the individuals (Gadais et al., 2018; Sallis et al., 2010). People may also adopt a healthy lifestyle as a way of maintaining their social esteem (Gadais et al., 2018; Reblin & Uchino, 2008). Ardic and Esin (2016) state that some basic variables such as health perceptions, relationships with family and friends, gender, type of family, and parental educational level influence health behavior, while stating that culture significantly mater for young generations' health behavior.

Despite the importance of a healthy lifestyle for young adults in Asia, and its accelerated space of changes due to cosmopolitism, research focusing on the same, specifically in addressing the availability of healthy lifestyle, its changes due to demographic characteristics of the young adults, and antecedents of the healthy lifestyle in the Asian context is seldom. Physical neighborhood environment (Gadais et al., 2018; Sallis et al., 2010), collective self-esteem (Gadais et al., 2018; Reblin & Uchino, 2008), and health consciousness (Chen, 2011) are identified as influences on a healthy lifestyle, but there is a paucity of research conducted in Sri Lanka. Hence this study focuses on the respective gap in research. Accordingly, this study aimed to investigate the antecedents of a healthy lifestyle for young adults in Sri Lanka. Neighborhood environment, collective self-esteem, and health consciousness are investigated as antecedents in this context.

Literature Review

Lifestyle

Lifestyle is simply "how one lives," to put it simply. Contrarily, "lifestyle" in marketing depicts how individuals, small social groups, and large social groupings behave when functioning as potential customers (Katz, 2013). As a result, the concept of lifestyle denotes a group of concepts very dissimilar from those of personality. The lifestyle has to do with how much money individuals make and how they utilize the same (Anderson & Golden, 1984). The scholars have employed the notion of lifestyle on four different levels: the national, global, positional or subcultural, and the individual level (Jensen, 2007).

The attitude, routines, or belongings associated with an individual or group can also be referred to as a lifestyle. Depending on an individual's eating habits, amount of activity, and behavior, their lifestyle can be either healthy or unhealthy. Individual happiness can be attained by a positive way of life, whereas melancholy might result from a negative way of life (Jacob et al., 2016).

Lifestyles can include anything, from action (such as choosing, acquisition, use, and consumption) to behavioral dominions (like housing, employment, and transportation) to factors that affect behavior, which are all incredibly diverse (Heijs et al., 2009). Jensen (2007) states that the concept of lifestyle has numerous shapes where social researchers have used it as a way of living the life or want to live the life whereas others used it as the sum of health-related factors and consumption. Because the lifestyle approach includes traits such individualized patterns of values, intentions, and preferences, it serves as a supplement to traditional sociodemographic difference through this medium. Individualization and cultural independence, among other socioeconomic shifts, are the driving forces behind the lifestyle concept's current success (Bootsma, 1995). It is important to investigate on the concept of lifestyle since it is predominant to understand and analyze the sustainable development problems of an economy (Jensen, 2007).

Healthy Lifestyle

According to the World Health Organization (WHO), health is explained as "a complete state of mental, bodily, and social well-being, not only the absence of disease," as of 1946 (World Health Organisation [WHO], 1948). With the aid of the above definition and various other derived explanations, scholars define healthy lifestyle in different perspectives. Some have considered it as energy-balanced behavior whereas others considered it as additive behavior. Energy-balanced behavior refers to physical activities, sedentary behavior, and healthy diet (e.g. Alamian & Paradis, 2009), whereas addictive behavior refers to alcohol consumption, smoking, and sleeping habits (e.g. van Nieuwenhuijzen et al., 2009). Rodelli et al. (2018) refer health as the collection of both aspects such as diet, sleep, physical activity, and absence of addictive behaviors. Gil et al. (2000) stated that healthy lifestyle is a combination of three basic subdimensions namely: "natural food consumption, life equilibrium, and health care." Nevertheless, prior researchers utilized food, physical activities, and alcohol behaviors as the aspects of a healthy lifestyle too (Giles & Brennan, 2015).

Individual behaviors and lifestyle decisions can effect health and enhance quality of life as stated by Kaplan (1991). Sadiq et al. (2019) explained that healthy lifestyle features can vary with the age category of the individuals. Further, Divine and Lepisto (2005) reveal that age appears as the predominant antecedent of a healthy lifestyle over the other demographic variables like gender education, etc., and individuals who maintain greater levels of healthy lifestyles are older. As they journey from infancy to adulthood, young people form behavioral patterns and make lifestyle decisions that could influence on both their current and future health (Sawyer et al., 2012). Compared to adults, younger adults are excessively affected by serious health and safety issues, examples include injuries, violence, and sexual behavior (Blum & Nelson-Mmari, 2004). They have a lower perception of a healthy lifestyle compared to the older generation (Arroyo et al., 2021). The healthy lifestyle of young adults is critical compared to that of other age groups. Young adulthood is a crucial period to create the foundations for an individual's health that will lead the behavioral practices during the rest of the time of their lives (Marques et al., 2019). Aside, a healthy lifestyle for young adults is critical in maintaining the strong and active labor force of an economy. However, Giles and Brennan (2015) indicate that they do not tend to engage in healthy lifestyles due to the fact that the cost and competitive forces are higher than the perceived benefits of adapting to such a lifestyle. The cornerstones of maintaining good health include a healthy diet, regular exercise, and enough sleep. Positive stress management lessens hormonal deterioration and wear-and-tear on the body. According to Gandhi et al. (2019), a healthy lifestyle has an impact on mental health in South India. Therefore, for a longer and more comfortable life, a healthy lifestyle is paramount. There are some aspects of a healthy lifestyle as given below.

• Eating Habits for a Healthy Lifestyle

The growth of cells and metabolism depend on an individual's cardiovascular, musculoskeletal, immunological, and other body systems receiving a steady supply of nutrients. A diversified diet is necessary to consume several vital forms of protein, vitamins, carbs, fats, and minerals. In order to manage weight and lower the risk of cardiovascular and other ailments, one must also be aware that portion control during meals is crucial (Sogari et al., 2018). This behavior can only be incorporated into a healthy lifestyle.

• Exercise Habits for a Healthy Lifestyle

If one does not burn off all of the calories that are included in meals, weight gain will eventually result. The chance of causing heart attacks, diabetes, and conceivably cancer rises when someone carry an extra weight. It is essential to stay active every day in order to maintain a permanent healthy weight. The US Department of Health and Human Services established the Physical Fitness Guidelines for Americans, which placed an emphasis on muscle-strengthening exercises like weight lifting and cardiovascular exercise like walking or jogging. It recommends aiming for 15 hours of exercise per week, but inactive persons should gradually increase this amount under the guidance of their doctor. Yoga is one of several workouts that can enhance flexibility and mobility for a pleasant daily life (Cobb-Clark et al., 2014).

• Sleep Habits for a Healthy Lifestyle

Cellular decay and renewal are delayed by daily metabolism, and the body repairs itself while you sleep. During this period of decreased physical activity, memory consolidation and appetite management take place. According to the National Sleep Foundation, a healthy lifestyle requires seven to nine hours of sleep per night (Kilani et al., 2013).

• Stress Reduction for a Healthy Lifestyle

The body of a person reacts to everyday stress by releasing hormones that prime the body for action. Muscular pain, migraines, sleep difficulties, and a host of other symptoms can develop if he or she does not relieve this state through relaxation. This cycle is broken by leading a stress-reduction-focused lifestyle before it reaches unhealthy levels.

Some of the activities that cut into free time are suggested to be reduced by the US Department of Health and Human Services. Achieving a release of stress through stretching, massages, yoga, and enjoyable exercise are all common methods which can be implemented. While other methods can include connecting with friends and family, taking time out to read, pursuing a hobby, or experiencing activities that make you feel good (Badger et al., 2019). Further,

Hacihasanoglu et al. (2011) state six important areas, namely, "self-actualization, health responsibility, physical activity, nutrition, interpersonal relations, and stress management" as aspects of a healthy lifestyle accordingly to the HPLP scale. They claim that a healthy lifestyle is reflected in the means of these six areas.

For this research, the author has chosen to focus and narrow down the research on healthy lifestyle due to its high importance in the world we live in today!

As per the above-discussed literature, it can be identified that there is a high tendency that people are moving toward a healthy lifestyle. However, given this setting, no one is aware of the circumstances in Sri Lanka because there is a paucity of research on the subject. Thus, the authors seek to discover this gap in this study through the following objective.

> Objective 1: To examine the nature of healthy lifestyles of young consumers in Sri Lanka.

According to the literature discussed above, young adults in Sri Lanka may have a high tendency to adopt a healthy lifestyle and accordingly the following hypothesis was developed;

> H_1: There is a high tendency to adopt a healthy lifestyle among young consumers in Sri Lanka.

Antecedents of a Healthy Lifestyle

Numerous factors influence healthy lifestyles worldwide. For example, demographic antecedents like gender, education and age (Divine & Lepisto, 2005), eating habits (Calvert et al., 2020), beliefs (Kelly et al., 2011), etc. The factors that are frequently referenced in literature and academia, however, are the physical neighborhood environment, societal self-esteem, and health consciousness. As a result, the author is using these three variables as independent variables in the current study.

The connection between the physical neighborhood environment and healthy lives has been discussed by a number of academics. According to several researchers' findings, a person's physical neighborhood environment determines how healthy their lifestyles are most of the time Sallis et al. (2010). Therefore, the physical neighborhood environment is the main focus of the current study as a factor in leading a healthy lifestyle.

Physical Neighborhood Environment

The physical environment is made up of all the various social and physical circumstances that surround a person and may have an impact on their existence. One's physical surroundings include both their indoor and outdoor settings. For instance, the health of a person depends on the quality of the air they breathe, the water they drink, and how exposed they are to noise pollution. An individual can better safeguard their health by being aware of potential hazards in their immediate physical environment (Wang et al., 2007).

Physical neighborhood environment refers to a certain area that is made up of elements that are present in the neighborhood. Natural circumstances, such as weather-related environmental circumstances, may be included. Additionally, there is a man-made environment, such as a recreation area (Wang et al., 2007).

The physical surroundings of the neighborhood are a well-known variable employed in investigations to ascertain different subjects. For instance, May C. Wang studied the physical neighborhood environment's characteristics to comprehend its connection to body mass index. The nearby neighborhood environment serves as a background to support physical activity, claim Chaudhury et al. (2016). One of the topics explored in this study was whether or not people who lived in neighborhoods with fast food businesses had unhealthier eating habits (Wang et al., 2007).

Physical Neighborhood Environment and Healthy Lifestyle

The implementation of a healthy lifestyle, including one's level of physical activity, can be impacted by aspects and traits of a person's neighborhood environment. A healthy city must have a clean, high-quality, and safe physical environment (De Leeuw, 2012). Ishak et al. (2018) show that neighborhood parks can promote a healthy lifestyle by reducing stress. Similarly, unhealthy lifestyles are encouraged by poorly designed neighborhoods (Allanah et al., 2010).

Sallis et al. (2010) looked into the measurement of the neighborhood environment and its relationship to the participation in physical activity. Sallis et al. (2010) and Gadais et al. (2018) also show that the physical neighborhood environment influences a healthy lifestyle.

The physical neighborhood environment can therefore be considered as a component that affects the adoption of a healthy lifestyle among young adults in Sri Lanka given the already deduced "Physical Activity" dimension of the healthy lifestyle previously discussed.

Physical neighborhood environment and a healthy lifestyle are two characteristics that may have a substantial relationship. For instance, a neighborhood with a place for people to go for jogs and engage in other forms of exercise will encourage people to go there and participate. A healthy lifestyle may follow as a result of this. We can even say that a neighborhood with higher crime rates wouldn't encourage people to go outside and exercise because of the dangers involved, despite the presence of a recreational area.

Several scales have emerged to measure the quality of the neighborhood environment to date. Elsawahli and Ali (2017) discovered social cohesion, physical activity, social interaction, walking, walking facilitation, walking barriers, convenience, accessibility, permeability, maintenance, and safety. The

"Physical Activity Neighborhood Environment Scale (PANES)" can be used to assess the relationship between the physical neighborhood environment and a healthy lifestyle. This is a tried-and-true scale that has been used in previous research (Sallis et al., 2010). PANES is being employed to assess ecological factors for walking, cycling, and other activities in different neighborhoods. It is thorough but concise enough to be used in multipurpose surveys. For the current study, the PANES is used to measure the variable "physical neighborhood environment" and its influence on a healthy lifestyle with the dimensions of "pedestrian infrastructure, land use mix access, recreational facilities, crime safety, and traffic safety" (Sallis et al., 2010). The fact that no published research has been done to measure the connection between the physical neighborhood environment and a healthy lifestyle among young adults in Sri Lanka is also identified as a contextual research gap in this study.

According to the previously mentioned literature, it can be determined that a neighborhood's physical environment has an impact on a healthy lifestyle. However, given this scenario, one cannot know Sri Lanka's situation because it has not been studied in the published literature; therefore, the author seeks to identify this gap in the literature review.

Social Support and Collective Self-esteem

Social support networks, which may include more assistance from family, friends, and the general community, are one of the factors that influence health (Wu & Sheng, 2019) Social support affects attitudes toward adopting a healthy lifestyle as well as the perceived difficulties of doing so (Kelly et al., 2011). According to the study of Reblin and Uchino (2008), contemporary research frequently demonstrates a strong correlation between social support from others and health protection. According to Koulierakis et al. (2022), social support influences whether people choose to eat healthily or unhealthily. Patients are more likely to maintain a healthy lifestyle when enough social support is offered (Tawalbeh et al., 2015).

In general, social support networks consist of the people a person spends the most of their time with, including their social circles. As a result, a person might relate to the impacts brought about by the affiliation of their distinct social groupings. These affects can, however, be either positive or detrimental (Barker, 2009).

Through collective self-esteem, one develops their social identity (how they view the group they belong to), which leads them to participate in group activities and adopt a lifestyle that is similar to that of their group (Luhtanen & Crocker, 1992). Self-esteem is influenced by relationships with those around them. For instance, Glendinning (1998) found that households with lower levels of inter-family activity are more likely to have members with low self-esteem. According to a study Jones et al. (2019) comparing domestic and overseas students, domestic students have greater overall mental health and self-esteem.

Collective Self-esteem and Healthy Lifestyle

Being a part of a social cluster causes an individual to develop traits and influences that reflect the group's overall views and ideals. It was also determined that belonging to a social group assists an individual in adopting a specific lifestyle that highlights characteristics of the associated social group. As a result, a social organization that prioritizes leading a healthy lifestyle can affect and shape the lifestyles of all of its members allowing each individual member to lead a healthy lifestyle. Social influence in terms of family influence and peer groups can create considerable pressure toward the healthy eating of adolescents (Calvert et al., 2020; Gilmour et al., 2020). According to Ridder et al. (2010), adolescents believe their parents can improve their healthy lifestyle through healthy meals, opportunities to participate in sports, and cycling. Reblin and Uchino (2008) and Gadais et al. (2018) also show that collective self-esteem influences the health behaviors of the people in such a community.

Feeling pride in being healthy and fit and becoming a role model of fitness is a self-esteem need of an individual (Chopra, 2022). Bowman and Hill (2011) and Stupnisky et al. (2013) emphasized that one's self-esteem is a robust predictor of both mental and physical health. According to Becerra et al. (2021), self-esteem acts as a salient factor that promotes the overall well-being of young adults. According to Chawak et al. (2020), self-esteem is related to aspects of a healthy lifestyle like a healthy diet and adequate sleep. Moreover, self-esteem is related to psychological distress and general mental health (Becerra et al., 2021; Jones et al., 2019).

Collective self-esteem will help in determining and measuring how much people value their membership in the social group and how much they are influenced to adhere to its rules (Luhtanen & Crocker, 1992). For instance, group self-esteem can be used to detect and measure if a person is cooperative, highly participative, and representative of the social group in terms of leading a healthy lifestyle.

The evaluations of the collective self-esteem scale are very personal, based on how the individual sees himself in the collectivist society (Luhtanen & Crocker, 1992). One component of group self-esteem is how well people think they fit into their social group (Luhtanen & Crocker, 1992). Moreover, collective self-esteem influences similar domains of a healthy lifestyle like job stress and subjective well-being (Choi, 2017; Du et al., 2017). We use a measurement scale which consists of four subscales; "membership esteem, private collective self-esteem, public collective, self-esteem, and importance to identity" developed by Luhtanen and Crocker (1992) in measuring collective self-esteem. In addition, it is noted that no published research has been done to estimate the connection between overall self-esteem and a healthy lifestyle among young adults in Sri Lanka.

Based on the above literature, it is determined that a healthy lifestyle is influenced by collective self-esteem; however, given the scenario, one cannot know the situation in Sri Lanka because it is not there in the published literature. As a result, the authors seek to address this gap in the current study.

Health Consciousness

The term "health consciousness" can be used to describe an attitude in which a person is aware of how healthy his or her diet and way of life are (Tan et al., 2022). As opposed to how it is commonly understood and defined, which is as taking an interest in your health (Batterham et al., 2016). Consequently, it is an element of personal cognition (Chen & Lin, 2018). Gonzaga (2014) proceeded with in-depth studies on health consciousness and identified three stages of health consciousness as mentioned below.

(1) The first phase of health consciousness focuses on symptom elimination.
(2) The second phase of health awareness extends beyond symptoms.
(3) The third phase of health consciousness expands on the second.

Gonzaga (2014) further emphasized that "The highest level of health consciousness is when taking consistent care of yourself becomes your service to humanity."

Health Consciousness and Healthy Lifestyle

Health is viewed more proactively by those who are health conscious. This means that a health-conscious lifestyle refers to the ability to make decisions in one's own life in favor of maintaining or even improving health, rather than simply being aware of the absence of disease (Kempen et al., 2012).

The association between health consciousness and a healthy lifestyle has been the subject of numerous earlier studies (Chen, 2011). According to the study, health consciousness is a broader phenomenon that represents a person's willingness to do something for his or her health and life, and it examines the extent of desire to participate in healthy behavior (Chen, 2011). Arroyo et al. (2021) state that more health-conscious consumers concern more about health-related attributes than conventional attributes like price and taste when consuming food. Further, health consciousness influences attitudes toward eating green and organic foods (Chen, 2009; Tan et al., 2022).

The influence of health consciousness toward various aspects of a healthy lifestyle has been investigated and found significant influence by different scholars. For instance, the intent to use wearable health devices (Srivastava et al., 2021), the intent to practice fitness applications (Damberg, 2022), healthy eating habits (Arroyo et al., 2021; Gilmour et al., 2020; Tan et al., 2022), health information search (Ahadzadeh et al., 2015, 2018), etc., are some instances. As a result, many young adults in Sri Lanka can incorporate health consciousness as a factor that influences a healthy lifestyle.

To measure the association between health consciousness and a healthy lifestyle, a scale was developed by Hong (2009) which is used for the current study. Health consciousness is measured with three dimensions which have been derived from past research and incorporated into the studies by Hong (2009). The dimensions of health consciousness are identified as: "self health awareness, personal responsibility, and health motivation."

A healthy lifestyle and health consciousness among young individuals in Sri Lanka have not been quantified in any published research, it is further noted. Considering the circumstances, one doesn't understand the circumstances in Sri Lanka since it has not been investigated in the existing literature, so the author wishes to identify a gap in the literature review. As per the literature, health consciousness has an impact on living a healthy lifestyle and the following objective is developed accordingly.

Objective 2: To assess whether physical neighborhood environment, collective self-esteem, and health consciousness differently influence a healthy lifestyle among young adults in Sri Lanka.

The following hypothesis was developed to achieve the aforementioned objective.

H_2: Physical neighborhood environment, collective self-esteem, and health consciousness differently influence a healthy lifestyle among young adults in Sri Lanka.

Methodology

The study is intended to look at the factors that contribute to young people in Sri Lanka living healthy lifestyles, and this calls for a quantitative analysis (Dewasiri et al., 2018; Shroff et al., 2024). The individuals in Sri Lanka's young generation are the subject of the analysis. The Western Province is chosen for the sample because it is the commercial center of Sri Lanka and has the highest percentage of the young population. Therefore, judgmental sampling is employed. A structured questionnaire was used to collect data from 658 participants in the study. The Five Point Likert Scale is used to assess all latent variables (1 – strongly agree, 5 – strongly disagree). Physical neighborhood, collective self-esteem, health consciousness, and a healthy lifestyle are measured through the scales of Sallis et al. (2010), Luhtanen and Crocker (1992), Hong (2009), and Hacihasanoglu et al. (2011), respectively.

Analysis and Findings

Exploratory factor analysis ensures that all measures of the latent variables are one-dimensional. Bartlett's Test of Sphericity, KMO test for sample adequacy, average variance extracted, and composite reliability were used to confirm convergent validity (Hair et al., 2012). Table 4.1 presents the findings.

All of the latent variables' Cronbach's alpha values were more than 0.7, confirming inter-item reliability as explained by Hair et al. (2012). The results are specified in Table 4.2.

Table 4.1. Results of the Convergent Validity.

Variable	KMO >0.5	BTS-Sig <0.5	CR >0.7	AVE >0.5
Collective self-esteem	0.812	0.000	0.856	0.598
Neighborhood (PANES)	0.791	0.000	0.806	0.706
Health consciousness	0.723	0.000	0.774	0.683
Healthy lifestyle	0.892	0.000	0.912	0.781

Table 4.2. Cronbach's Alpha Values.

Variable	No of Items	Cronbach's Alpha (>0.70)
Collective self-esteem	16	0.779
Neighborhood (PANES)	17	0.801
Health consciousness	11	0.731
Healthy lifestyle	48	0.939

As long as the AVE values of the respective constructs are greater than the square of the correlation values of the respective rows and columns, discriminant validity (see Table 4.3) is guaranteed (Fornell & Larcker, 1981).

The first hypothesis states that a one-sample T-test can determine the level of healthy living among young consumers in Sri Lanka. The findings in Tables 4.4a and 4.4b demonstrate that leading a healthy lifestyle is prevalent and statistically significant.

Table 4.3. Values for Discriminant Validity.

	Collective Self-Esteem	Neighborhood	Health Consciousness	Healthy Lifestyle
Collective self-esteem	0.598			
Neighborhood	0.278	0.706		
Health consciousness	0.228	0.481	0.683	
Healthy lifestyle	0.302	0.378	0.421	0.781

A Cross-Sectional Study of Sri Lanka   77

Table 4.4a. Descriptive Statistics.

	N	Minimum	Maximum	Mean	Std. Deviation
HLS_Mean	658	2.50	4.70	4.50	0.502
Valid N (listwise)	658				

Table 4.4b. One-Sample Test.

	T	Df	Sig. (2-tailed)	Mean difference	95% Confidence Interval of the Difference Lower	Upper
HLS_Mean	5.678		0.000	0.2000	0.1294	0.2806

Antecedents of Healthy Lifestyle of Young Generation in Sri Lanka

The second hypothesis of the study is tested employing multiple regression analysis to achieve the study's second objective. Tables 4.5a and 4.5b show the results (b).

The model summary (Table 4.5a) shows that 52.4% of the healthy lifestyle is explained by antecedents such the physical neighborhood environment, societal self-esteem, and health consciousness. The adjusted R-squared value is 0.524.

Table 4.5a. Model Summary.

Model	R	R Squared	Adjusted R Squared	Std. Error of the Estimate
1	0.562[a]	0.527	0.524	0.12768

[a] Predictors: (Constant), NB_mean, CSE_mean, HC_mean.
[b] Dependent Variable: HLS_mean.

Table 4.5b. Coefficients[a].

Model		Unstandardized Coefficients B	Std. Error	Standardized Coefficients Beta	t	Sig
1	(Constant)	0.314	0.061		4.623	0.000
	NB_mean	0.122	0.012	0.170	6.532	0.000
	CSE_mean	0.164	0.018	0.281	9.237	0.000
	HC_mean	0.238	0.027	0.312	8.512	0.000

[a] Dependent Variable: HLS_mean.

According to Table 4.5b, all the antecedents of healthy lifestyle are significant. The highest contribution to a healthy lifestyle of the young generation in Sri Lanka is given by health consciousness, collective self-esteem, and physical neighborhood environment, respectively. It reveals that health consciousness represents the most significant factor determining the healthy lifestyle of Sri Lanka's young generation.

Discussion

The primary goal of the study is to investigate the origins of the young generation in Sri Lanka's healthy lifestyle. The article is focused on two distinct goals. The youthful generation in Sri Lanka will first have their level of healthy lifestyle assessed, and then the antecedents of a healthy lifestyle will be examined while the salient component for a healthy lifestyle is identified. The results of the current survey show that young people in Sri Lanka are more concerned with leading healthy lives. It exhibits the similar pattern observed in other Asian nations, such as South India, as discovered by Gandhi et al. (2019). However, it is contradictory to the findings of Arroyo et al. (2021).

According to the findings of Wang et al. (2007), Allanah et al. (2010), Ishak et al. (2018), and Chaudhury et al. (2016), the current study discloses that the physical neighborhood environment significantly influences the healthy lifestyle of the young generation. Further, by extending the findings of some scholars, for instance, Tawalbeh et al. (2015), Jones et al. (2019), Koulierakis et al. (2022), and Becerra et al. (2021), our findings suggest that collective self-esteem is a significant antecedent for the healthy lifestyle of the young generation. Further, by extending the findings of Ahadzadeh et al. (2015, 2018), Gilmour et al. (2020), Arroyo et al. (2021), and Tan et al. (2022), this study discloses that health consciousness of the young consumers significantly impacts on their healthy lifestyle.

By extending the knowledge in this area, the current study shows that health consciousness, collective self-esteem, and physical neighborhood environment are simultaneously explaining the healthy lifestyle of the young generation by 52%. It further extends the current knowledge that health consciousness is the main antecedent followed by collective self-esteem and physical neighborhood environment, respectively.

Conclusion, Implications, and Future Directions

The main contribution of the current study is assessing the healthy lifestyle of the young generation in the Sri Lankan context, addressing the research scarcity in the South Asian context. Further, investigating the antecedents, namely, health consciousness, collective self-esteem, and physical neighborhood environment, simultaneously is the other contribution of the study. The scholars' attention has not been given to such a kind of investigation so far despite its significance.

The current study is useful for managers in the corporate sector. As young consumers are more concerned about their healthy lifestyle, managers in certain industries such as food and beverages, hotels and restaurants should adopt their products and services in line with the healthy lifestyle. Further, being aware that health consciousness, collective self-esteem, and physical neighborhood environment are the main antecedents to the healthy lifestyle, the corporates can make use of them when motivating young consumers to first behave in terms of the healthy lifestyle and then to purchase healthy products and services.

However, as the current study mainly addresses these restrictions with regard to young consumers, future research can also look into how they apply to other generations. Furthermore, since the current version selects the sample in a biased manner, this study can be expanded to include the entire nation. Another researcher may conduct another research to assess the young people in Sri Lanka's healthy lifestyle. Exploring other antecedents for healthy lifestyle is also another fertilized research area.

References

Ahadzadeh, A. S., Sharif, S. P., & Ong, F. S. (2018). Online health information seeking among women: The moderating role of health consciousness. *Online Information Review*, *42*(1), 58–72.

Ahadzadeh, A. S., Sharif, S. P., Ong, F. S., & Khong, K. W. (2015). Integrating health belief model and technology acceptance model: An investigation of health-related internet use. *Journal of Medical Internet Research*, *17*(2), 45–55.

Al-Jawaldeh, A., & Abbass, M. M. (2022). Unhealthy dietary habits and obesity: the major risk factors beyond non-communicable diseases in the eastern mediterranean region. *Frontiers in Nutrition*, *9*, 1–21.

Alamian, A., & Paradis, G. (2009). Clustering of chronic disease behavioral risk factors in Canadian children and adolescents. *Preventive Medicine*, *48*(5), 493–499.

Allanah, L., Ashley, K., & Farley, E. (2010). Diabetes and the built environment: Contributions from an emerging interdisciplinary research programme. *University of Western Ontario Medical Journal*, *79*(1), 20–22.

Anderson, W. T., Jr, & Golden, L. L. (1984). Lifestyle and psychographics: A critical review and recommendation. *Advances in Consumer Research*, *11*(1), 405–411.

Ardic, A., & Esin, M. N. (2016). Factors associated with healthy lifestyle behaviors in a sample of Turkish adolescents: A school-based study. *Journal of Transcultural Nursing*, *27*(6), 583–592.

Arroyo, P. E., Liñan, J., & Vera-Martínez, J. (2021). Who really values healthy food? *British Food Journal*, *123*(2), 720–738.

Badger, J., Quatromoni, P. A., & Morrell, J. S. (2019). Relationship between stress and healthy lifestyle factors of college students. *Health Behavior and Policy Review*, *6*(1), 43–55.

Barker, V. (2009). Older adolescents' motivations for social network site use: The influence of gender, group identity, and collective self-esteem. *CyberPsychology and Behavior*, *12*(2), 209–213.

Batterham, R. W., Hawkins, M., Collins, P. A., Buchbinder, R., & Osborne, R. H. (2016). Health literacy: Applying current concepts to improve health services and reduce health inequalities. *Public Health*, *132*, 3–12.

Becerra, M. B., Arias, D., Cha, L., & Becerra, B. J. (2021). Self-esteem among college students: The intersectionality of psychological distress, discrimination and gender. *Journal of Public Mental Health, 20*(1), 15–23.

Blum, R. W., & Nelson-Mmari, K. (2004). The health of young people in a global context. *Journal of Adolescent Health, 35*(5), 402–418.

Bootsma, H. G. (1995). The influence of a work-oriented life style on residential location choice of couples. *Netherlands Journal of Housing and the Built Environment, 10*(1), 45–63.

Bowman, N. A., & Hill, P. L. (2011). Measuring how college affects students: Social desirability and other potential biases in college student self-reported gains. *New Directions for Institutional Research, 2011*(150), 73–85.

Calvert, S., Dempsey, R. C., & Povey, R. (2020). A qualitative study investigating food choices and perceived psychosocial influences on eating behaviors in secondary school students. *British Food Journal, 122*(4), 1027–1039.

Chaudhury, H., Campo, M., Michael, Y., & Mahmood, A. (2016). Neighbourhood environment and physical activity in older adults. *Social Science and Medicine, 149*, 104–113.

Chawak, S., Chittem, M. S. A., Varghese, D., & Epton, T. (2020). Predictors of health behaviors among Indian college students: An exploratory study. *Health Education, 120*(2), 179–195.

Chen, M. F. (2009). Attitude toward organic foods among Taiwanese as related to health consciousness, environmental attitudes, and the mediating effects of a healthy lifestyle. *British Food Journal, 111*(2), 165–178.

Chen, M. F. (2011). The joint moderating effect of health consciousness and healthy lifestyle on consumers' willingness to use functional foods in Taiwan. *Appetite, 57*(1), 253–262.

Chen, M.-F., & Lin, N. P. (2018). Incorporation of health consciousness into the technology readiness and acceptance model to predict app download and usage intentions. *Internet Research, 28*(2), 351–373.

Choi, T. J. (2017). The influence of collective self-esteem on teachers' job stress. *Journal of Fisheries and Marine Sciences Education, 29*(3), 732–745.

Chopra, K. (2022). Maslow's theory for preventive healthcare in India – A content analysis approach. *International Journal of Pharmaceutical and Healthcare Marketing, 16*(1), 40–54.

Cobb-Clark, D. A., Kassenboehmer, S. C., & Schurer, S. (2014). Healthy habits: The connection between diet, exercise, and locus of control. *Journal of Economic Behavior & Organization, 98*, 1–28.

Damberg, S. (2022). Predicting future use intention of fitness apps among fitness app users in the United Kingdom: The role of health consciousness. *International Journal of Sports Marketing & Sponsorship, 23*(2), 369–384.

De Leeuw, E. (2012). Do healthy cities work? A logic of method for assessing impact and outcome of healthy cities. *Journal of Urban Health, 89*(2), 217–231.

De Soysa, I., & Lewin, O. L. (2018). Gender empowerment, inequalities and the prevalence of adult female obesity: An empirical analysis using new data, 1990–2013. *Scandinavian Journal of Public Health, 47*(10), 1–12. https://doi.org/10.1177/1403494818807568

Dewasiri, N. J., Rana, S., & Kashif, M. (2021). Editorial – Theory building in marketing: Rationalizing South Asian perspective. *South Asian Journal of Marketing*, *2*(1), 1–4. https://doi.org/10.1108/SAJM-03-2021-071

Dewasiri, N. J., Weerakoon, Y. K. B., & Azeez, A. A. (2018). Mixed methods in finance research: The rationale and research designs. *International Journal of Qualitative Methods*, *17*, 1–13.

Divine, R. L., & Lepisto, L. (2005). Analysis of the healthy lifestyle consumer. *Journal of Consumer Marketing*, *22*(5), 275–283.

Du, H., King, R. B., & Chi, P. (2017). Self-esteem and subjective well-being revisited: The roles of personal, relational, and collective self-esteem. *PLoS One*, *12*(8), e0183958.

Elsawahli, H., & Ali, A. S. (2017). Measured neighbourhood environmental factors correlate with active lifestyle among elderly. *Open House International*, *42*(1), 87–94.

Fornell, C., & Larcker, D. F. (1981). Evaluating structural equation models with unobservable variables and measurement error. *Journal of Marketing Research*, *18*(1), 39–50.

Gadais, T., Boulanger, M., Trudeau, F., & Rivard, M. C. (2018). Environments favorable to healthy lifestyles: A systematic review of initiatives in Canada. *Journal of Sport and Health Science*, *7*(1), 7–18.

Gandhi, S., Gurusamy, J., Ragupathy, S. K., Damodharan, D., Ganesan, V., & Marimuthu, P. (2019). Healthy lifestyle behavior and personal control in people with schizophrenia with healthy controls: A cross-sectional comparative study. *Asian Journal of Psychiatry*, *45*, 95–98.

Giles, E. L., & Brennan, M. (2015). Changing the lifestyles of young adults. *Journal of Social Marketing*, *5*(3), 206–225.

Gil, J. M., Gracia, A., & Sanchez, M. (2000). Market segmentation and willingness to pay for organic products in Spain. *The International Food and Agribusiness Management Review*, *3*(2), 207–226.

Gilmour, A., Gill, S., & Loudon, G. (2020). Young adolescents' experiences and views on eating and food. *Young Consumers*, *21*(4), 389–402.

Glendinning, A. (1998). Family life, health and lifestyles in rural areas: The role of self-esteem. *Health Education*, *98*(2), 59–68.

Gonzaga, M. A. (2014). Listening to the voices: An exploratory study of the experiences of women diagnosed and living with breast cancer in Uganda. *Pan African Medical Journal*, *16*(1), 1–5.

Hacihasanoglu, R., Yildirum, A., Karakurt, P., & Saglam, R. (2011). Healthy lifestyle behvaiour in university students and influential factors in eastern Turkey. *International Journal of Nursing Practice*, *17*(1), 43–51.

Hair, J. F., Ringle, C. M., & Sarstedt, M. (2012). Partial least squares: The better approach to structural equation modeling? *Long Range Planning*, *45*(5–6), 312–319.

Heijs, W., Carton, M., Smeets, J., & Van-Gemert, A. (2009). The labyrinth of lifestyles. *Journal of Housing and the Built Environment*, *24*(3), 347–356.

Hong, H. (2009). Scale development for measuring health consciousness: Reconceptualization. In *Paper Presented at the 12th Annual International Public Relations Research Conference*. Holiday Inn University of Miami Coral Gables.

Ishak, S. A., Hussein, H., & Jamaludin, A. A. (2018). Neighbourhood parks as a potential stress reliever: Review on literature. *Open House International, 43*(4), 52–64.

Jacob, M. E., Yee, L. M., Diehr, P. H., Arnold, A. M., Thielke, S. M., Chaves, P. H., & Newman, A. B. (2016). Can a healthy lifestyle compress the disabled period in older adults? *Journal of the American Geriatrics Society, 64*(10), 1952–1961.

Jayasuriya, N. A. (2016). Sri Lankan consumer attitudes towards healthy meals. *Journal of Marketing and Consumer Research, 24*, 69–79.

Jensen, M. (2007). Defining lifestyle. *Environmental Sciences, 4*(2), 63–73.

Jones, C. P., Lodder, A., & Papadopoulos, C. (2019). Do predictors of mental health differ between home and international students studying in the UK? *Journal of Applied Research in Higher Education, 11*(2), 224–234.

Kaplan, R. M. (1991). Health-related quality of life in patient decision making. *Journal of Social Issues, 47*(4), 69–90.

Katz, S. (2013). Active and successful aging. Lifestyle as a gerontological idea. *Recherches sociologiques et anthropologiques, 44*(44-1), 33–49.

Kelly, S. A., Melnyk, B. M., Jacobson, D. L., & O'Haver, J. A. (2011). Correlates among healthy lifestyle cognitive beliefs, healthy lifestyle choices, social support, and healthy behaviors in adolescents: Implications for behavioral change strategies and future research. *Journal of Pediatric Health Care, 25*(4), 216–223.

Kempen, E. L., Muller, H., Symington, E., & Van Eeden, T. (2012). A study of the relationship between health awareness, lifestyle behaviour and food label usage in Gauteng. *South African Journal of Clinical Nutrition, 25*(1), 15–21.

Kilani, H., Al-Hazzaa, H., Waly, M. I., & Musaiger, A. (2013). Lifestyle habits: Diet, physical activity and sleep duration among Omani adolescents. *Sultan Qaboos University Medical Journal, 13*(4), 510–519.

Koulierakis, G., Dermatis, A., Vassilakou, N.-T., Pavi, E., Zavras, D., & Kyriopoulos, J. (2022). Determinants of healthy diet choices during austerity in Greece. *British Food Journal, 124*(9), 2893–2910.

Luhtanen, R., & Crocker, J. (1992). A collective self-esteem scale: Self-evaluation of one's social identity. *Personality and Social Psychology Bulletin, 18*(3), 302–318.

Marques, A., Peralta, M., Santos, T., Martins, J., & de Matos, M. G. (2019). Self-rated health and health-related quality of life are related with adolescents' healthy lifestyle. *Public Health, 170*, 89–94.

Rana, S., Udunuwara, M., Dewasiri, N. J., Kashif, M., & Rathnasiri, M. S. H. (2022). Editorial: Is South Asia ready for the next universe – Metaverse? Arguments and suggestions for further research. *South Asian Journal of Marketing, 3*(2), 77–81. https://doi.org/10.1108/SAJM-10-2022-141

Rathnasiri, M. S. H. (2021). Impact of perceived service quality on customer satisfaction: With special reference to ABC fast food restaurant Chain in Sri Lanka. *International Journal of Advances in Engineering and Management, 3*(9), 261–267.

Reblin, M., & Uchino, B. N. (2008). Social and emotional support and its implication for health. *Current Opinion in Psychiatry, 21*, 201–205.

Ridder, M. A. M., Heuvelmans, M. A., Visscher, T. L. S., Seidell, J. C., & Renders, C. M. (2010). We are healthy so we can behave unhealthily: A qualitative study of the health behavior of Dutch lower vocational students. *Health Education, 110*(1), 30–42.

Rodelli, M., De Bourdeaudhuij, I., Dumon, E., Portzky, G., & DeSmet, A. (2018). Which healthy lifestyle factors are associated with a lower risk of suicidal ideation among adolescents faced with cyberbullying? *Preventive Medicine, 113*, 32–40.

Sadiq, M. A., Rajeswari, B., & Ansari, L. (2019). Segmentation of Indian shoppers in the context of organic foods. *South Asian Journal of Business Studies, 9*(2), 167–192.

Sallis, J. F., Kerr, J., Carlson, J. A., Norman, G. J., Saelens, B. E., Durant, N., & Ainsworth, E. (2010). Evaluating a brief self-report measure of neighborhood environments for physical activity research and surveillance: Physical Activity Neighborhood Environment Scale (PANES). *Journal of Physical Activity and Health, 7*(4), 533–540.

Sawyer, S. M., Afifi, R. A., Bearinger, L. H., Blakemore, S. J., Dick, B., Ezeh, A. C., & Patton, G. C. (2012). Adolescence: A foundation for future health. *The Lancet, 379*(9826), 1630–1640.

Shroff, S. J., Paliwal, U. L., & Dewasiri, N. J. (2024). Unraveling the impact of financial literacy on investment decisions in an emerging market. *Business Strategy & Development, 7*(1), 1–14. https://doi.org/10.1002/bsd2.337

Sogari, G., Velez-Argumedo, C., Gómez, M. I., & Mora, C. (2018). College students and eating habits: A study using an ecological model for healthy behavior. *Nutrients, 10*(12), 1–16.

Srivastava, N. K., Chatterjee, N., Subramani, A. K., Akbar Jan, N., & Singh, P. K. (2021). Is health consciousness and perceived privacy protection critical to use wearable health devices? Extending the model of goal-directed behavior. *Benchmarking: An International Journal, 29*(10), 3079–3096.

Stupnisky, R. H., Perry, R. P., Renaud, R. D., & Hladkyj, S. (2013). Looking beyond grades: Comparing self-esteem and perceived academic control as predictors of first-year college students' well-being. *Learning and Individual Differences, 23*, 151–157.

Tan, B. C., Lau, T. C., Sarwar, A., & Khan, N. (2022). The effects of consumer consciousness, food safety concern and healthy lifestyle on attitudes toward eating "green". *British Food Journal, 124*(4), 1187–1203.

Tawalbeh, L. I., Tubaishat, A., Batiha, A. M., Al-Azzam, M., & AlBashtawy, M. (2015). The relationship between social support and adherence to healthy lifestyle among patients with coronary artery disease in the North of Jordan. *Clinical Nursing Research, 24*(2), 121–138.

Taymoori, P., Moeini, B., Lubans, D., & Bharami, M. (2012). Development and psychometric testing of the Adolescent Healthy Lifestyle Questionnaire. *Journal of Education and Health Promotion, 1*(1), 1–20.

Van-Nieuwenhuijzen, M., Junger, M., Velderman, M. K., Wiefferink, K. H., Paulussen, T. W., Hox, J., & Reijneveld, S. A. (2009). Clustering of health-compromising behavior and delinquency in adolescents and adults in the Dutch population. *Preventive Medicine, 48*(6), 572–578.

Wang, M. C., Kim, S., Gonzalez, A. A., MacLeod, K. E., & Winkleby, M. A. (2007). Socioeconomic and food-related physical characteristics of the neighbourhood environment are associated with body mass index. *Journal of Epidemiology & Community Health, 61*(6), 491–498.

Watson, R. R., & Zibadi, S. (2018). *Lifestyle in heart health and disease* (1st ed.). Elsevier.

World Health Organization. (1948). *Summary reports on proceedings minutes and final acts of the international health conference held in New York from 19 June to 22 July 1946.* https://apps.who.int/iris/handle/10665/85573

Wu, F., & Sheng, Y. (2019). Social support network, social support, self-efficacy, health-promoting behavior and healthy aging among older adults: A pathway analysis. *Archives of Gerontology and Geriatrics, 85,* 1–15.

Chapter 5

Artificial Intelligence and Augmented Reality: A Business Fortune to Sustainability in the Digital Age

Henry Jonathan[a], Hesham Magd[a] and Shad Ahmad Khan[b]

[a]Modern College of Business and Science, Oman
[b]University of Buraimi, Oman

Abstract

Artificial intelligence and augmented reality are two key tools gaining importance in the digital era due to their wide range of applications in different fields and sectors. Industry 4.0 lays emphasis principally on the technology used to help the business remain competitive and sustainable. Sustainable development goals are another important objective of the UN which has laid responsibility for every business to support addressing the global challenges. Purpose: This chapter essentially aims to present the standpoint of artificial intelligence and augmented reality in meeting the sustainability perspective of organizations. Information about the study is gathered through secondary approaches, critically reviewing published literature, scientific reports, and statistical data accessible through business reports, and corporate websites. Further analyzed to present the perspectives of the authors in the study. Globally artificial intelligence market size is predicted to reach $190 billion by 2025, while the funding for startups doubled during the period 2011–2020 globally. The investment in artificial intelligence is going to reach $500 by 2024 resulting in substantial revenue returns. The augmented reality market size could reach $97 billion by 2028. Artificial intelligence today is increasingly used in many fields and is attracting multiple applications in many sectors such as manufacturing, retail, education, IT, and health care and has also contributed to sustainable development the same time by providing energy conservation options, optimization, and reduction of resources, minimizing wastage, offering timely assistance on maintenance schedules, practices which are enabling organizations to reach closer to sustainability and transformation.

Navigating the Digital Landscape, 85–105

Copyright © 2024 Henry Jonathan, Hesham Magd and Shad Ahmad Khan

Published under exclusive licence by Emerald Publishing Limited

doi:10.1108/978-1-83549-272-720241005

Keywords: Sustainable development; artificial intelligence; technology; digital; transformation; business; industry

Introduction

The current 21st century unprecedented is earmarked as the age of digital technology, embracing the fourth industrial revolution. Artificial intelligence (AI) and augmented reality (AR) surface as the main components to accomplish industry 4.0 objectives principally complimenting the manufacturing sector (Devagiri et al., 2022; Magd et al., 2022). Together they occupy a conspicuous place among the technological components to facilitate digital transformation in the work environment (Reis et al., 2018). Indeed, AI is becoming a driving force in combination with other technological tools to lead digitalization and digital transformation.

AR is a subset of AI and has also gained importance from its wide applications and its capability to offer a digitally interactive work environment. As a result, there is an increasing investment perceived in AI and AR tools to diversify their applications in different sectors to amplify digital transformation. Statistical reports indicate the global AI market is expected to reach $190 billion by 2025, while this would increase GDP by 26.1% in China and 14.5% in the United States of America by 2030. The global AI market by the year 2021 was $327.5 billion indicating the funding for AI from startups worldwide has doubled from 2011 to 2021 which reached $36 billion in 2020 (Statista.com). Anonymous reports also show funding and capital investment in AI technological tools can potentially double annual economic output in some South Asian countries. Further, independent research analysis from corporates such as Accenture, Forbes, Deloitte, MIT Management Sloan school, etc., reports that AI technology would enter almost all major global markets and business applications in the coming years.

Enabling AI technology applications along with AR can potentially encourage developing economies to boost digitalization and digital transformation of the business process. Industries such as manufacturing, health care, and automobile have recently started incorporating AI-enabled applications in business processes to assist through inspection, design, maintenance schedules, etc., as well as provide efficient customer service and satisfaction (Sahu et al., 2021; Wan et al., 2020). There are also growing research studies published on the topics related to AI and AR applications in different sectors and fields, which shows the exploring phenomena of the technology tools globally. Few studies are explored to understand the role of AI and AR applications in achieving sustainability of the business environment in different sectors (Szajna & Kostrzewski, 2022), which are very important for organizations for improving organization performance and sustainable growth.

Organizations are prioritizing developing business models to adapt their operations to facilitate achieving the sustainable development goals of the UN. Both small and larger firms have to develop mechanisms to ensure that business operations are grounded on sustainability which is very crucial to maintain the economy (Di Vaio et al., 2020). Moreover, sustainable development is gaining an overwhelming approach in every economy, since organizations and businesses are expected to orient their business approach and process toward protecting the environment and addressing global challenges (Chladek, 2019). While sustainability is demanded to be at the core of every business in the current scenario, orientation toward environmental protection probably fetches multiple benefits to organizations from bringing more customer/consumer satisfaction to a firm's business trend.

There is also an increasing awareness among corporate businesses to engage more in sustainable business practices benefitting economic, social, and environmental entities. Likewise, also link the organization's business process toward sustainable approaches which are inevitable for every organization and economy to meet sustainable development goals. Obviously, in the current age of digitalization, organizations might be very much required to make efforts to remain competitive in the present global market to sustain their businesses (Rafi, 2023), which should be balanced against the technology tools to keep pace with the current digital era.

Despite there are substantial studies targeting the topic of digital transformation and sustainability concepts in organizations and businesses. Those categorically emphasize the importance of technological tools like AI, machine learning (ML), virtual reality (VR), AR, etc., supplementing the fourth industrial revolution. From this notion, we understand in the era of digitalization, sustainability and sustainable development goals of the UN are very critical for organizations to improve performance and remain competitive in the global market. Therefore, this chapter will present an overview of the role AI and AR is currently playing in various sectors toward digitalization and digital transformation of businesses. The study will also cover addressing the association between the two technology tools and sustainability and further will review the ways these digital tools are explored by organizations globally for achieving organizational sustainability.

Theoretical Context

Era of Digital Technology Tools

The current era is the age of digital technology inviting organizations and businesses to imbibe technology and innovation into their operations. This has quite obviously introduced the concept of digitalization and digital transformation to all work cultures. Thereby eventually has enforced organizations to use digital technology tools such as AI, Internet of Things (IoT), ML, etc., to advance in a technology-driven society. Presumably, these technology applications can assist in responding to the various challenges of the environment and help in meeting the sustainable development goals for organizations (Joppa, 2015; Vinuesa et al., 2020).

It's essential to draw attention to the fact that there are different definitions and meanings of digital technology described in the literature, few from technology-based companies. Digital technology implies the "use of wide range of technologies, tools, services, and applications using various types of hardware and software." The tools include the use of computers, digital television, radio, mobile phones, robots, etc. (Brečko & Ferrari, 2016; Rice, 2003; Tulinayo et al., 2018).

The use of technology tools has paved the way for digital applications more precisely which led to the digitalization process in the work process triggering a digital transformation in all walks of life. Within this fusion of digital technology, different technology-enabled tools have evolved recently in the last few decades, most prominent of them such as AI, ML, VR, AR, and IoT have seen tremendous growth in the last decade (Cheng et al., 2018). Particularly there has been more emphasis on AI and AR technology prospects at its applications in industries such as manufacturing, service, hospital, and education as well (Kumar et al., 2021; Liu et al., 2020).

AI-enabled technologies are gaining increasing applications in the field of energy use, to minimize wastage, and balance the supply of energy based on demand, in addition, can be explored in managing renewable energy (Soon & Hui, 2022). Moreover, sustainability has become the prime goal across every business and organization and business planners are more concerned with the use of digital technology tools to boost business prospects in conjunction with sustainable development goals. As a result, investment in AI toward sustainable initiatives is bound to gain height by 2030. Rasp et al. (2018) and Reichstein et al. (2019) describe AI technology as expanding its usage in climate change monitoring, climate modeling, and environment studies (Hino et al., 2018). Galaz et al. (2021) disclose that AI-enabled technologies are currently being explored in the environmental field, agriculture, and marine resources for assisting in monitoring, predicting, and decision-making during adverse conditions.

AI and AR

AI originates from the combined fields of computer science and engineering, but there are also other fields like cognitive science, philosophy, neuroscience, etc., which influence the technology (Richter et al., 2019). The definition of AI is diverse, but John McCarthy 1956 first coined the term AI in defining it as "the science and engineering of making intelligent machines, especially intelligent computer programs. It is related to the similar task of using computers to understand human intelligence, but AI does not have to confine itself to biologically observable methods." However, the birth of AI was first unraveled by Alan Turning in 1950 who pioneered the field of computer science (IBM, 2020). Over the years AI-associated tools have made tremendous ingress into many sectors since then, and today is the prime component of fourth industrial evolution to lead digitalization and transformation (Collins et al., 2021).

AR is a recent technology tool that works on the principle of overlaying computer-generated virtual images in a real-world situation to portray the images for enabling real-world interaction (Dey et al., 2018). AR is defined as a "newer technological system in which virtual objects are added to the real world in

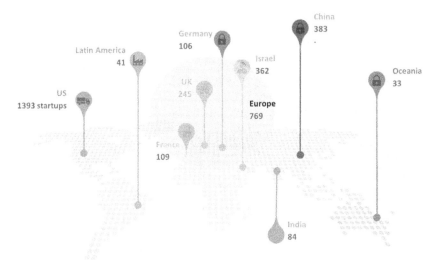

Artificial intelligence's global influence from the startup applications in different sectors

Fig. 5.1.   Artificial Intelligence's Global Influence From Applications
in Different Fields (Fabian, 2018).

real-time during the user's experience" (Cipresso et al., 2018). The origin of AR goes back to the 1960s and has gradually started to expand its applications into various fields such as education, engineering, entertainment and gaming, retail, and architecture (Dey et al., 2018; Dow et al., 2007; Lin & Hsu, 2017), medicine (De Buck et al., 2005), maintenance (Schwald & De Laval, 2003), and psychological treatments (Juan et al., 2005) (Fig. 5.1).

Study Framework

The study is one of the significant works on the topic of digitalization and digital transformation currently drawing attention in 4.0. The chapter mainly targets the role of digital technology tools, particularly AI and AR in driving businesses and organizations toward sustainability, where the authors have presented an overview of the position both two technologies stand on the roadmap of sustainable development goals in different fields and sectors. Information and data on digital technology tools and the role of AI and AR are gathered from multiple sources such as referring literature published by various researchers, analytical studies by corporate organizations, business analysts, and reports from planners, government, and nongovernmental sectors. Further, the authors have critically reviewed the published work and have prepared the chapter to present the findings of the study from the author's perspective.

Discussion

Scope of AI and AR in Business

AI has wider uses for businesses in today's world, which is the prime mover of digitalization and transformation. The application of AI currently is visible in all fields, and sectors covering all aspects of business such as marketing, sales, customer support services, administration, data management, etc. Moreover, AI is not a technology replacement but rather acts as a supporting tool for improving functions that are done by human intervention through various subsets like ML, deep learning, etc. With the onset of Industry 4.0, AI and the subdisciplines have gained wide usage in almost every sector and field; however, some sectors like IT, finance, transport, marketing, and healthcare are maximizing AI applications in their operations. This could lead to increased spending on AI-enabled applications and according to some reports, the global investment might reach $500 billion by 2024.

Studies from PwC reveal that AI technology can cause a steep rise to the global economy which might account for $16 trillion by 2030, and the Middle Eastern countries are likely to get a 2% share from the economic hike. While reports from McKinsey show AI can result in fetching $13 trillion to the global economic output by the end of 2030. These figures indicate that technology most importantly AI-enabled applications are going to get priority in every business operation primarily to substitute digitalization on one side, and the other hand to assist businesses and organizations to remain competitive. Despite these initiatives, increased spending on technology is also regarded as an investment toward sustainable development, because organizations and businesses are required to adopt sustainable practices to meet sustainable development goals (Fig. 5.2).

In the digital age, AI and its subdisciplines like AR are being used in multiple ways by different companies ranging from IT to service sectors. One of the promising fields in AI technologies that have gained advancement in recent years was the medical field, assisting in multiple ways such as virtual diagnostics, examination, consultations, etc. (Haleem et al., 2019). Besides, AI technology is also used in fields like geology (Lez'er et al., 2019), mechanical engineering (Patel et al., 2021), ML applications in manufacturing and processing industries (Fahle et al., 2020) in addition to many other uses in science and daily life.

Similarly AR along with other digital technology has gained wide usage, especially in the technology sector. According to market research reports, the global AR market size has increased from $ 4.16 billion in 2020 to $ 6.12 billion in 2021 and is projected to reach $ 97.76 billion by the year 2028, and such a tremendous increase would lead AR to be the future version of the internet. Currently, AR is playing a significant role in businesses like retail, design and modeling, industrial field services, training and education, and repair and maintenance, but the future of this technology seems to expand to multiple fields and applications. Some of the areas that are extensively using AR technology include shopping, travel, real estate, food services, health care, marketing, education, sports, training, navigation, gaming, etc., which are mostly accessed through user

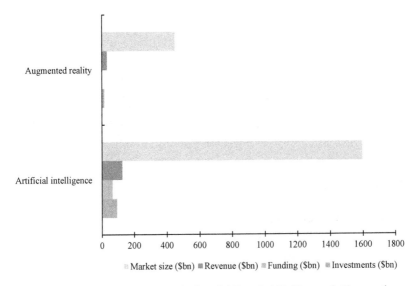

Fig. 5.2. Comparative Analysis of AI and AR Toward Competing Size, Revenue, Funding, and Investments Predictable Up to 2030.[1]

devices like smartphones, apps, and tablets. Worldwide there are around 1.73 billion users actively using AR through smartphones itself (Fig. 5.3). Interestingly, AR technology has also been explored in space applications to assist astronauts in providing rightful instructions on the international space station (Fig. 5.4).

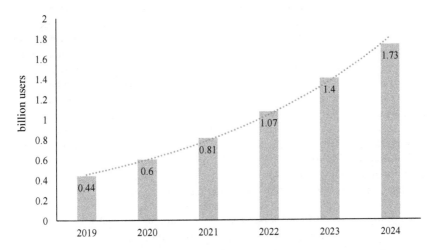

Fig. 5.3. The Exponential Growth of Augmented Reality Usage During the Last Decade (Alsop, 2022).

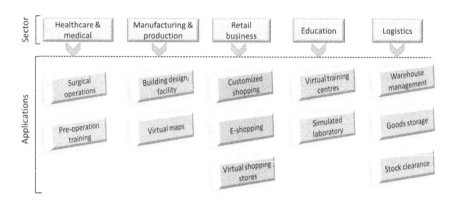

Fig. 5.4.   Use Cases of Augmented Reality Applications in Different Sectors in the Digital Age (Johnson, 2022).

Theoretical Models of AI Applications in Marketing

AI has been gaining quite popularity in every sector more than any other technology tool due to its versatility and diverse applications. Principally, many sectors are exploring the much precision digital technology tools like AI and how they work in different scenarios through developing theoretical models. These models work together by assimilating a set of data which involves the recognition of patterns through an algorithm calculation to make predictions and decision-making that are very important at the time of solving complex problems. These prediction models are provided as outputs without any human interference. In today's competitive business, AI models are a very important application area in marketing, as many companies are in the process of digital transformation of their business operations, AI technology can enhance customer satisfaction, and improve operating efficiency through different platforms helping the companies to make automated decisions from data analysis. Besides, AI models are facilitating in development of digital marketing trends, where customer data are gathered to provide purchasing options based on their buying preferences. Moreover, AI in the marketing sector is also capable of providing solutions between customers and marketers apart from making connections with customer data and future marketing trends. AI renders marketing solutions to various companies through ML, big data and analytics, and AI marketing platforms and tools. Some of the more specific cases that AI is currently helping marketing are:

• Data analytics: AI helps in gathering and scanning through large amounts of marketing data from various sources more easily and effortlessly, saving the time required for the manual sorting of information.

- Natural language processing: AI supports marketing in creating content for customers on production information, where customers can get assistance through customer service bots, and personalization contacts.
- Automated decision-making: The use of AI in generating automated decision-making helps the marketing team to plan appropriate marketing strategies based on past data on user preferences.
- Real-time personalization: A customer experience can be achieved through the webpage, social media posts, and email preferences before or after buying products.

Among the roles AI plays in the marketing component, it is very productive in improving the customer experience, efficient data processing of customer preferences, purchases, feedback on marketing strategies, etc., decision-making, assists in online purchases, and helps the e-commerce industry in developing good brand association in the consumer market. Apart from the many roles and uses of AI technology in assisting marketing through the theoretical models, it is also very instrumental in supporting marketers in strategic planning of marketing activities such as segregating data that helps orient a firm's vision (Huang & Rust, 2017). Other principal areas AI models can render service to the marketing component are product management, pricing management, promotion of products, use of drones and cobots in packaging, delivery, tracking dispatch orders, etc. (Verma et al., 2021).

AI technology particularly in marketing provides far-reaching advantages to companies in meeting the established goals and visions of firms, maintaining the privacy of data in compliance with standards, reliability of data sources on customer and firms trends, supports in maintaining the quality of data concerning time, consistency, relevance, transparency, accuracy, and totality.

The Growth Potential of AI-Enabled Technology Tools in Different Sectors – Augmented Reality, Virtual Reality, and Machine Learning

AR and VR in industries: AI subset technologies like AR, VR, and ML are making tremendous routes into every sector and field currently in the present industrial revolution. AR and VR are two twin technologies that are making significant progress across many organizations mainly in IT-enabled companies. AR is referred to as an "enhanced, interactive version of a real-world environment achieved through digital visual elements, sounds, and other sensory stimuli via holographic technology." This technology fundamentally works on creating digital features to the real-world view to create a better design for the environment. Such a technology feature can be applied to the type of field or business needed to create an understanding of the real-world environment. AR technology can be incorporated into employer training in organizations to enhance the learning experience on different professional skills. Presently many industries and sectors have already started using AR in their business operations, such as:

- Retail: Employees can use AR for onboarding and training sessions. It aids new employees in future interactions such as sales training, sales floor tours, and preparing for a retail setting. AR can also assist clients in testing things before purchase or learning how to use them in their environments. Delivering relevant information in a real-world environment can increase customer engagement or assist customers to solve problems.
- Manufacturing: AR can provide the workers and employees step-by-step instructions on the work process. That assistance can provide workers with better performance with reduced errors.
- Healthcare: Medical and healthcare sectors can get greatly benefitted from the AR technology application in anatomical examination and surgeries.
- Military: AR can also potentially help by integrating into the combat training exercises to create simulations of real wartime situations, with the help of combat military forces can evaluate the response time, and the force needed based on the combat strength.
- Automobile: AR technology is extensively being used in the automobile industry in bringing new technology and advancement in customer afford-ability and comfort. The automotive industry is integrating AR in the designing and developing of automobiles from the prototypes for real-world settings. During the manufacturing process, many concerns related to testing and design features are improved by avoiding repeating operations saving time, resources, and manpower. In addition, AR technology is also helpful in fetching better sales, improving employee communication, enhancing the driving experience by incorporating GPS and head-up displays for improving visibility, and finally in maintenance and after-sales services. Large conglomerate automotive companies like BMW, Jaguar land rover, Mercedes, and Audi are maximizing the use of AR and VR in the production and manufacturing process.

Apart from these, the twin technologies AR and VR are also in great demand in some of the large industrial sectors like construction, automotive, tourism, architecture, interior design, learning and development, real estate, entertainment, sports, social, marketing, education, e-commerce, healthcare, furniture, fire and emergency rescue services, recreation, fitness and wellbeing, journalism, law enforcement, etc. (Fig. 5.5).

ML Application Tool in Industries

ML is a subset of AI and computer science that works with the use of data and algorithms to mimic the functions of human learning, thereby improving accuracy. In other words, it is a set of coded algorithmic languages which directs a computer to learn from either experience or the analysis of data. Such functionary role of computers will help many industries and companies in making predictions or outcomes depending on the nature of business operations. Regardless of the type of industry or nature of the organization, ML is likely to benefit organizations in the area of automation, an affinity for improvement, efficient data

Fig. 5.5.   Principal Applications Sectors of AR and VR in the Present Scenario (Top 14 Industries That Use Virtual Reality Applications to Redefine User Experience. https://www.holopundits.com/blog/2021/03/top-14-industries-that-use-virtual-reality-applications-to-redefine-user-experience.html).

handling, less dependence on human interaction, and diversified applications. The different sectors that are currently embracing ML technologies include the financial sector, genetics, and genomics, healthcare, retail, education, manufacturing, marketing, agriculture, etc. While the impact of ML on industries is expanding rapidly, how it helps or assists each business process differs from sector to sector in manufacturing ML is applied in quality control, automation, and customization of products for customers. In the retail business and marketing, it is used in data analysis for making decisions on product pricing. Personalization and robotics will become more common in executing tasks in the retail business sector. Whereas in the medical and healthcare sector, ML is going to mainly assist in disease diagnosis, treatment, and prevention process. Medical practitioners can take the help of ML for providing personalized treatment, early diagnosis, and accurate medication based on the patient's medical history (Fig. 5.6).

In the marketing component, ML is used at different stages, from the purchase phase through online marketing where the ML tool would capture the customer activities on browsing online purchase websites that will give a clue to the companies on the user behavior and preferences and later optimizing the products for display according to the choice. While such a process generates huge amounts of data on user preferences, companies can use the data for customizing the content for an advertisement based on personalization patterns. Overall in the end, with ML-enabled applications in marketing, the technology tool can render reduced or decreased costs on companies' expenditure by diverting the marketers' time to more productive tasks. Moreover, ML can potentially help companies to

Fig. 5.6. Machine Learning-Enabled Technology Applications in Different Sectors and Functions Executed in Each Sector.

understand user preferences more precisely and offer suitable purchase choices, including content optimization and new customer segmentation.

Focus of AI and AR on Business Sustainability and Growth

The sustainable development goals of the UN are an important milestone every business and organization should pledge to achieve. With the world facing challenges such as climate change, environmental pollution degradation, natural resource depletion, etc., conservation of the environment and resources is an important part of every business and organization's operations (Laurent, 2021). The sustainable development goals of the UN pledge that businesses and organizations should develop mechanisms and means to adopt sustainable practices to minimize wastage and energy conservation.

AI and AR together are considered the present century fortunes to the industrial world and for years researchers and analysts assert that if explored judiciously, they can potentially contribute to sustainable development in multiple ways such as assisting businesses in predicting errors, planning, etc. (Strous et al., 2020). Particularly sustainability is going to become the futuristic trend for business and for organizations to boost their prospects', technology plays a key role. Indeed, digital technology such as AI can help organizations in various tasks like design, execution, and planning efficiently which can lead to resource conservation, waste reduction, and management. While the prime objectives of the UN SDGs are to facilitate economies to embrace renewable energies, AI usage can mediate countries in the transition from fossil fuel-intensive energy to renewable energies effectively and efficiently.

Businesses and organizations that are dependent on renewables can manage their business more profitably through AI interface by predicting production estimates, diagnosing breakdowns, predicting errors, scheduling maintenance, timely guidance, etc. In addition, AI and AR are also currently being explored in the agriculture, transport, traffic management, and manufacturing sector in different capacities (Filho et al., 2023). According to studies by Vinuesa et al. (2020), incorporating AI in business can help achieve as much as 79% of sustainable development goals facilitating a circular economy and sustainable cities. Surprisingly AI applications are positively impacting many sectors especially the energy sector by providing the rightful information on maintenance, inspection, and predicting optimized consumption thereby reducing energy use and mitigating environmental impact. In the supply chain and logistics sector, AI technology is providing substantial support in reducing carbon emissions by optimizing transport, avoiding transit delays, etc. Notwithstanding, there are several ways AI technology is facilitating companies and businesses toward achieving sustainability in a small-scale dimension (Fig. 5.7). Intense application areas of AI followed by other digital technologies are already in adoption in some of the companies like Apple, Google, Amazon, IBM, Facebook, Baidu, Alibaba, Microsoft, JD.com, Tencent, etc. With the help of AI and other forms of AI applications, smaller companies are now able to move toward the path of sustainable development in their business which has changed the small-scale business landscape.

There are many use cases related to the subsets of AI, for example, ML has helped Google data centers reduce energy consumption by 40% by identifying efficient energy-optimizing options that have eventually reduced the carbon

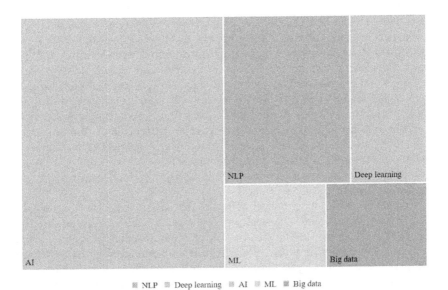

🔲 NLP   🔲 Deep learning   🔲 AI   🔲 ML   🔲 Big data

Fig. 5.7.   Range of Applications With AI-Enabled Technology in Adoption by Different Global Companies.

footprint of the company. Another promising area of AI and its forms are findings of potential users in the food industry, fishing, water resources management, and agriculture sector demonstrating novel applications in each of these sectors. In the food industry, food waste generated is tracked using computer vision (a subset of AI) helping the industry to identify waste sources and minimize and reduce costs. Companies like Winnow Vision Japan (food waste technology) could successfully reduce food wastage by using an AI interface in their business operation that has saved an equivalent of 36 million meals ending up in landfills.

Other companies such as Tokyo Hilton Bay and catering company ISS have started to use interface their business using AI in reducing food waste and avoiding hunger which is goal 2 of SDGs. In the fishing industry, ML applications have helped the fishing industry to keep control of overfishing by tracking suspicious fishing boats in ocean hot spot areas. The global fishing watch company has tied up collaboration with Google, sky truth, and Oceana to regulate unsustainable, illegal, and unregulated fishing in ocean waters. Among other use cases, in agriculture AI forms such as ML, image recognition, and predictive modeling through technology apps to estimate crop production according to demand, while ML provides weather forecast for suitable crop planting, analyze yields, etc., helping millions of farmers in harvesting accurately without any time delays.

Image recognition technology in another way helps the agriculture sector in detecting plant disease, pests, nutrition status of soil, etc., to assist farmers in soil management for better yields. Moreover, ML application provides real-time images of plant and cropland, generating vital information about the plant and crop status which can be shared with farmers, agricultural scientists, and researchers instantly for evaluating crop growth. All these application areas of AI and its subsets are considerably reducing the wastage of resources, time, and crop losses subsequently supporting in increasing the yield. In the field of water resources and management, domestic and commercial water use leads to many million gallons of water getting wasted annually through leakages and faulty water connection systems. A company (named Wint) specializing in water management is using AI for detecting water leakages both at small- and large-scale dimensions, leading to conserving water from unnecessary wastage in commercial buildings. From this AI-enabled interface, reducing water wastage has considerably saved expenditure on consumption, parallelly contributing to reducing the burden on depleting water resources.

Emphasizing the specific role AI plays in sustainability and sustainable development in companies, AI-enabled applications tend to leverage the three pillars of sustainable development targeting environmental protection, social influence, and economic impact. These trilogies are optimized by AI more critically in sectors such as agriculture, energy, natural resources, automobile sector, etc., apart from other sectors like healthcare, automotive, tourism, and education. Moreover, with the responsibility of meeting the sustainable development goals of the UN by the year 2030, a set target for every nation, technology tools like AI and its enabled subsets receive much recognition in streamlining and optimizing resource use, time, space, manpower, reduce wastage while providing efficient and effective suggestions and predictions in management. For example, AI usage at the current rate and in the future could lead companies to reduce approximately 2.6–5.3 gigatons of greenhouse gas emissions which accounts for 5%–10% of the total emissions globally. Further, there are many ways AI is currently helping companies achieve sustainability at different stages such as in processing, procurement, packaging, transporting, waste reduction, marketing, etc. In the retail business and marketing, AI-generated computer vision systems can potentially address the issue of defects in products at the manufacturing stage. Installing AI vision-enabled quality control systems at the production line can route defective products getting into packaging units. Globally wastage from the return of products from defective or consumer dissatisfaction is leading to the accumulation of 4.7 million metric tons of carbon dioxide, which can be reduced to a significant amount with the use of an AI-enabled monitoring system. Another area that AI has the scope to strengthen sustainability in the marketing field is by promoting digital marketing concepts, trends, and strategies, which in one way is leading to a reduction in greenhouse gas emissions and reducing the carbon footprint of companies implementing them. Digital marketing can reduce transportation, and enables users or customers to choose products that are manufactured locally without compromising on quality, and these measures indirectly reduce carbon emissions from long-distance air or land transportation of goods.

Technology Tools in the Digital Era for Sustainable Transformation of Business

The present age is the era of digitalization, tagged with Industry 4.0. Characteristically in this era, all businesses and organizations are immersed in digital technology tools, intending to move toward digital transformation. Digital transformation refers to the practice that uses digital technology tools to improvise or modify the existing business process, method, culture, and customer experience to meet the changing business and market requirements. Digital technology tools form the important elements that contribute to the digital transformation process in businesses and such digital-enabled businesses use a wide range of technology applications to improve the work process, quality, output value, improve customer experience and satisfaction concurrently to sustain business and profitability.

Currently, in the Industry 4.0 framework, technology utilization and automation are the key focus areas aimed to bring digital transformation and digitalization to organization operations. Among them, AI, AR, IoT, ML, deep learning, etc., are some of the tools having extensive use in almost many fields, and sectors contributing largely toward digitalization and transformation (Frank et al., 2019). Further, there are many reports published by researchers and business analysts who expressed that adopting digital technology has led to progression in business growth and improved business prospects. In other words, incorporating digitalization into organization operations offers multiple benefits to business such as reducing cost, avoiding wastages, improving operating efficiency, and enhancing productivity all possible through effective planning through applications of technological tools. Besides, digital technology offers opportunities for improving economies generating employment, and increasing efficiency in transactions, particularly in the banking sector (Zuo et al., 2021). Also, many organizations are on the desperate path of sustainable development, digitalization and transformation are presumably seen as the best pathways for achieving sustainability in business. Subsequent studies also prove that digitalization and transformation create a sense of willingness and interest among customers to prefer a business with such companies (Fig. 5.8).

Sustainable transformation of business is an important activity for every economy to achieve sustainable development goals. In this pursuit, organizations in Europe have introduced a concept referred to as sustainable digitalization to bring digitalization into the economy to lead sustainability in businesses across the European region. The concept works on three fundamental approaches to achieve sustainable transformation of business which are sustainable business-to-business digitalization, incorporating green technologies for a circular economy, and policy for enabling innovation and regulatory framework. The mechanism used in sustainable business-to-business digitalization intends to incorporate technology tools to transform business operations from analog to digital platforms, ideally converting the nondigital businesses to digitally enabled sectors.

In contrast, some organizations are taking a proactive role toward reducing resource use, lowering energy consumption, and adopting models for efficiency by adopting big data, AI, blockchain, and additive manufacturing to emphasize circular economy which can bring a positive impact on the environment, society,

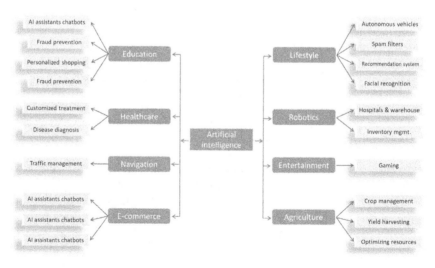

Fig. 5.8.   Artificial Intelligence in Different Sectors and
Corresponding Applications Areas.

and economic fronts of sustainability. Manufacturing industries currently are aiming toward the circular economy concept for enabling resource conservation, reducing wastage, and efficient management of inputs and outputs to embrace sustainability transformation in business. Confirming this, digital technology tools such as AI, blockchain, AR, IoT, and other digital interface applications positively impact businesses and organizations promoting environmental, societal, and economic sustainability (Schneider, 2019; Vial, 2021).

Conclusion

AI and AR are two promising digital technologies gaining wide applications in many sectors, leading businesses toward digitalization and transformation. This chapter attempts to explore the role of AI and AR in leading businesses and organizations on the road to digitalization and transformation. The study categorically emphasizes the influence of digital technology tools specifically AI and AR on the path of achieving sustainability.

Sustainable development goals of the UN have invariably laid responsibility on every business, organization, and government across the globe, and achieving them is critical for sustaining businesses amid global challenges. Typically, digital technology tools such as AI and AR are a few of them making entry into every business and sector far and wide, and organizations are exploring a wide range of these tools for transforming operations to digital platforms. Besides, analysts, researchers, and planners perceive that digitalization and digital transformation can significantly help organizations march toward sustainability and contribute to sustainable development goals. In response, sectors such as manufacturing, healthcare, education, retail, service, entertainment, automobiles, etc., are some of the few that started interfacing their business with tools like AI and AR which has made a tremendous positive impact on growth and sustainability.

Further, AI and AR have also found applications in fields like agriculture, water resources, fisheries, navigation, sports, aviation, etc., assisting in energy conservation, waste reduction, optimizing resources, stabilizing outputs, etc., eventually contributing toward the betterment of the environment, society, and economy. In conclusion, the path to sustainability is a challenging path for businesses and organizations, transforming every facet of the business process toward sustainable practices needs the intervention of technology, regulatory mechanism, and administrative guidance to support sustainability initiatives. Toward achieving those objectives, AI and AR as technology tools can hasten the process of sustainable transformation of business in all dimensions.

Future Scope of Research and Direction

Much of the study presented in the chapter examines the role of digital technology tools like AI and AR impacting the different fields and sectors. While AI has a principal technology tool that has been incorporated into different industries for some time, other subsets like AR, VR, and ML are a few other AI-enabled technologies that are getting accelerated in many businesses and fields. In this chapter, no distinction is being made on any of these technology tools in any particular field, regardless of all these technological tools being known to make significant progress in diversified fields. However, there is a need to understand the role these technologies play in different sectors across different geographic regions. As the success, growth, and integration into business operations are largely dependent on the funding and investment potential of each country, in that sense there is a disparity in the extent and level to which these technology tools are incorporated. Therefore, future studies and research should orient in identifying the determinant factors of the different technological tools like AI, AR, VR, and ML that would probably influence the growth, progress, and extent of integration into business operations in different economies.

References

Alsop, T. (2022). Number of mobile augmented reality (AR) active user devices worldwide from 2019 to 2024. www.Statista.com. https://www.statista.com/statistics/1098630/global-mobile-augmented-reality-ar-users/

Brečko, B., & Ferrari, A. (2016). In R. Vuorikari & Y. Punie (Eds.), *The digital competence framework for consumers.* Joint Research Centre Science for Policy Report. EUR 28133 EN. https://doi.org/10.2791/838886

Cheng, F., Zhang, H., Fan, W., & Harris, B. (2018). Image recognition technology based on deep learning. *Wireless Personal Communications, 102*(2), 1917–1933.

Chladek, N. (2019). *Why you need sustainability in your business strategy.* Harvard Business School. https://online.hbs.edu/blog/post/business-sustainability-strategies

Cipresso, P., Giglioli, I. A. C., Raya, M. A., & Riva, G. (2018). The past, present, and future of virtual and augmented reality research: A network and cluster analysis of the literature. *Frontiers in Psychology, 9*, 2086. https://doi.org/10.3389/fpsyg.2018.02086

Collins, C., Dennehy, D., Conboy, K., & Mikalef, P. (2021). Artificial intelligence in information systems research: A systematic literature review and research agenda. *International Journal of Information Management, 60*, 102383.

De Buck, S., Maes, F., Ector, J., Bogaert, J., Dymarkowski, S., Heidbuchel, H., & Suetens, P. (2005). An augmented reality system for patient-specific guidance of cardiac catheter ablation procedures. *IEEE Transactions on Medical Imaging, 24*, 1512–1524. https://doi.org/10.1109/TMI.2005.857661

Devagiri, J. S., Paheding, S., Niyaz, Q., Yang, X., & Smith, S. (2022). Augmented reality and artificial intelligence in the industry: Trends, tools, and future challenges. *Expert Systems With Applications.* 118002.

Dey, A., Billinghurst, M., Lindeman, R. W., & Swan, J. E., II (2018). A systematic review of 10 years of augmented reality usability studies: 2005 to 2014. *Frontiers in Robotics and AI, 5*, 37. https://doi.org/10.3389/frobt.2018.00037

Di Vaio, A., Palladino, R., Hassan, R., & Escobar, O. (2020). Artificial intelligence and business models in the sustainable development goals perspective: A systematic literature review. *Journal of Business Research, 121*, 283–314.

Dow, S., Mehta, M., Harmon, E., MacIntyre, B., & Mateas, M. (2007). Presence and engagement in an interactive drama. In *Conference on Human Factors in Computing Systems – Proceedings* (pp. 1475–1484).

Fabian. (2018). Global artificial intelligence landscape | including database with 3,465 AI companies. https://medium.com/}@bootstrappingme/global-artificial-intelligence-landscape-including-database-with-3-465-ai-companies-3bf01a175c5d

Fahle, S., Prinz, C., & Kuhlenkötter, B. (2020). Systematic review on machine learning (ML) methods for manufacturing processes – Identifying artificial intelligence (AI) methods for field application. *Procedia CIRP, 93*, 413–418.

Filho, W. L., Yang, P., Eustachio, J. H. P. P., Azul, M. A., Gellers, J. C., Gielczyk, A., Dinis, M. A. P., & Kozlova, V. (2023). Deploying digitalisation and artificial intelligence in sustainable development research. *Environment, Development and Sustainability, 25*, 4957–4988. https://doi.org/10.1007/s10668-022-02252-3

Frank, A. G., Dalenogare, L. S., & Ayala, N. F. (2019). Industry 4.0 technologies: Implementation patterns in manufacturing companies. *International Journal of Production Economics, 210*, 15–26. https://doi.org/10.1016/j.ijpe.2019.01.004

Galaz, V., Centeno, M. A., Callahan, P. W., Causevic, A., Patterson, T., Brass, I., Baum, S., Farber, D., Fischer, J., Garcia, D., McPhearson, T., Jimenez, D., King, B., Larcey, P., & Levy, K. (2021). Artificial intelligence, systemic risks, and sustainability. *Technology in Society, 67*, 101741.

Haleem, A., Javaid, M., & Khan, I. H. (2019). Current status and applications of artificial intelligence (AI) in medical field: An overview. *Current Medicine Research and Practice, 9*(6), 231–237. https://doi.org/10.1016/j.jbusres.2020.08.019

Hino, M., Benami, E., & Brooks, N. (2018). Machine learning for environmental monitoring. *Nature Sustainability, 1*(10), 583–588.

Huang, M. H., & Rust, R. T. (2017). Technology-driven service strategy. *Journal of the Academy of Marketing Science, 45*(6), 906–924.

IBM. (2020). What is artificial intelligence (AI)? https://www.ibm.com/topics/artificial-intelligence

Johnson, J. T. (2022). Digital twinning use cases strengthen with AR, VR. https://www.techtarget.com/searchcio/tip/Digital-twinning-use-cases-strengthen-with-AR-VR

Joppa, L. N. (2015). Technology for nature conservation: An industry perspective. *Ambio, 44*(Suppl. 4), 522–526. https://doi.org/10.1007/s13280-015-0702-4

Juan, M. C., Alcaniz, M., Monserrat, C., Botella, C., Baños, R. M., & Guerrero, B. (2005). Using augmented reality to treat phobias. *IEEE Computer and Graphics Applications, 25*, 31–37. https://doi.org/10.1109/MCG.2005.143

Kumar, A., Yadav, S. S., Kumar, S., & Johri, P. (2021, March). Augmented reality systems in gaming and multimedia. In *2021 International Conference on Advance Computing and Innovative Technologies in Engineering (ICACITE)* (pp. 333–338). IEEE.

Laurent, E. M. (2021). Can artificial intelligence effectively support sustainable development? In E. Mercier-Laurent, M. Ö. Kayalica, & M. L. Owoc (Eds.), *Artificial intelligence for knowledge management. AI4KM 2021. IFIP advances in information and communication technology* (Vol. 614). Springer. https://doi.org/10.1007/978-3-030-80847-1_10

Lez'er, V., Semeryanova, N., Kopytova, A., & Kvach, I. (2019). Application of artificial intelligence in the field of geotechnics and engineering education. In *E3S Web of Conferences* (Vol. 110, p. 02094). EDP Sciences.

Lin, C. H., & Hsu, P. H. (2017). Integrating procedural modeling process and immersive VR environment for architectural design education. In *MATEC Web of Conferences* (Vol. 104). Les Ulis: EDP Sciences. https://doi.org/10.1051/matecconf/201710403007

Liu, Y., Rai, R., Purwar, A., He, B., & Mani, M. (Eds.). (2020). Machine learning applications in manufacturing. *Journal of Computing and Information Science in Engineering, 20*(2), 020301.

Magd, H., Jonathan, H., Khan, S. A., & El Geddawy, M. (2022). Artificial intelligence – The driving force of Industry 4.0. *A Roadmap for Enabling Industry 4.0 by Artificial Intelligence*, 1–15.

Patel, A. R., Ramaiya, K. K., Bhatia, C. V., Shah, H. N., & Bhavsar, S. N. (2021). Artificial intelligence: Prospect in mechanical engineering field – A review. *Data Science and Intelligent Applications*, 267–282.

Rafi, T. (2023). *Why sustainability is crucial for corporate strategy*. Weforum https://www.weforum.org/agenda/2022/06/why-sustainability-is-crucial-for-corporate strategy/

Rasp, S., Pritchard, M. S., & Gentine, P. (2018). Deep learning to represent subgrid processes in climate models. *Proceedings of the National Academy of Sciences of the United States of America, 115*, 9684–9689. https://doi.org/10.1073/pnas.1810286115

Reichstein, M., Camps-Valls, G., Stevens, B., Jung, M., Denzler, J., & Carvalhais, N. (2019). Deep learning and process understanding for data-driven earth system science. *Nature, 566*, 195–204. The National Energy Research Supercomputing Center in Lawrence Berkeley National Laboratory, Berkeley, CA, USA.

Reis, J., Amorim, M., Melão, N., & Matos, P. (2018). Digital transformation: A literature review and guidelines for future research. In Á. Rocha, H. Adeli, L. P. Reis, & S. Costanzo (Eds.), *Trends and advances in information systems and technologies. WorldCIST'18. Advances in intelligent systems and computing* (Vol. 745). Springer. https://doi.org/10.1007/978-3-319-77703-0_41

Rice, M. (2003). Information and communication technologies and the global digital divide: Technology transfer, development, and least developing countries. *Comparative Technology Transfer and Society, 1*(1), 72–88.

Richter, O. Z., Juarros, V. I. M., Bond, M., & Gouverneur, F. (2019). Systematic review of research on artificial intelligence applications in higher education: Where are the educators? *International Journal of Educational Technology in Higher Education, 16*(6).

Sahu, C. K., Young, C., & Rai, R. (2021). Artificial intelligence (AI) in augmented reality (AR)-assisted manufacturing applications: A review. *International Journal of Production Research, 59*(16), 4903–4959. https://doi.org/10.1080/00207543.2020.1859636

Schneider, S. (2019). The impacts of digital technologies on innovating for sustainability. In N. Bocken, P. Ritala, L. Albareda, & R. Verburg (Eds.), *Innovation for sustainability. Palgrave studies in sustainable business in association with future earth*. Palgrave Macmillan. https://doi.org/10.1007/978-3-319-97385-2_22

Schwald, B., & De Laval, B. (2003). An augmented reality system for training and assistance to maintenance in the industrial context. *Journal of WSCG, 11*.

Soon, O. Y., & Hui, L. K. (2022). *Making artificial intelligence work for sustainability*. Technology. https://technologymagazine.com/ai-and-machine-learning/making-artificial-intelligence-work-for-sustainability

Statista.com. (2023). *Artificial intelligence (AI) startup funding worldwide from 2011 to 2021 (in billion U.S. dollars), by quarter.* https://www.statista.com/statistics/943151/ai-funding-worldwide-by

Strous, L., Johnson, R., Grier, D. A., & Swade, D. (Eds.). (2020). *Unimagined futures – ICT opportunities and challenges* (Vol. 555). Springer AICT.

Szajna, A., & Kostrzewski, M. (2022). AR-AI tools as a response to high employee turnover and shortages in manufacturing during regular, pandemic, and war times. *Sustainability*, *14*, 6729. https://doi.org/10.3390/su14116729

Tulinayo, F. P., Ssentume, P., & Najjuma, R. (2018). Digital technologies in resource constrained higher institutions of learning: A study on students' acceptance and usability. *International Journal of Educational Technology in Higher Education*, *15*(1), 1–19.

Verma, S., Sharma, R., Deb, S., & Maitra, D. (2021). Artificial intelligence in marketing: Systematic review and future research direction. *International Journal of Information Management Data Insights*, *1*(1), 100002.

Vial, G. (2021). Understanding digital transformation: A review and a research agenda. *Managing Digital Transformation*, 13–66.

Vinuesa, R., Azizpour, H., Leite, I., Balaam, M., Dignum, V., Domisch, S., Felländer, A., Langhans, S. D., Tegmark, M., & Fuso Nerini, F. (2020). The role of artificial intelligence in achieving the sustainable development goals. *Nature Communications*, *11*(1), 1–10.

Wan, J., Li, X., Dai, H. N., Kusiak, A., Martínez-García, M., & Li, D. (2020). Artificial-intelligence-driven customized manufacturing factory: Key technologies, applications, and challenges. *Proceedings of the IEEE*, *109*(4), 377–398.

Zuo, L., Strauss, J., & Zuo, L. (2021). The digitalization transformation of commercial banks and its impact on sustainable efficiency improvements through investment in science and technology. *Sustainability*, *13*(19), 11028. https://doi.org/10.3390/su131911028

Chapter 6

A Qualitative Inquiry Into Preference of Bahraini Fashion Designers Towards Fashion Shows Versus Digital Fashion Shows, and Factors Influencing Their Choice

Nidhi Goyal

Royal University for Women, Bahrain

Abstract

As the areas of fashion marketing are transforming, fashion show research needs to be recognised, to understand its prevalence, changing form and influence on the consumer behaviour. The paper studied the promotion strategies for the brand and products of fashion designers in Bahrain, in particular the fashion shows, its digital versions, and the factors influencing their choice. The study was conducted using the qualitative method and the detailed semi-structured qualitative interview method was employed and sample of designers and a prominent modeling agency were selected by purposive sampling technique. In-depth interviews with designers were structured to understand the fashion industry, participation in fashion shows and preference of mode of fashion show. Interviews were conducted with the modeling agency, to understand the prevalence of fashion shows, and the execution and demand of organising fashion shows. The data gathered were supported by the relevant secondary data and document analysis and presented. In the study both the forms of the fashion show viz., live and digital are discussed and compared. The digital fashion show and similar forms as short films, videos, on social media seem to be more promising, with minimum requirement of set design, wider reach, economic, ease of execution. The research suggests that physical and digital fashion shows have their advantages and disadvantages, with the choice ultimately based on the brand's goals and resources. As technology advances and the fashion

Navigating the Digital Landscape, 107–118
Copyright © 2024 Nidhi Goyal
Published under exclusive licence by Emerald Publishing Limited
doi:10.1108/978-1-83549-272-720241006

industry changes, digital fashion shows are likely to play an increasingly important role in the future.

Keywords: Bespoke; consumer behaviour; digital media; fashion show; fashion marketing; social media

Introduction

Throughout the history of fashion, fashion shows have played an important role in the business promotion and brand awareness. Additionally, it has acquired cultural significance in our society today. In society, fashion shows serve many purposes: entertainment, communication of important creative messages, subversion, political statements and career launches. The fashion show has acquired cultural significance within our society. The connection between the public, the media and the consumer has been permanently changed by digital media. A brand or designer no longer has to rely on the press to showcase their products to target audience. With technological advancements and digital media, brands showcase their products directly to the consumer, tapping into discontent within the industry about seasonal time (Min et al., 2015; Silva & Bonetti, 2021; Stark, 2018).

Fashion business in Bahrain comprised a number of local brands, local bespoke and designers. Fashion is a multi-billion dollar industry, where many different fields provide employment opportunities, such as design, production, distribution, marketing, retailing, advertising, consulting, etc. Fashion is among the fastest growing industries in the four regions of Gulf Corporation Council (GCC). The fashion design industry is thriving in the GCC, particularly with a supplementary Islamic clothing industry that deals with clothes such as *abayas* and *jalabiyas*. Fashion business in the region is primarily on a traditional manufacturing set up with the prevalence of bespoke clothing; however, with waves of e-commerce on the rise, it is evolving rapidly. Since perhaps 20 years ago, fashion has been modest and there haven't been any fashion weeks or presentations. Fashion events in the form of runway presentations and after party are marketplace icons. With the media coverage, and social media abundance, fashion events have been playing a crucial role (Pinchera & Rinallo, 2019).

As the areas of fashion marketing are transforming, research on fashion show needs to be recognised, to understand its prevalence, execution and changing form. A fashion show is a way for a designer to introduce a new collection, which starts with an inspiration, and presenting idea or concept. Fashion shows are not only a presentation of garments but also a performance like a theatre. Evolving from the streets of Paris in 1800s in the earliest days, fashion shows have been significantly influencing the fashion systems. Today with digital technology, a new era of live streaming of fashion films has become viral. Through digital media, its accessibility is no more restricted and can be experienced by almost everyone. Fashion shows, even though are theatrical or magical, are also supposed to be commercial. In the contemporary context, with the live streaming of the show, buying by the consumer has become faster and easier. The way the fashion industry is evolving, the communication of fashion collection is also revolutionising (Stark, 2018).

The fashion industry is rapidly changing, and new technologies are emerging for designing, production and marketing, and various solutions in terms of sustainability and wider consumer reach have been achieved (Bertola & Teunissen, 2018; Nobile et al., 2021). The innovations in fashion industry pertaining to the digital intervention can be classified into four categories: (1) digital design and e-prototyping, (2) digital business and promotion, (3) digital human and metaverse and (4) digital apparel and smart e-technology (Sayem, 2022). Smartphones have made it possible for fashion consumers to use their mobile devices for shopping and other social activities (Drapers, 2019). The research in the area of fashion business promotion often focused on popular modes like advertisements (Lee et al., 2021) and marketing on social media (Boerman & Müller, 2022). Fashion shows have been of research interest, with perspective to its history, and importance of fashion shows as marketplace icons and staging concepts (Mendes, 2021; Pinchera & Rinallo, 2021; Strömberg, 2019). This paper starts with an overview of the drivers of expanding fashion industry in Bahrain and illustrates a comparison between actual/live fashion show and digital/recorded fashion shows, as an important marketing activity by Bahraini designers. The paper makes an attempt to contribute to the research in Arab's world pertaining to the fashion industry, particularly the Kingdom of Bahrain, from theory and practical perspectives.

Methodology

Around the middle of the 2000s, the Gulf Cooperation Council (GCC) saw a rapid increase in internet usage. The consumers in the GCC are some of the most technologically sophisticated and connected worldwide. Is the high usage of digital technology resulting in designers expanding the power of fashion shows for their businesses and recognition globally? For the purpose of this study, we used a qualitative research approach under a descriptive research design. The qualitative inquiry helps to understand in a detailed way, with effective analysis of the results, thus the researcher could explore the drivers of fashion industry and fashion shows in Bahrain (Moran-Ellis et al., 2020). The detailed semi-structured qualitative interview method was employed and sample of designers and a prominent modeling agency were selected by purposive sampling technique. In-depth interviews with designers were structured to understand the fashion industry, participation in fashion shows and preference of mode of fashion show. Similarly, interview was conducted with the modeling agency, to understand the prevalence of fashion show, execution and demand of organising fashion show. These interviews were conducted as one-to-one online while ensuring complete confidentiality. Each interview lasted around 15–20 min. The data gathered were supported by the relevant secondary data and document analysis. An analysis of the data was carried out qualitatively, and the results were presented.

Findings and Discussion

In the first section of the research work, an overview of the fashion industry in Bahrain and important drivers contributing towards the industry expansion were studied. The next section of the study focusses on the runway fashion presentation, where obstacles faced by the fashion designers to organise or participate in the fashion show were studied. Also, an attempt was made to establish a comparison between the conventional fashion show and the digital version, being organised in Bahrain and acceptability by the designers.

Understanding Bahrain Fashion Industry

Before mall-culture, most people got their clothes stitched in the *souq* in Manama (capital, Bahrain). In middle eastern cities, *souq* is a traditional market and also very popular tourism attraction. More than a commercial place, *souq* is actually an important social, cultural and recreational centre. Manama *souq*, Bab Al Bahrain, Muharraq *souq* are among the popular *souq*s in Bahrain, especially for fabric retailing and bespoke clothing (Alraouf, 2012). Arab countries primarily appear as oil-based economy; however, other sectors, among which apparel design and production have been gaining popularity. The apparel design and production operate on a standard rather conventional system, without a significant industrial production. It was in the late 1980s that fashion designers first came into being. As the US.-Bahrain Free Trade Agreement (FTA) gained momentum in the 2000s, mall culture grew and fashion retail business thrived (MOIC, 2021; USTR, 2021).

Effect of the US-Bahrain Free Trade Agreement on the Textile and Apparel Industry

A 10-year free trade agreement was signed between the US and Bahrain in August 2006. With the improvement in trade in goods between the US and Bahrain, the purpose of the agreement was to improve economic relations between the two countries and to establish free trade between them. Other consumer industries, including apparel, were affected by it. Manufacturing units for fabrics and garments were established during this period, viz., MRS Fashion, Noble garment Factory, Ambattur Clothing International (apparel manufacturers) and West-Point Home Bahrain (home furnishing unit). As a result of the US.-Bahrain FTA, the bilateral trade relations significantly improved and both countries seen tangible benefits as a result (Saxena, 2014).

- A 47% increase in imports from Bahrain from 2005 (pre-FTA), along with a 190% increase in exports from Bahrain, were recorded in 2014.
- Aluminum ($181 m), woven apparel ($107 m), mineral fuel (oil) ($95 m), fertilisers ($91 m) and miscellaneous textile articles ($64 m) were the five largest imports categories, in the year 2013.

- The apparel and textile sector contributed 27% to US exports and invested $250 million in the sector.

On 31 July 2016, FTA expired and negatively affected the textile and garment industries in Bahrain. A few closed down and others, shifted the apparel manufacturing factories to Jordan, Oman and other places (Bair et al., 2016; Suri, 2017).

The State of the Global Islamic Economy Report 2020–2021 projects that the modest clothing market will grow from its current $277 billion valuation to $311 billion by 2024 (Benissan, 2021). In Bahrain, males wear a long, white, clothing called a *Thowb*. Further, women wear, an *Abaya*, which is the traditional dress, consisting of a long black, floor length dress that covers the arms. Women wear a *Hijab*, a scarf on their head to cover hair, which can be black or any other color/s. Some women cover themselves even more and wear a *Nikab* that only allows the eyes to be seen (Condora, 2013). Contemporary traditional and modest fashion has been rising and will always be in demand, in not only in Bharain also in MENA region as well, as suggested by the respondent. With the aim of expanding in the region outside Bahrain, designers create modest contemporary wear not only for women consumer in Bahrain but also outside of their target market, indicating a growing designer and consumer base. Atelier Kubra Al Qaseer, founded in 1987, as '*Alsaafa*', is one of the prominent names in Bahrain's Fashion Industry in traditional and haute coutureKubra Al Qaseer, the first fashion designer in Bahrain, is the owner.

'Bahrain has always been very creative since a long time ago. The fashion industry has grown a lot. On global platform it is in the nascent stage', respondent suggested during the interview. A land steeped in artistry has a number of fashion brands owned by especially Bahrini Women. One of the modern and popular names among the upcoming designer is Haya Khalifa is creative director in Naseem AlAndalos, a couture brand. She has presented Naseem AlAndalos in multiple international shows in Paris, London and Dubai and also received the award of best Arab fashion designer by the Arab Sat Festival in Egypt (Martensson, 2017). Like Haya, Areej Alhaikh is another upcoming designer, best known for traditional Bahrini collection of *Jalabiya* as well as for modern wear. Annada, NS by Noof, Noon by Noor, Rawan Maki Design House are among the renowned brands pioneering the fashion industry (StartupMGZN, 2019). Having a number of established fashion brands primarily owned by Bahrini women also has a significant implication to a fact that here women constitute 49% of the total workforce (BNA, 2021).

Fashion Runway Events: Popularity, Acceptance and Mode

Fashion runway event is one of the marketing or sales promotion activities that has been appreciated by all the designers and is considered as a cultural event (Kalbaska et al., 2019; Skov et al., 2009). In this section, following themes have been developed based on the research question – 'What is the attitude of designers in Bahrain towards the fashion runway as the marketing event?' One of the key observations while developing these themes was that undoubtedly, fashion runway is an essential part of the global industry and contributes to the cultural and economic aspects; however, with a limited target market in the region and also the increase in modest fashion events across the globe, Bahraini designers have a mixed attitude towards it.

Bahrain Fashion Week, which included one local designer, organised the country's first fashion show in 2008. The Bahraini government persistently pays attention to fashion industry to provide more revenue and employment opportunities to its population. For instance, His Excellency Dr. Hassan Abdullah Fakhro, Minister of Industry and Commerce, supported to organise the Bahrain International Design Week (BIDW, 2013). However, prior to it, public events featuring fashion runway presentations were hardly ever planned. In 2015, Arab Fashion Council (AFC) was formed, and Arab Fashion Week was organised, in Dubai. By way of the AFC, the fashion industry is anticipated to expand jobs in the private sector, expand tourism to become a more metropolitan country and aid in reducing the region's reliance on oil. It's important to note that the AFC, which represents the fashion industry of 22 Arab nations, is the largest non-profit organisation in the world. In addition, the Dubai Islamic Fashion Week, Vogue Fashion Dubai Experience and Fashion Forward focus on modest and Islamic clothing. Other countries across the MENA region also introduced fashion events, but those are their own. *The runway events are extremely good platform to launch new designers!* suggested by most of the respondents.

Bahrain is an island country with a population of 1.58 million people (as of 2021), with more than 800,000 foreigners (53%) (Nationsonline, n.d.). Such a small consumer base can easily be covered. *Our buyers prefer to meet us personally or in exhibition where we showcase and sell items, instead of fashion shows.*

Another small point, but important to highlight that in the region is that models for the photoshoot, video shoot and runway events are available through limited agencies and as well as freelance models.

> We are primarily being engaged for photoshoots and video shoots, as there is high prevalence of digital marketing. Designers in the region prefer to develop e-content, said the respondent from the modeling agency. The magical drama of the actual runway can never be replaced by the digital one, as to organise a professional audience attracting show, it requires experts, latest resources like camera, VR technology and can prove to be expensive, he added

Furthermore, Bahrain's government is persistently interested in creating more revenue and employment opportunities for its citizens through the fashion industry. For example, Medpoint-design, a successful organisation, has been hosting expo and fashion shows/fashion week in Bahrain (Medpoint-design a, n.d.). The first virtual show was organised in 2020 by Medpoint, under the event name 'Global Women Virtual Fashion Forum & Show' and the digital show was aired on YouTube and it provided a massive opportunity to a large number of clothing as well accessories designers amidst COVID-19. The experience of the fashion show was presented as the fashion videos that were presented with designer details and other visual effects. The eight days of fashion shows presented the innovative event and showed a huge participation from the famous fashion designers from New York, France/Paris Fashion Week, Italy, Morocco, Kingdom of Bahrain, Oman, KSA, UAE, Kuwait, Egypt, Jordan, Lebanon, Turkey, Sudan, India, Tunisia, Australia, Iraq, Portugal and Nepal (Medpoint-design b, n.d.). It was interesting as live comments on the live feeds appeared in real time, with viewers posting their thoughts on the show. The entire recording of the event was done in a limited time span.

In order to reach the right client at the right time, more of these tests and trials with virtual shows should be undertaken! The details about the digital consumption in Bahrain have been discussed in the next section. It is clear that fashion runways will continue to be crucial, but they must offer the proper balance of virtual and real presentations.

Digital Shows: Pros and Cons

It can be said that COVID-19 pandemic also brought opportunity to the fashion industry and gave birth to the digital runway shows. The year 2020 can be referred to indicate the infancy stage of the digital fashion shows. While physical fashion shows are still important for creating brand awareness and showcasing new collections, digital fashion shows offer several advantages, including:

- ability to reach a wider audience,
- reduce costs,
- provide greater flexibility in terms of scheduling and production,
- more shoppable, so viewers can purchase designs directly from the show.
- Sustainability is one of the most promising aspects of digital fashion that holds a lot of potential.

However, a lack of audience engagement can be con, possibly due to the lack of compelling cinematic and theatrical storytelling. The audience is able to see the clothing up close and experience the energy of the live event.

Consumers Who Are Digitally Savvy and More Instagrammable

Bahrain demonstrates a strong consumer base of the apparel. Between 2023 and 2028, Bahrainis are predicted to continuously spend 194.4 million USD on clothing and footwear (+22.59%). By 2028, fashion-related spending is expected to amount to 1.1 billion USD. It is expected that the market will grow by 1.79% annually from 2023 to 2027 (CAGR 2023–2027). With a market volume of US$367.40m in 2023, women's apparel is the market's largest segment (Statista, 2021). The digital adoption and consumption is very high. A high percentage of digital consumption appears to be promising to support the fashion retail industry. Further, there are a number of fashion online sites, such as Ounass, Farfetch, Asos and Namshi and a few others that have made their marks in

Bahrain and indicate online shopping being preferred by the consumer. As consumer study was out of the scope of the objective of the research thus, details provided are limited.

Fashion runway presentation is indeed an important part of the fashion industry, globally. However, with the advent of technology, fashion show also seems to be changed. It was discussed above that the virtual/you tube fashion show gained a lot of popularity. Similarly, with a high percentage of population using internet and social media like Instagram, Facebook, twitter, Tumblr, etc., are actively being used (Amed, 2015). This section highlights the dominance of the online social media platform like Facebook and Instagram and influence in fashion industry.

Social media is a very promising platform for creating brand awareness (Chu et al., 2013; Sumarliah et al., 2021). In the contemporary digital context, designers in Bahrain, however, as not very interested in fashion shows especially due to logistics, but prefer to share fashion show photo shoot process, back stage action and fashion videos with the brand's online followers.

> It is possible to create original material using the internet and social media platforms without relying on outside sources. Customers who are following me can access the promotional photo shoots and videos and then contact on 'whats app' for orders, said respondent

Further, social media influencers also significantly influence the purchasing decision of the consumer. Such influencers are primarily present on Instagram actively and affect the purchase intention (Sokolova & Kefi, 2020). Secondly, in comparison to the Facebook, it is Instagram, which seems to be a favored platform for many reasons, viz., perfect visual display, ease of uploading information, ease of usage, complete control on data, cobranding with influencers (Amed, 2013).

Conclusion

The research helped to understand and explain the fashion business in Bahrain, and how it has changed in relation to how marketing uses digital technology and customer behaviour. The aim of the article was to trace how rapidly the fashion show in Bahrain has been evolving and with the very high percentage of the consumer using internet, the shows are filmed and can be watched on the internet.

The growing prominence as an emerging potential market for fashion retail in the Kingdom is contributed to the factors like strong consumer demand, tourism expansion and leisure spending all favor fashion retail. In the research study, key drivers of the fashion industry viz., government initiatives and prevalence of bespoke clothing were elaborated. Acceptance and prevalence of digital fashion presentation is gaining popularity in a big way thus, opening new platforms for both established and upcoming designers for showcasing their collections and brand marketing. Such innovative digital practices are indeed challenging the conventional fashion promoting practices. However, the digitised marketing route is defining the new generation of fashion designers who want to promote their creativity on the global platform.

The traditional methods of presenting fashion have always been difficult to execute, due to logistics arrangements, availability of resources, fashion event organizers and experts; however, at the same time, digital presentation has gained momentum in the region, supported by tech-savvy generation and a very high digital consumption. This has influenced the fashion designers to showcase their creative aspects in terms of digital presentations, fashion films, photo shoots and others that help the designers to connect with the regional as well as the global buyer, irrespective to the cultural barriers what had been prevalent in the past. The other aspect to highlight in the paper is from the consumer perspective in Bahrain, where consumers experience the digital fashion presentations as interactive, accessible and lie within the cultural domain. But there will be question exists that, will fashion shows still be there? Do digital fashion shows have future potential? The fashion sector benefits from the gradual transition to digital technology since it allows for the satisfaction of consumer needs while also benefiting designers. The issues related to social and logistics are pertinent to the show production. However, the magic of fashion show, including the pose and parade, will still remain unmatched.

Growing interest of fashion designers with bespoke prevalence in social media to market the collection clearly connects the growing popularity of social media for fashion buying. Retailing using the conventional model of brick and mortar appears to be difficult especially for the new or start-ups because of logistics and financial implications. As with the brick-and-mortar set-up, the customer reach is limited, and inventory is another problem. It can be seen that the relationship of a designer and consumer has changed significantly, due to the digital context. With the fashion video, live streaming or even a photo shoot being uploaded on social media, consumer can make buying decision and place order faster. Connecting and catering to the individual customer is way much faster.

Overall, the research suggests that both physical and digital fashion shows have their advantages and disadvantages, and the choice between the two ultimately depends on the goals and resources of the fashion brand. However, with the rise of technology and the changing landscape of the fashion industry, it is likely that digital fashion shows will continue to play an increasingly important role in the future.

Limitation of the Study

According to the scope of the research and location, it was difficult to collect a large enough sample of fashion designers, which limited the generalizability of the findings. Further, as the study was conducted in Bahrain, fashion designers from different regions may have different preferences for fashion shows versus digital shows. As the research has focused on designers from one region may not capture this variation.

Future Scope of the Study

There are several potential areas for future research on fashion designers' preferences for fashion shows versus digital shows. As technology continues to evolve, it will be important to understand how new technologies could be incorporated into fashion shows and how this might impact designers' preferences. Secondly, while much of the current research has focused on designers' preferences, it would be valuable to also explore the preferences of consumers. This could include investigating how consumers engage with digital fashion shows. Thirdly, different regions and cultures may have different preferences for fashion shows versus digital shows. Future research could explore these differences and how they might impact the fashion industry as a whole. Further, future research could explore how digital fashion shows might be a more sustainable alternative.

By investigating these areas, future research can contribute on how the fashion industry is evolving and what the future of fashion shows might look like.

Disclosure Statement

No possible conflicts of interest were disclosed by the author.
Funding: The research received no external funding.

References

Alraouf, A. A. (2012). A tale of two SOUQS: The paradox of Gulf urban diversity. *Open House International, 37*(2), 72–81. https://doi.org/10.1108/OHI-02-2012-B0009

Amed, I. (2013). *Fashion's made-for-Instagram moments.* Business of Fashion. https://www.businessoffashion.com/opinions/news-analysis/fashions-made-for-instagram-moments/. Accessed on April 20, 2023.

Amed, I. (2015). *Why Stage Fashion Shows?* Business of Fashion. http://www.businessoffashion.com/articles/week-in-review/why-stage-fashion-shows. Accessed on June 15, 2021.

Bair, J., Frederick, S., & Gereffi, G. (2016). *Bahrain's position in the global apparel value chain: How the U.S.-Bahrain FTA and TPLs shape future development options.* Technical Report.

Benissan, E. (2021). *Muslim consumers want luxury. They just can't find it.* Vogue Business. https://www.voguebusiness.com/fashion/muslim-consumers-want-luxury-they-just-cant-find-it. Accessed on June 24, 2021.

Bertola, P., & Teunissen, J. (2018). Fashion 4.0. Innovating fashion industry through digital transformation. *Research Journal of Textile and Apparel, 22*(4), 352–369. https://doi.org/10.1108/RJTA-03-2018-0023

BIDW. (2013). Bahrain International Design Week 2013. Debuts at Bahrain International Exhibition Centre (n.d.), Bahrain International Design week. http://bidw.co/News.html. Accessed on March 10, 2021.

BNA. (2021). *Bahraini women account for 49% of workforce, surpassing global average.* https://www.bna.bh/en/Bahrainiwomenaccountfor49ofworkforcesurpassingg lobalaverage.aspx?cms=q8FmFJgiscL2fwIzON1%2BDm8Al69Gr3qLP1N DGtwssmU%3D. Accessed on December 20, 2021.

Boerman, S. C., & Müller, C. M. (2022). Understanding which cues people use to identify influencer marketing on Instagram: An eye tracking study and experiment. *International Journal of Advertising, 41*(1), 6–29. https://doi.org/10.1080/02650487. 2021.1986256

Chu, S. H., Kamal, S., & Kim, Y. (2013). Understanding consumers' responses toward social media advertising and purchase intention toward luxury products. *Journal of Global Fashion Marketing, 4*(3), 158–174. https://doi.org/10.1080/ 20932685.2013.790709

Condora, J. (Ed.). (2013). *Encyclopedia of national dress: Traditional clothing around the world.* ABC-CLIO. ISBN: 978-0-313-37636-8.

Drapers. (2019, May 1). *Gen Z and Millenials.* Drapers Online. https://www. drapersonline.com/business-operations/special-reports/gen-z-and-millennials/ 7035593.article

Kalbaska, N., Sádaba, T., & Cantoni, L. (2019). Editorial: Fashion communication: Between tradition and digital transformation. *Studies in Communication Sciences, 18*(2), 269–285. https://doi.org/10.24434/j.scoms.2018.02.005

Lee, S. H., Liang, Y., Chen, Y., Mahdi, A., & Qin, J. (2021). Can consumers' visual attention be predictable? A saliency modelling-based approach on fashion advertisements. *International Journal of Fashion Design, Technology and Education, 14*(3), 253–262. https://doi.org/10.1080/17543266.2021.1925354

Martensson, S. (2017). This new Bahraini brand will add edge to your evening look. https://en.vogue.me/fashion/haya-khalifa-interview/. Accessed on April 20, 2021.

Medpoint-Design a. (n.d.). *Wow expo & Abaya fashion show.* http://medpoint-design. com/web/wow-expo-abaya-fashion-show/. Accessed on April 28, 2021.

Medpoint-Design b. (n.d.). *Global women virtual fashion forum & show.* http:// medpoint-design.com/web/global-women-virtual-forum/. Accessed on April 28, 2021.

Mendes, S. (2021). The Instagrammability of the runway: Architecture, scenography, and the spatial turn in fashion communications. *Fashion Theory, 25*(3), 311–338. https://doi.org/10.1080/1362704X.2019.1629758

Min, S., Koo, H. S., & DeLong, M. (2015). Differences of information management between fashion show video and fashion film: Focusing on cases of channel. *Research Journal of Textile and Apparel, 19*(1), 73–83. https://doi.org/10.1108/ RJTA-19-01-2015-B008

MOIC. (2021). *BH-US free trade agreement.* https://www.moic.gov.bh/en/Tiles/ ForeignInvestment/free-trade-area-agreement. Accessed on April 28, 2021.

Moran-Ellis, J., Alexander, V. D., Cronin, C., Dickinson, M., Fielding, J., Sleney, J., & Thomas, H. (2020). *Triangulation and Integration: Processes, Claims and Implications. Qualitative Research, 6,* 45–59. https://doi.org/10.1177/146879410 6058870

Nationsonline. (n.d.). *Bahrain.* https://www.nationsonline.org/oneworld/bahrain.htm. Accessed on September 22, 2021.

Nobile, T. H., Noris, A., Kalbaska, N., & Cantoni, L. (2021). A review of digital fashion research: Before and beyond communication and marketing. *International Journal of Fashion Design, Technology and Education*, *14*(3), 293–301. https://doi.org/10.1080/17543266.2021.1931476

Pinchera, V., & Rinallo, D. (2019). *Marketplace icon: The fashion show* (pp. 479–491). Consumption Markets & Culture. https://doi.org/10.1080/10253866.2019.1703699

Pinchera, V., & Rinallo, D. (2021). Marketplace icon: The fashion show. *Consumption, Markets and Culture*, *24*(5), 479–491. https://doi.org/10.1080/10253866.2019.1703699

Sayem, A. S. M. (2022). Digital fashion innovations for the real world and metaverse. *International Journal of Fashion Design, Technology and Education*, *15*(2), 139–141. https://doi.org/10.1080/17543266.2022.2071139

Saxena, A. (2014). Key US-Bahrain FTA 'has no expiry date'. https://www.bilaterals.org/?key-us-bahrain-fta-has-no-expiry. Accessed on 28 April 2021.

Silva, E. S., & Bonetti, F. (2021). Digital humans in fashion: Will consumers interact? *Journal of Retailing and Consumer Services*, *60*. https://doi.org/10.1016/j.jretconser.2020.102430

Skov, L., Skjold, E., Moeran, B., Larsen, F., & Csaba, F. (2009). *The fashion show as an art form*. Department of Intercultural Communication and Management, Copenhagen Business School. https://research.cbs.dk/en/publications/the-fashion-show-as-an-art-form. Accessed on September 22, 2021.

Sokolova, K., & Kefi, H. (2019). Instagram and YouTube bloggers promote it, why should I buy? How credibility and parasocial interaction influence purchase intentions. *Journal of Retailing and Consumer Services*, *53*. https://doi.org/10.1016/j.jretconser.2019.01.011

Stark, G. (2018). *The fashion show: History, theory and practice*. Bloomsbury Publishing Plc. ISBN: 978-1-4725-6848-9.

StartupMGZN. (2019). *Here are 20 women-owned Bahraini brands you should know of and support!* https://www.startupmgzn.com/english/features/here-are-20-women-owned-bahraini-brands-you-should-know-of-and-support/. Accessed on December 10, 2021.

Statista. (2021). Apparel-Bahrain. https://www.statista.com/outlook/cmo/apparel/bahrain. Accessed on 20 April 2021.

Strömberg, P. (2019). Industrial Chic: Fashion shows in readymade spaces. *Fashion Theory*, *23*(1), 25–56. https://doi.org/10.1080/1362704X.2017.1386503

Sumarliah, E., Usmanova, K., Mousa, K., & Indriya, I. (2021). E-commerce in the fashion business: The roles of the COVID-19 situational factors, hedonic and utilitarian motives on consumers 'intention to purchase online'. *International Journal of Fashion Design, Technology and Education*. https://doi.org/10.1080/17543266.2021.1958926

Suri, M. (2017). Implications of U.S.-Bahrain free trade agreement on textile and apparel industry in Bahrain. *International Journal of Arts and Commerce*, *6*(6), 36–45.

USTR. (2021). *Bahrain free trade agreement*. https://ustr.gov/trade-agreements/free-trade-agreements/bahrain-fta. Accessed on April 28, 2021.

Chapter 7

Students Perspective Toward Online Teaching in Higher Education During COVID-19: A Cross-Sectional Analysis

Pooja Kansra

Lovely Professional University, India

Abstract

Coronavirus illness is an irresistible infection instigated by a newfound coronavirus. Social distancing was identified as the most effective preventive measure, and it has shifted the teaching to online mode. The present study explored the various perceptions held by students while attending the classes during COVID-19. Primary data have been obtained for the fulfillment of the objective of the study. The data were analyzed with descriptive and inferential statistics. It was exhibited that students specified that online teaching provides real-world skills followed by financial benefits, active learning, recorded lectures, comfortable, ease of access, safe, flexible timings, interactive, and build self-confidence. However, various challenges in online classes were less interaction, technical issues, network issues, lack of self-discipline, social isolation, family distractions, difficult e-learning tools, etc. Logit regression provided that willingness to attend online classes in post COVID-19 was associated with age, gender, IT skills, prior experience, and location. Application of e-learning posed several challenges and possibilities throughout the entire field of education throughout the pandemic. The study suggested the need to address the various challenges faced by the students on immediate basis. It was recommended that training programs can help to prepare the students to take the benefits of digital education platforms.

Keywords: Pandemic; COVID-19; students; digital platform; e-learning; higher education

Navigating the Digital Landscape, 119–127
Copyright © 2024 Pooja Kansra
Published under exclusive licence by Emerald Publishing Limited
doi:10.1108/978-1-83549-272-720241007

Introduction

The infectious disease coronavirus sickness (COVID-19) is recognized as a "Public Health Emergency." According to the World Health Organization (WHO), coronavirus can be reduced with social separation, contact tracing, testing, and isolation (Matrajt & Leung, 2020). Social distancing has been known as the utmost precautionary measure proposed by healthcare providers, advisories, and regulatory bodies worldwide (Coroiu et al., 2020; Wilder & Freedman, 2020). One of the most obvious developments brought about by the present pandemic was the shift of people from traditional to online employment (Ling & HO, 2020). COVID-19 has brought a biggest disruption in the education sector in the country and embattled 1.6 billion students in 190 or more nations. As a result of the shutting down of schools and colleges all around the world, about 94% of the world's student population has been impacted (Aristovnik et al., 2020).

As stated by the UNESCO, in April 2020 around 90% of the global student population was affected by the current pandemic and in June 2020 around 67% of student's population was directly affected by the pandemic (Jena, 2020). However, large proportion of students was affected in India due to nationwide lockdown. The complete nationwide lockdown made educational institutions to put a full stop on the physical delivery of classes and conducted the internships, examinations, and classes online (Jena, 2020; Sundarasen et al., 2020; Toquero, 2020). The teachers were instructed and directed to teach through platforms available online such Zoom, Google Meet, Google classroom, etc. COVID-19 led to the adoption of innovative teaching tools for continual delivery of classes (Adnan & Anwar, 2020; Crawford et al., 2020; Jandric et al., 2020).

COVID-19 ushered in a digital revolution in higher education, increasing the use of online lecture delivery, teleconferencing, online examinations, and virtual interactions between teachers and students (Bao, 2020; Dhawan, 2020; Jandric et al., 2020; Kapasia et al., 2020). However, online learning is biased for poor and marginalized students (Mishra et al., 2020). The shift from traditional classroom to online instruction during the COVID-19 epidemic was not a seamless one, and it presented a number of difficulties for the educators, the students, and their families (Kim, 2020; Setiawan & Taiman, 2020). This growth in online learning is familiar for the teachers but not for the students (Leonard & Guha, 2001; Sepulveda & Morrison, 2020). Thus, it is crucial to comprehend the students' perceptions of online education in light of the current epidemic. Understanding views and perceptions of the students will help to utilize the online learning platform effectively and will improve the learning outcomes. Therefore, present study explored the various challenges, perceptions, and willingness of the students to attend online classes in post COVID-19. The study contributed to the current literature about students' overall experiences and perceptions of online instruction. To accomplish the objective, chapter has been organized into four major parts. "Introduction" talked about the current situation of the online teaching during COVID-19. "Research Methodology" deals with material and methods adopted to examine the various experiences, perceptions, and future willingness to attend classes online. "Results" describes the empirical results of the study.

"Implications" discusses the various implications of the study. "Conclusion" summarizes the discussion along with policy implications.

Research Methodology

Research Design

The present study was descriptive and cross-sectional in nature and has been conducted in Punjab.

Sample Size and Sampling Technique

A primary survey has been used for the collection of data. A sample of 150 respondents was included for the present study. The data have been collected as per the purposive sampling.

Study Instrument

The data have been collected with the help of a self-constructed questionnaire. The questionnaire includes demographic information of the respondents, various benefits, challenges faced while attending the classes, and willingness of the students to attend online classes in post COVID-19.

Statistical Analysis

The analysis of the data has been made with the help of descriptive and inferential statistics. Logit binary regression was applied to identify the various determinants of willingness to join online classes by students. The dependent variable in the Logit regression was measured as 1 if the student is willing to attend the online classes in post COVID-19 and 0 otherwise. However, various socioeconomic variables were included as independent variables.

Results

Table 7.1 exhibited the demographic information of the students and it was observed that majority of the respondents were male. However, age-wise analysis has shown that 40% of the respondents were up to 20 years of age and 60% of them were 20 years and above. It was found that 55% of the students were from the PG classes and 45% from UG classes. 41% of the students belong to the rural areas and 59% belong to urban areas. The income-wise classification has shown that 31% of them have a monthly income of Up to ₹30,000, 27% ₹30,000–₹40,000, 23% ₹40,000–₹50,000, and only 19% with an income of ₹50,000 and above. The study shows that 21% of the students were from public institutions and 79% were from the private institutions. The study found that 35% of the students have used the mobile device for attending the classes and 65% have

Table 7.1. Demographic Profile of Students.

Variables	N (%)
Gender	
Male	84 (56)
Female	66 (44)
Age	
Up to 20 years	60 (40)
20 years and above	90 (60)
Education	
UG	67 (45)
PG	83 (55)
Location	
Rural	62 (41)
Urban	88 (59)
Monthly income	
Up to ₹30,000	46 (31)
₹30,000–₹40,000	41 (27)
₹40,000–₹50,000	35 (23)
₹50,000 and above	28 (19)
Type of institute	
Public	32 (21)
Private	118 (79)
Device used for attending classes	
Mobile	52 (35)
Laptop	98 (65)
Proficiency in IT skills	
Low	46 (31)
Moderate	83 (55)
High	21 (14)
Platform used for attending classes?	
Zoom	82 (55)
Google classrooms	45 (30)
Google meet	23 (15)
Prior experience of online classes	
Yes	50 (33)
No	100 (67)

Source: Survey results.

used laptops for attending the classes. However, it was noticed that 55% of the respondents have moderate, 31% low, and 14% had high proficiency in IT. It was seen that greater part of the respondents have attended online classes through Zoom (55%) followed by Google classrooms (30%) and Google meet (15%). It has been observed that 33% of the students have some form of experience of the online classes and 67% of the students have never attendant any classes online.

Table 7.2 demonstrated the benefits of attending classes online due to COVID-19. It has been observed that first benefit perceived by students regarding the online classes is that it increases the real-world skills (Mean = 4.38, SD = 0.36) followed by financial benefits (Mean = 4.00, SD = 0.14), breaks the monotony of classroom teaching (Mean = 3.94, SD = 0.26), can be recorded for future reference (Mean = 3.94, SD = 0.26), comfortable (Mean = 3.95, SD = 0.23), ease of access online resources (Mean = 3.91, SD = 0.76), online classes are safe (Mean = 3.88, SD = 0.07), learning at your own pace (Mean = 3.83, SD = 0.67), flexible timings (Mean = 3.78, SD = 0.08), and more interactivity in classes and build self-confidence (Mean = 3.71, SD = 0.05).

Table 7.3 revealed the various challenges associated with the online classes. It was found that the first challenge perceived by students was reduced interaction with the teachers (Mean = 4.12, SD = 0.62), lot of technical issues (Mean = 4.09, SD = 0.37) followed by lot of network issues (Mean = 4.03, SD = 0.11), less communication with classmates (Mean = 3.94, SD = 0.92), lack of self-discipline (Mean = 3.94, SD = 0.57), social isolation (Mean = 3.81, SD = 0.05), online learning is not effective (Mean = 3.73, SD = 0.02), lot of family distractions (Mean = 3.69, SD = 0.12), too challenging e-learning tools (Mean = 3.45, SD = 0.12), need good management skills (Mean = 338, SD = 0.35), and need an active learner (Mean = 3.02, SD = 0.36).

Table 7.2. Benefits of Attending Online Classes During COVID-19.

S. No.	Variable	Mean	SD
1	Ease to access online resources	3.91	0.76
2	Learning at own pace	3.83	0.67
3	Online classes are safe	3.88	0.07
4	Online classes can be recorded for future reference	3.97	0.07
5	Online classes are comfortable	3.95	0.23
6	More interactivity in classes	3.77	0.75
7	Flexible timings	3.78	0.08
8	Breaks monotony of classroom teaching	3.94	0.26
9	Online classes have financial benefits	4.00	0.14
10	Online classes build self-confidence	3.71	0.05
11	Online classes increase real-world skills	4.38	0.36

Source: Survey results.

Table 7.3. Challenges of Online Classes During COVID-19.

S. No.	Variable	Mean	SD
1	Reduced interaction with the teachers	4.12	0.62
2	Lot of technical issues	4.09	0.37
3	Lot of network issues	4.03	0.11
4	Less communication with classmates	3.94	0.92
5	Lack of self-discipline	3.92	0.57
6	Social isolation	3.81	0.05
7	Online learning is not effective	3.73	0.02
8	Lot of family distractions	3.69	0.12
9	Too challenging eLearning tools	3.45	0.91
10	Need good management skills	3.38	0.35
11	Need an active learner	3.02	0.36

Source: Survey results.

Table 7.4 describes the determinants of the willingness of the students to attend online classes in the post COVID-19. It was found that education, income, and type of institute were not significant. Age ($p < 0.10$) was significantly associated with the willingness to attend classes online in the future. On the basis of the regression coefficient, it can be concluded that younger students were more likely to join the online teaching than of elders. Gender ($p < 0.01$) was significantly related to the willingness to do online teaching in post COVID-19. The coefficient of gender shows that female respondents were more likely to attend the online classes in future as compared to male respondents. The knowledge of the IT skills directly influences the student's willingness to attend classes in post COVID-19. Prior experience of online classes ($p < 0.10$) was significantly associated with the willingness to attend classes online in the future. Location of the students was found significant ($p < 0.01$) thus it can be observed that students from rural areas were less willingness to attend the classes online in future. However, income, education, experience, and type of institute were not found significant.

Implications

The present study has copious implications on extending the online education in the country. It can uphold the public authority, educationists, and policy planners to plan and understand the various issues experienced while attending classes by the student during current pandemic. COVID-19 has made a great deal of changes in the online teaching and learning framework and forced to apply innovative teaching tools in limited time. In the event that the pandemic

Table 7.4. Willingness for Attend Online Teaching in Post COVID-19.

Variable	Coefficient	Std. Error	z-Statistic	Prob.
C	2.824	3.298	0.856	0.392
Age	−1.747*	0.926	−1.887	0.059
Education	0.177	0.981	0.180	0.857
Gender	4.300***	1.074	4.005	0.000
Income	−0.074	0.490	−0.151	0.880
IT skills	2.107***	0.651	−3.235	0.001
Prior experience of online classes	2.018**	1.051	1.921	0.055
Location	−2.665**	1.057	−2.520	0.012
Type of institute	−0.578	0.965	−0.599	0.549
Model summary				
McFadden R-squared	0.811	Mean dependent var		0.527
S.D. dependent var	0.501	S.E. of regression		0.190
Akaike info criterion	0.381	Sum squared resid		5.099
Schwarz criterion	0.562	Log likelihood		−19.609
Hannan-Quinn criter.	0.455	Deviance		39.218
Restr. Deviance	207.517	Restr. log likelihood		−103.759
LR statistic	168.300	Avg. log likelihood		−0.131

Source: Primary survey.

*** Significant at 1%, ** Significant at 5%, * Significant at 10%.

remaining parts for a more extended period, it might change the training framework from offline o online. Online teaching can help to increase the penetration of education in the country with more reach and less cost. Therefore, it is fundamental to adjust the progressions which occurred in the training framework presented by COVID-19. The need is to prepare the students for the new normal with a holistic approach and continuous support, training, and development. Teachers should also embrace the change and learn from the experiences brought by COVID-19. The present study has its own limitations. A sample of 150 students has been used to analyze the results. Due to small sample, it may be difficult to analyze the generalizations of the findings for the future research. As the present study has been conducted in Punjab and the result may change in a different socioeconomic set up.

Conclusion

Thus, it was clearly visible from the above discussion that students have faced several challenges while attending online classes during COVID-19. It was analyzed that majority of the respondents were from private institutions and used mobile phone for attending classes. It was demonstrated that students specified that online teaching provides real-world skills followed by financial benefits, active learning, recorded lectures, comfortable, ease of access, safe, flexible timings, interactive, and build self-confidence. However, various challenges in online classes were less interaction, technical issues, network issues, lack of self-discipline, social isolation, family distractions, difficult e-learning tools, etc. It was seen that greater part of the respondents have attended online classes through Zoom followed by Google classrooms and Google meet. The willingness to attend online classes in post COVID-19 was associated with age, gender, IT skills, prior experience, and location. The study suggested the need to prepare the students for new normal with a continuous support, training, and mentorship so that they can utilize the various lessons learned during online classes. The study suggested the need for correct measures of the various problems experienced by the students during the online classes in pandemic. There is a need for the continuous feedback from the students to lessen the impact of the many challenges faced by them. It was found that students neither consider online classes to be as identical as of offline classes nor simpler. In the future, researchers should make effort to analyze the various challenges faced by the teachers while teaching online as it will give better insights to the policymakers and educators to devise various strategies to improve the online teaching. The time calls to prepare the students for the new normal with a holistic approach and continuous support, training, and development.

References

Adnan, M., & Anwar, K. (2020). Online learning amid the COVID-19 pandemic: Students' perspectives. *Online Submission*, *2*(1), 45–51.

Aristovnik, A., Kerzic, D., Ravselj, D., Tomazevic, N., & Umek, L. (2020). Impacts of the COVID-19 pandemic on life of higher education students: A global perspective. *Sustainability*, *12*(20), 8438.

Bao, W. (2020). COVID-19 and online teaching in higher education: A case study of Peking University. *Human Behavior and Emerging Technologies*, *2*(2), 113–115.

Coroiu, A., Moran, C., Campbell, T., & Geller, A. C. (2020). Barriers and facilitators of adherence to social distancing recommendations during COVID-19 among a large international sample of adults. *PLoS One*, *15*(10), e0239795.

Crawford, J., Butler-Henderson, K., Rudolph, J., Malkawi, B., Glowatz, M., Burton, R., & Lam, S. (2020). COVID-19: 20 countries' higher education intra-period digital pedagogy responses. *Journal of Applied Learning & Teaching*, *3*(1), 1–20.

Dhawan, S. (2020). Online learning: A panacea in the time of COVID-19 crisis. *Journal of Educational Technology Systems*, *49*(1), 5–22.

Jandrić, P., Hayes, D., Truelove, I., Levinson, P., Mayo, P., Ryberg, T., ... Jackson, L. (2020). Teaching in the age of Covid-19. *Postdigital Science and Education, 2*(3), 1069–1230.

Jena, P. K. (2020). Impact of Covid-19 on higher education in India. *International Journal of Advanced Education and Research (IJAER), 5*(3), 77–81.

Kapasia, N., Paul, P., Roy, A., Saha, J., Zaveri, A., Mallick, R., & Chouhan, P. (2020). Impact of lockdown on learning status of undergraduate and postgraduate students during COVID-19 pandemic in West Bengal, India. *Children and Youth Services Review, 116*, 105194.

Kim, J. (2020). Learning and teaching online during Covid-19: Experiences of student teachers in an early childhood education practicum. *International Journal of Early Childhood, 52*(2), 145–158.

Leonard, J., & Guha, S. (2001). Education at the crossroads: Online teaching and students' perspectives on distance learning. *Journal of Research on Technology in Education, 34*(1), 51–58.

Ling, G. H., & Ho, C. M. (2020). Effects of the coronavirus (COVID-19) pandemic on social behavior's: From a social dilemma perspective. *Technium Social Sciences Journal, 7*(1), 312–320.

Matrajt, L., & Leung, T. (2020). Evaluating the effectiveness of social distancing interventions to delay or flatten the epidemic curve of coronavirus disease. *Emerging Infectious Diseases, 26*(8), 1740.

Mishra, N., Tandon, D., Tandon, N., & Gupta, I. (2020). Online teaching perceptions amidst Covid-19. *JIMS8M: The Journal of Indian Management & Strategy, 25*(3), 46–53.

Sepulveda, E. P., & Morrison, A. (2020). Online teaching placement during the COVID-19 pandemic in Chile: Challenges and opportunities. *European Journal of Teacher Education, 43*(4), 587–607.

Setiawan, F., & Taiman, T. (2020). The impact of the lockdown status on student learning during the Covid-19 pandemic. *Syntax Literate; Jurnal Ilmiah Indonesia, 5*(11), 1311–1324.

Sundarasen, S., Chinna, K., Kamaludin, K., Nurunnabi, M., Baloch, G. M., Khoshaim, H. B., ... Sukayt, A. (2020). Psychological impact of Covid-19 and lockdown among university students in Malaysia: Implications and policy recommendations. *International Journal of Environmental Research and Public Health, 17*(17), 6206.

Toquero, C. M. (2020). Challenges and opportunities for higher education amid the COVID-19 pandemic: The Philippine context. *Pedagogical Research, 5*(4).

Wilder, S. A., & Freedman, D. O. (2020). Isolation, quarantine, social distancing and community containment: Pivotal role for old-style public health measures in the novel coronavirus (COVID-19) outbreak. *Journal of Travel Medicine, 27*(2), 1–20.

Chapter 8

Extending the Technology Acceptance Model as Predictor to Explore Student's Intention to Use an Online Edtech Platform in India

Jitendra Singh Rathore and Neha Goyal

Banasthali Vidyapith, India

Abstract

Today the research area on technology acceptance is mainly dependent on the theory of technology acceptance model (TAM). The TAM was used in this study primarily for the purpose of providing a basis for determining the impact of various external variables on the adoption of edtech platforms. The TAM is a theory of information systems that suggests steps for learners to take as they adopt and use new technologies. The primary TAM variables for adoption of edtech platforms are evaluated in this study: perceived usefulness (PU) and perceived ease of use (PEOU) by using the factors – perceived enjoyment (PE), information quality, electronic-word of mouth (e-WOM), perceived compatibility, computer self-efficacy and objective usability. By analyzing and defining the relationship between the external variables with respect to the adoption of edtech platform among students, we hope to contextualize the TAM model. The end result provides a clearer understanding of TAM and its growth as a useful model for technology adoption studies and for clarifying the relationship between the uptake of edtech platforms and technological acceptability. The study employed a qualitative methodology and selected publications and research papers about the adoption of technology. These were then carefully assessed, analyzed and scrutinized for the terms of how students adopted edtech platforms. It was proposed that the adoption of an edtech platform may result from proper training in technology usage and its application to real-world scenarios.

Navigating the Digital Landscape, 129–148
Copyright © 2024 Jitendra Singh Rathore and Neha Goyal
Published under exclusive licence by Emerald Publishing Limited
doi:10.1108/978-1-83549-272-720241008

Keywords: TAM; Edtech platform adoption; external factors; perceived usefulness; perceived ease of use

List of Abbreviations

ATT—Attitude
AU—Actual usage
BI—Behavioral intention
CE—Competitive environment
CSE/SE—Computer self-efficacy/Self-efficacy
ELS—Electronic learning system
E-WOM—Electronic word of mouth
JR—Job-relevance
PBC—Perceived behavioral control
PC—Perceived compatibility
PE—Perceived enjoyment
PEC—Perception of external control
PEOU—Perceived ease of use
PU—Perceived usefulness
RA—Relative advantage
RD—Result demonstrability
SN—Subjective norms
TAM—Technology acceptance model
T&D—Training and development
T/L—Teaching and learning
TPB—Theory of planned behavior
TRA—Theory of reasoned action
UF—User friendly

Introduction

Due to the growth of information and communication technology (ICT), greater numbers of people are engaging in online learning exercises. As per Cheng (2012), the comparison between traditional and online classroom-based instruction shows online education-based studying more adaptable and broadens the education landscape because there are no time or location restrictions. Although online learning has several limitations, but still online education is considered a potential replacement for traditional classroom instruction (Liu et al., 2010). One of the best models is the technology acceptance model (TAM) for examining questions of technology acceptance and rejection (Davis, 1986, 1989). Granić and Marangunić (2019) stated that numerous studies have confirmed the TAM's validity, and the model has emerged as the fundamental for comprehending the variables that predict users' intentions to adopt a technology. The TAM model is frequently utilized to assess user's readiness to adopt a technology, but very few studies have known to influence student's adoption of technology for learning purposes. Many underdeveloped countries are still in the early stages of online education, despite the fact that numerous educational technologies have gained popularity in western nations (Cakır & Solak, 2015). In India, there is shortage of policies regarding edtech platforms. So, between policy and reality, there is a gap (Xue & Churchill, 2019). In 2020, the Indian government authorized a national education policy intended to implement adjustments in Indian education system as it stands (Kalyani, 2020). As an outcome, several online edtech platforms were created and utilized and this is the first time, learner-related variables would be deeply investigated.

In order to elaborate on the initial TAM model, this study investigates possible antecedents of technology use from the standpoint of the students and find prospective elements that may influence learners' intentions to utilize an online edtech platform used in India. In terms of implementing online education, the study findings may have practical consequences for both practitioners and scholars. The results of this study may provide ideas for improving the layout of online learning environments.

Various ideas were created to investigate how people use technology and to demonstrate their capacity to do so based on behavioural science theories and how they affect technology usage. Each of these theories has developed over time and resulted from the extensions of the others. The following 10 important and well-known hypotheses are examined:

The findings in Table 8.1 showed that learner's intentions to utilize and ATTs about technology were equally influenced by perceived usefulness (PU) and felt enjoyment. However, it was determined that ATT and reported ease of use were unrelated.

Table 8.1. Models of Technology Acceptance.

Model	Constructs	Authors
Theory of Reasoned Action (TRA)	Behaviour, Intention, Subjective Norms (SN), Attitude (ATT)	Fishbein and Ajzen (1975)
Theory of Planned Behaviour (TPB)	Behaviour, Intention, Subjective Norms (SN), Attitude (ATT), Perceived Behavior Control (PBC)	Ajzen (1985)
Innovative Diffusion Theory (IDF)	Reasoned Action (RA), Complexity, Compatibility, Trialability, Observability	Roger (1995)
Technology Acceptance Model (TAM)	Perceived ease of use (PEOU), Attitude (ATT), Intention to use and actual usage	Davis (2011)
Technology Acceptance Model (TAM 2)	You Perceived ease of use (PEOU), Subjective Norms (SN), Job Relevance, Output Quality	Venkatesh and Speier (2000)

Literature Review

Chesti Lazrina Md Lazim (2021) showed the findings that how well the TAM model explained the items that affected individuals' readiness to engage in online learning. The balancing of PU and perceived ease of use (PEOU) had influenced student's accepting behaviour towards edtech platforms. This connection supports the original TAM concept, which postulated that Attitude would be directly influenced by PU and PEOU. Alamri et al. (2020) proved that the utility of an electronic learning system (ELS) is what determines a person's willingness to use it for their activities. Ameen (2014) explained that the technology acceptance of user is based on two important factors, that is, PU and PEOU. In 2014, Alatawi et al. resulted that the association between PEOU and PU is strong and significant which highlights how crucial it is for the system to be viewed as user friendly (UF) and simple to use for it to be considered valuable by its users. According to Landry et al. (2006) and Theng (2008), students may view an e-learning system as a helpful learning aid if they perceive it to be user-friendly.

Technology Acceptance Model

In 2012, it was suggested that an edtech platform intended use is significantly influenced by PEOU as per investigated by Premchaiswadi and Porouhan. Ronnie et al. (2011) findings were consistent with earlier studies. TAM is a solid theoretical model with applicability to the setting of online learning (Table 8.2). According to Durvasula et al. (1993) although the majority of consumer behaviour models were created in western nations, it is crucial to assess their viability in other cultural contexts. As per this study, testing the applicability of TAM model in different cultures is crucial.

Theory of reasoned action (TRA) served as the framework for the theory of planned behaviour (TPB) (Ajzen, 2006), which was later expanded to include the decomposed TPB and TRA as given by Ajzen and Fishbein in 1980 and by Taylor and Todd (1995). In 1986 according to Davis, an outgrowth of TRA that also has an outgrowth to TAM2 was made possible in part by information systems explained by Venkatesh and Davis in the year 2000. A succinct account of the theories and models that came before the TAM's emergence is necessary to better comprehend the circumstances underlying its evolution. Liu et al. (2010) investigated that many studies have used TAM to anticipate student's intentions to use the virtual learning society and the findings of these research suggested that TAM could accurately forecast and explain how people will adopt information system or technology. Yoon and Kim (2007) according to this research study, user's perceptions of ease should be taken into account when determining how effectively they recognize and use information technology (edtech platform or technology). Selim (2003) reported that enjoyment as a key component in addition to perceive usability and convenience of use.

In the year 2003, it was proved that around 60% of publications using the TAM model investigated extrinsic parameters explained by Legris and other authors.

Table 8.2. Researches Based on TAM Model With Different External Factors.

No.	Author(s) and Year	Topic	Findings and Results
1.	Malhotra and Galletta (1999)	Extending the TAM to account for social influence	TAM has emerged as one of the influential models used in IS research. Social influence plays a critical role in IS acceptance and usage. Users' education and involvement in the system decision making can improve acceptance and usage of new system.
2.	Venkatesh and Davis (2000)	A theoretical extension of the technology acceptance model: four longitudinal field studies	It emerged that there is interactive effect between job relevance and output quality in determining perceived usefulness.
3.	Pijpers et al. (2001)	Understanding senior executives' use of IT and the Internet	External variables such as demographics, managerial, knowledge in IT, company and IT characteristics have effects on PU and PEOU.
4.	Amoako-Gyampah and Salam (2004)	An extension of the TAM in an ERP implementation environment	TAM was extended by adding a belief construct (shared belief) and two external variables (training and communication).
5.	Chung and Tan (2005)	Validating the extended TAM perceived playfulness in the context of information-searching websites	The results indicate that PU had a stronger effect on Attitude towards using than PEOU.
6.	Kulviwat et al. (2007)	Towards a unified theory of consumer acceptance technology	The study result support the fact that PEOU has a positive influence on actual use of a system. That pleasure and arousal have positive influence on attitude.

(Continued)

Table 8.2. (*Continued*)

No.	Author(s) and Year	Topic	Findings and Results
7.	Bertrand and Bouchard (2008)	Applying the TAM to virtual reality (VR) with people who are favourable to its use	Intention to use VR is predicted only by perceived usefulness.
8.	Venkatesh and Bala (2008)	TAM and a research agenda on interventions	The determinants of PU will not influence PEOU and vice versa. There is potential relationship between interventions and PU and PEOU which offers an important future research direction. Experience is an important moderating variable in IT/system adoption and usage.
9.	Park (2009)	An analysis of the TAM in understanding university students BI to use e-learning	TAM is good model to understand users' acceptance of e-learning. Self-efficacy, subjective norms and system accessibility are important constructs that affect both BI and attitude.
10.	Celik and Yilmaz (2011)	Extending the TAM for adoption of e-shopping by consumers in Turkey	There is the need for further theoretical and experimental studies in order to expand the classical TAM. TAM must be revised in line with new developments in information technologies.
11.	Hanadi et al. (2012)	IT acceptance by university lecturers	PU has no influence on IT acceptance. But PEOU, PC, computing and management supports influence IT acceptance.

12.	Punnoose (2012)	Determinants of intention to use e-learning Bangkok, Thailand	Only three out of the five personality trait extraversion, conscientiousness and neuroticism variables turned out to be significant in the final model.
13.	Al-Adwan et al. (2013)	Exploring students' acceptance of e-learning using TAM in Jordanian universities	TAM is a useful theoretical base to predict and understand users' intentions to use a system. PU had no significant influence on students' attitude. PEOU significantly influenced both attitude and PU.
14.	Chiome (2013)	e-Infrastructure acceptance in e-health, e-learning and e-agriculture in Zimbabwe: the quest for the user acceptance variable	PU, trust and self-efficacy were found to have influence on user acceptance behaviour as identified by the previous studies. Group influence also in user acceptance behaviour in Zimbabwe.
15.	Vogelsang et al. (2013)	A qualitative approach to examine TAM	The qualitative approach allows for a theory building process. TAM is a valid and robust model which is able to display different effects of user and usage types.
16.	Sharma and Chandel (2013)	TAM for the use of learning through websites among students in Oman	The study validates the previous TAM results. PU and PEOU have positive effects on BI. Quality and self-efficacy of the system have positive relationship with the BI. Attitude and BI relate positively. TAM is a powerful and reliable predictive model that may be used in various contexts.

Factors Influencing the Behavioural Intention of Students

Ahmed et al. investigated a study in 2011 and resulted that PU and PEOU predict student's Attitude towards technology acceptance and Attitude of student influence the behavioural intention (BI) of students (Sujeet & Jyoti, 2013). Mun and Hwang (2003) proved from the empirical research that BI has direct and significant relationship with actual usage (AU) of technology. This study proves that edtech platform increases productivity and easy to use in nature quality makes users Attitude positive. Positive Attitude creates positive behaviour towards technology and induce the users for the actual adoption of technology. Bansal (2010) investigated that PU is positively influenced by PEOU. This study proved that it is very crucial for the edtech platforms to be viewed as UF and simple to use before users may find it valuable.

According to Katz et al. (1955), electronic-word of mouth (e-WOM) has demonstrated to have a significant impact on user buying decision. This study proved that the positive reviews, suggestions and feedback about edtech platform have increased the probability of adopting these platforms. Bronner and De Hoog (2011) proved that e-WOM helps people make better buying decisions as information from the e-WOM may play a significant role in how online shoppers choose which things to buy. As per this study, it is resulted that even though e-WOM information is supportive but it is crucial to determine which e-WOM information could influence user's buying intention for edtech platforms(technology).

Agarwal et al. (2000) believed that the computer self-efficacy (CSE) played a crucial contribution in understanding how each person responds to technology. According to research conducted by various authors, that is, Gong et al. (2014), Abdullah and Ward (2016) and Ibrahim et al. (2018) revealed that users with high CSE have a strong perception of PU and PEOU. Punnoose examined a study which was conducted in 2012 and explained that another critical element in the utilization of e-learning is self-efficacy (SE).

In the year 2000, a study conducted by Ryan and Deci explained that intrinsic motivation-based enjoyment is measured by how much a technology is enjoyed without consideration to any performance-related results. Rafiee and Abbasian-Naghneh (2019) explained that the enjoyment construct which is the frequently used factor in technology acceptance studies in the field of e-learning. Similarly, in 2019, a study took place by Al-Rahmi et al. which found that enjoyment is related to PEOU, PU and intention. So there is a positive relation between technology acceptance and enjoyment.

Rogers (1995) investigated that individuals will encounter a technology more valuable and likely to utilize it if they believe that it is consistent and in accordance to their compatibility. Hence it is proved that there is a positive influence between technology acceptance and compatibility.

According to Jaber (2016), a prior study on e-learning found a strong relationship between the content knowledge and PEOU. Similarly, Alsabawy et al. (2016) discovered a positive relationship between the perceived value of an ELS

Table 8.3. Research Gap and Objectives for the Study.

Research Gap	Research Objective
There seems to be a paucity of literature on the adoption of edtech platforms in the Indian context.	The objective of this study is to determine and evaluate the external factors that influence acceptance and resistance to achieve a successful implementation of edtech platforms

and the quality of the material it contains. According to this study, information quality positively affects PU and PEOU in terms of technological acceptability.

Table 8.3 gives a detailed understanding of the research gap and objective that is carried out in the study.

Proposed Conceptual Framework

Perceived usefulness (Table 8.4, Fig. 8.1) is defined by Davis through a study conducted in 1989 stated that 'the amount to which a person believes that using technology would improve their performance or productivity is the basis for a technology's PU'. PEOU means that using technology requires no work (Davis, 1989; Teo & Jarupunphol, 2015). It opines that the interaction and use of technology will be free from intellectual pressure and enable a person to adopt the technology. Kaplan (1972) defined attitude as a propensity to react favourably or unfavourably to an occurrence. Prior research on the acceptability of e-learning has suggested that BI to use e-learning is determined by attitude. It has been

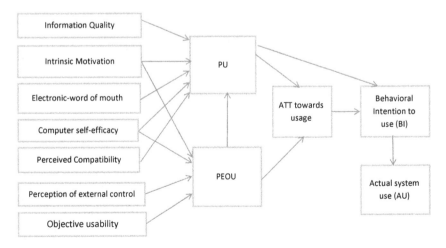

Fig. 8.1.   Proposed Conceptual Framework.

Table 8.4. Conceptual Framework Factors and Constructs.

Independent Variables	External Factors	Explaining the Conceptual Framework's Independent Variable Factors
Perceived usefulness (PU)	*Information quality*	As per Cho et al. (2009) and Wongvilaisakul and Lekcharoen (2015), utilizing e-learning to look for information that is updated to make it easier for the student to understand and could be vital for learning. McKinney et al. (2002) explained that the phrase 'user's belief on the quality of information offered on a website' is another way to describe information quality (IQ). According to Liu et al. (2010), the degree to which the user receives complete, accurate and timely information across the electronic service interface is what constitutes information quality. Jaber (2016) explained provisions e-learning study discovered a substantial link between information quality and perceived usability. Similarly, according to Alsabawy et al. (2016) and Damnjanovic et al. (2015), there is a correlation between the PU of an e-learning system and the information quality (IQ) of the system.
	Intrinsic motivation	Ryan and Deci (2000) defines 'intrinsic motivation' is the practice of a task for its own intrinsic rewards rather than for secondary benefits. Davis et al. (1992) investigated that the components from intrinsic motivational perspective should be included in the TAM because PU and PEOU were both extrinsic motivational aspects that are connected to a system's utility value. The study of Abdullah and Ward (2016) proved that intrinsic motivation factor significantly impacted PU and PEOU. These studies proved that intrinsic motivation factor positively influences both PU and PEOU and considered as potential significant predictor for learner's BI in adopting edtech platform.

Table 8.4. *(Continued)*

Independent Variables	External Factors	Explaining the Conceptual Framework's Independent Variable Factors
	Electronic-word of mouth (e-WOM)	As per Buttle (1998), word of mouth means influencing consumer attitudes and actions towards products and services through the exchange of marketing information among users. With the emergence of the internet, e-WOM has proved its importance. According to Cheung (2014) and Park et al. (2007), it is investigated that when evaluating the quality of e-WOM information, the descriptions are thought to provide unbiased and supportive information for the consumer's purchasing decision. Cheung and Thadani (2012) thought that the quality of e-WOM was a direct factor in PU. Erkan and Evans (2016) demonstrated that consumers report better perceived informational value when the PU is strongly correlated with the quality of e-WOM information.
	Computer self-efficacy (CSE)	Numerous researches have been conducted, according to Yussuff (2009), to ascertain the relationship between CSE and technology acceptance as a psychological attribute. Technology adoption and PEOU are both influenced by CSE. Research took place by Abdullah and Ward in year 2016 explained that CSE is the initial and most often utilized variable to extend TAM in the area of ELS.
	Perceived compatibility (PC)	Research of Rogers took place in 2003 examined that compatibility is the extent to which an invention is seen as being in line with the requirements, values and prior experiences of the target user. Kristensen (2016) and Wu and Wang (2005) explained that several research

(Continued)

Table 8.4. *(Continued)*

Independent Variables	External Factors	Explaining the Conceptual Framework's Independent Variable Factors
		resulted consumer's perception of technological compatibility has a positive and considerable influence on how useful they believe the technology to be. Therefore, this study investigated that there is a significant and positive relationship between PC and PU in adoption of e-learning (edtech platform).
Perceived Ease of Use (PEOU)	*Intrinsic motivation*	Van der Heijden investigated a study in 2004 defined perceived enjoyment (PE) as the limit to which the service or activities of the online ELS are seen as enjoyable, without consideration of any performance consequences. Kanwal and Rehman (2017) explained that PE has positive impact on PEOU. Similarly, PE has a positive relationship with PU (Chang et al., 2017) of e-learning. Venkatesh and Spier (2000) explained that PU and PEOU are considered as extrinsic motivation and PE is regarded as an internal driving force behind technological utilization and can be applied to determine how a person intends to use technology. Previous research has demonstrated that PE has an extensive impact on how users perceive the PEOU and PU of virtual learning. When students are aware that using an ELS is fun, they are more likely to have a positive impact on the utility and usability of such system.
	Computer self-efficacy (CSE)	According to Compeau and Higgins (1995), CSE is a measure of a person's view of his or her ability to use computer technology. So, if a person thinks they have a high level of computer technology competency, they are more likely to use the edtech platform. According to a study

Table 8.4. *(Continued)*

Independent Variables	External Factors	Explaining the Conceptual Framework's Independent Variable Factors
		examined by Abdullah and Ward in 2016, there is a strong association between CSE and both PU and PEOU, as determined by a statistical study of 107 research on the adoption of e-learning. The study therefore presupposes that students who score highly on CSE are more likely to use an ELS (edtech Platform).
	Perception of expected control (PEC)	A study conducted by Venkatesh and other authors in 2003 stated that PEC define as 'the degree to which an individual believes that organizational and technical resources exist to support the use of system'. Nanthida (2011) explained that external control is reliant on the knowledge that is at hand, the accessibility of pertinent resources, the dexterity with which new skills and contemporary technologies are applied, and the proficiency needed to complete a certain activity. Therefore, the degree of control in carrying out particular activities will considerably rise if students have access to particular resources and a larger body of information. External control is the best predictor of reported EOU, according to earlier studies. According to this study, students who had access to the necessary hardware, software and support for using the technology found it to be both pleasant and simple to use.
	Objective usability	Objective usability means how well a system works and can be used and how that affects how easy it is to use. Nanthida (2011) objective usability plays an important role in positively affecting a user's PEOU in using a system.

discovered that BI is mostly influenced by attitudes (Chu & Chen, 2016; Hussein, 2017; Teo, 2012; Teo et al., 2017; Zogheib et al., 2015). Behavioural intention to use (BI) Walker and Pearson (2012) opined that the degree to which an individual is consciously willing to carry out or refrain from carrying out a specific activity is known as their behavioural goal to employ fresh knowledge. Intention is a dependent variable that forecasts how effectively a specific skill will be applied, which will ultimately result in the development of an attitude.

Analysis and Interpretation

The result indicated that researchers have different opinions on the theoretical assumptions and practical implications of the TAM. As per the analysis of the data, various factors, that is, social influence, job relevance, information/output quality, system characteristics, training, PU, PEOU, experience, subjective norms, SE, system accessibility, perceived compatibility and trust are important factors for TAM model.

Similarly, various research studies prove that information quality, intrinsic motivation, e-WOM, CSE, perceived compatibility, perception of external control (PEC) and objective usability are another important external factor which positively related to the adoption of edtech platforms. But there is still need to evaluate other external factors also that influence the use of TAM in education sector.

Managerial Implications

In the context of edtech platforms, the existence of information quality, intrinsic motivation, e-WOM, CSE, perceived compatibility, PEC, objective usability based upon PU and PEOU are important factors. Edtech platforms should ensure that the information provided to edtech users is accurate, relevant and updated. For these data quality management systems and processes, quality control measures and training and support should be provided to people involved in implementing online education. The user's inherent desire to use and enjoy the use of technology is also very important factor. The technology of edtech platforms should be engaging and provides a sense of accomplishment or enjoyment. For this incorporating gamification technique, rewards and recognition programs into the design of the technology are being done.

Edtech platforms should actively monitor and manage online reviews and social media mentions of their products or services. Platforms are realizing this by responding promptly to negative reviews, and leveraging positive reviews for marketing purposes. Many users lack belief in using technology, so edtech platforms should provide training and support to users to help them build their CSE. Other ways to build this is user-friendly interfaces, clear instructions and tutorials, and providing access to technical support. Edtech platforms technology should be compatible with the user's existing systems and processes. The customization features, allowing users to adjust settings and preferences, providing clear feedback are also important to generate sense of control and autonomy in users. Also, the platforms should adopt best practices in user interface design, conducting user testing and incorporating user feedback into the design processes.

Conclusion and Recommendation

Since technology has developed into a tool that promotes access to and usage of current information resources to boost productivity and development, the BI to use and acceptance of edtech platforms in education largely depends on their proper use. In order to describe the process required for the acceptance of modern technology, this research took into account variables from four categories: user characteristics, system characteristics, organizational characteristics and other variables. In the twenty-first century, effective use of technology is necessary for efficient access to and utilization of edtech platforms in teaching/learning process. The difficulty in demonstrating expertise in this area, which could lead to antipathy towards technology, has been recognized as the primary barrier inhibiting the adoption of modern technology. Understanding technology acceptance will lead to better prediction of the use of edtech platform. The study shows that the higher the magnitude of CSE, PU and PEOU by users, the higher will be their intention to accept the technology. CSE is very influential in facilitating user's acceptance of the system. In addition, perceived enjoyment (PE) is an important factor concerning PU, PEOU and intention to use technology. The construct Attitude led to positive relationship in student's intention to use technology. The construct compatibility is considered the main predictor in finding the user's intention to use technology. This study shows that on the basis of TAM model, the test result of e-WOM is valid and reliable.

References

Abdullah, F., & Ward, R. (2016). Developing a general extended TAM for e-learning (GETAMEL) by analyzing commonly used external factors. *Computers in Human Behavior, 56*, 238–256. https://doi.org/10.1016/j.chb.2015.11.036

Agarwal, R., Sambamurthy, V., & Stair, R. M. (2000). Research report: The evolving relationship between general and specific computer self-efficacy—An empirical assessment. *Information Systems Research, 11*(4), 418–430. https://doi.org/10.1287/isre.11.4.418.11876

Ahmed, T. S., Kamal, M. B., Nik Suryani, A., & Tunku, B. T. A. (2011). Investigating students' ATT and intention to use social software in higher institution of learning in Malaysia. *Multicultural Education & Technology Journal, 5*(3), 194–208.

Ajzen, I. (1985). *From intention to actions: A theory of planned behavior*. Springer Verlag.

Ajzen, I. (2006). *The TPB*. http://sphweb.bumc.bu.edu/otlt/MPH-Modules/SB/SB721-Models/SB721Models3.html

Ajzen, I., & Fishbein, M. (1980). *Understanding ATTs and predicting social behaviour*. Prentice-Hall.

Al-Adwan, A., Al-Adwan, A., & Smedley, J. (2013). Exploring student's acceptance of e-learning using the technology acceptance model in Jordanian universities. *International Journal of Education and Development Using ICT, 9*(2).

Alamri, M. M., Almaiah, M. A., & Al-Rahmi, W. M. (2020). Social media applications affecting students' academic to: A model developed for sustainability in higher education. *Sustainability, 12*, 6471. https://doi.org/10.3390/su12166471

Alatawi, F. M. H., Dwivedi, Y. K., Williams, M. D., & Rana, N. P. (2014). *Exploring technological factors influencing knowledge management systems adoption in Saudi Arabian public sector: A validation of extended TAM model.* I-Gov Workshop, 12–13 June 2013 (pp. 82–97). Brunel University.

Alsabawy, A. Y., Cater-Steel, A., & Soar, J. (2016, November). Determinants of PU of e-learning systems. *Computers in Human Behavior, 64*, 843–858.

Ameen, F. (2014). *A user acceptance of web personalization systems: Model validation using S.E.M: A PLS-PM approach with moderating effects.* Iris Publishing.

Amoako-Gyampah, K., & Salam, A. F. (2004). An extension of the technology acceptance model in an ERP implementation environment. *Information & Management, 41*(6), 731–745.

Bansal, G. (2010). Continuing e-book use: Role of environmental consciousness, personality and past usage. *AMCIS 2010 Conference Proceedings*, 1–11.

Bertrand, M., & Bouchard, S. (2008). Applying the technology acceptance model to VR with people who are favorable to its use. *Journal of cyber Therapy & Rehabilitation, 1*(2), 200–210.

Bronner, F., & DeHoog, R. (2011). Vacationers and eWOM: who posts, and why, where, and what? *Journal of Travel Research, 50*(1), 15–26.

Buttle, F. A. (1998). Word of mouth: Understanding and managing referral. *Journal of Strategic Marketing, 6*(3), 241–254.

Cakır, R., & Solak, E. (2015). ATT of Turkish EFL learners towards e-learning through Tam model. *Procedia – Social and Behavioral Sciences, 176*(C), 596–601.

Celik, H. E., & Yilmaz, V. (2011). Extending the technology acceptance model for adoption of e-shopping by consumers in Turkey. *Journal of Electronic Commerce Research, 12*(2), 152.

Chang, C.-T., Hajiyev, J., & Su, C.-R. (2017, August). Examining the students BI to use e-learning in Azerbaijan? The general extended technology acceptance model for e-learning approach. *Computer Education, 111*, 128–143.

Cheng, Y. (2012). Effects of quality antecedents on e-learning acceptance. *Internet Research, 22*(3), 361–390.

Cheung, R. (2014). The influence of electronic word-of-mouth on information adoption in online customer communities. *Global Economic Review, 43*(1), 42–57.

Cheung, C. M., & Thadani, D. R. (2012). The impact of electronic word-of-mouth communication: A literature analysis and integrative model. *Decision Support Systems, 54*(1), 461–470.

Chiome, C. (2013). *E-infrastructure acceptance in e-health, e-learning and e-agriculture in Zimbabwe: The quest for the user acceptance variable.*

Cho, V., Cheng, T. C. E., & Lai, W. M. J. (2009, September). The role of perceived user interface design in continued usage intention of self-paced e-learning tools. *Computer Education, 53*(2), 216–227. [42].

Chu, T. H., & Chen, Y. Y. (2016). With good we become good: Understanding e-learning adoption by theory of planned behavior and group influences. *Computers & Education, 92,* 37–52.

Chung, J., & Tan, F. (2005). *Validating the extended technology acceptance model: Perceived playfulness in the context of information-searching websites.*

Compeau, D. R., & Higgins, C. A. (1995). Computer self-efficacy: Development of a measure and initial test. *MIS Quarterly,* 189–211.

Damnjanovic, V., Jednak, S., & Mijatovic, I. (2015). *Factors affecting the effectiveness and use of Moodle: Students' perception.* Interact.

Davis, F. D. (1986). *A TAM for empirically testing new end-user information systems: Theory and results.* PhD dissertation, MIT Sloan School of Management.

Davis, F. D. (1989). PU, PEOU, and user acceptance of information technology. *MIS Quarterly, 13,* 319–340.

Davis, F. D. (2011). *Foreword in technology acceptance in education: Research and issues.* Sense Publishers.

Davis, F. D., Bagozzi, R. P., & Warshaw, P. R. (1989). User acceptance of computer technology: A comparison of two theoretical models. *Management Science, 35*(8), 982–1003.

Davis, F. D., Bagozzi, R. P., & Warshaw, P. R. (1992). Extrinsic and intrinsic motivation to use computers in the workplace. *Journal of Applied Social Psychology, 22*(14), 1111–1132.

Durvasula, S., Andrews, J. C., Lysonski, S., & Netemeyer, R. G. (1993). Assessing the cross-national applicability of consumer behaviour models: A model of ATT toward advertising in general. *Journal of Consumer Research, 19*(4), 626–636.

Erkan, I., & Evans, C. (2016). The influence of eWOM in social media on consumers' purchase intentions: An extended approach to information adoption. *Computers in Human Behavior, 61*(11), 47–55.

Fishbein, M., & Ajzen, I. (1975). *Belief, attitude, intention and behavior: An introduction to theory and research.* Addison-Wesley.

Gong, M., Xu, Y., & Yu, Y. (2014). An enhanced TAM for web based learning. *Journal of Information Systems Education, 15*(4), 365–374.

Granić, A., & Marangunić, N. (2019). TAM in educational context: A systematic literature review. *British Journal of Educational Technology, 50*(5), 2572–2593.

Hanadi, A. Z., Samar, B. M., & Hasan, A. Z. A. (2012). Information technology acceptance by university lecturers: Case study at applied. *European Scientific Journal,* (10), 8.

Hussein, Z. (2017). Leading to intention: The role of attitude in relation to technology acceptance model in e-learning. *Procedia Computer Science, 105,* 159–164.

Ibrahim, R., Leng, N. S., Yusoff, R. C. M., Samy, G. N., Masrom, S., & Rizman, Z. I. (2018). E-learning acceptance based on TAM (TAM). *Journal of Fundamental and Applied Sciences, 9*(4), 871–889. https://doi.org/10.4314/jfas.v9i4s.50

Jaber, O. A. (2016). *An examination of variables influencing the acceptance and usage of e-learning systems in Jordanian higher education institutions.* Ph.D. dissertation, London School Commerce, Cardiff Metropolitan University.

Kalyani. (2020, October). An empirical study on NEP 2020 [national education policy] with special reference to the future of Indian education system and its effects on the S stakeholders. *Journal of Management Engineering and Information Technology (JMEIT), 7*(5).

Kanwal, F., & Rehman, M. (2017). Factors affecting e-learning adoption in developing countries–Empirical evidence from Pakistan's higher education sector. *IEEE Access, 5*, 10968–10978.

Kaplan, K. J. (1972). On the ambivalence-indifference problem in attitude theory and measurement: A suggested modification of the semantic differential technique. *Psychological Bulletin, 77*(5), 361.

Katz, E., Lazarsfeld, P. F., & Roper, E. (1955). *Personal influence.* Free Press.

Kristensen, S. M. (2016). *Understanding factors influencing Danish consumer's intention to use m-payment at point-of-sale'.* Doctoral dissertation, Msc thesis, Aarhus University.

Kulviwat, S., Bruner, G. C., II, Kumar, A., Nasco, S. A., & Clark, T. (2007). Towards a unified theory of consumer acceptance technology. *Psychology and Marketing, 24*(12), 1059–1084.

Landry, B. J. L., Griffeth, R., & Hartman, S. (2006). Measuring student perceptions of blackboard using the TAM. *Decision Science Journal of Innovative Education, 4*(1), 8799.

Lazim, C. S. L. M., Ismail, N. D. B., & Tazilah, M. D. A. K. (2021, April). Application of tam (tam) towards online learning during covid-19 pandemic: Accounting students perspective. *International Journal of Business, Economics and Law, 24*(1). ISSN 2289-1552 2021.

Legris, P., Ingham, J., & Collerette, P. (2003). Why do people use information technology? A critical review of the TAM. *Information Management, 40*(3), 191–204.

Liu, I., Chen, M., Sun, Y., Wible, D., & Kuo, C. (2010). Extending the TAM model to explore the factors that affect intention to use an online learning community. *Computers & Education, 54*(2), 600–610.

Malhotra, Y., & Galletta, D. F. (1999, January). Extending the technology acceptance model to account for social influence: Theoretical bases and empirical validation. *Proceedings of the 32nd annual Hawaii international conference on systems sciences. 1999. HICSS-32 abstracts and CD-ROM of full papers* (p. 14). IEEE.

McKinney, V. R., Yoon, K., & Zahedi, F. (2002). The measurement of Webcustomer satisfaction: An expectation and disconfirmation approach. *Information Systems Research, 13*(3), 296–315.

Mun, Y. Y., & Hwang, Y. (2003). Predicting the use of web-based information systems: Self-efficacy, enjoyment, learning goal orientation, and the TAM. *International Journal of Human-Computer Studies, 59*(4), 431–449.

Nanthida, J. B. (2011). *Altering user perceptions of applications: How system design can impact playfulness and anxiety.* https://ideals.illinois.edu/bitstream/handle/2142/24139/Barranis_Nanthida.pdf?sequence=

Park, S. Y. (2009). An analysis of the technology acceptance model in understanding University student's behavioral intention to use e-learning. *Educational Technology & Society, 12*(3), 150–162.

Park, D. H., Lee, J., & Han, I. (2007). The effect of on-line consumer reviews on consumer purchasing intention: The moderating role of involvement. *International Journal of Electronic Commerce, 11*(4), 125–148.

Pijpers, G. G. M., Bemelmans, T. M. A., Heemstra, F. J., & Montforr, K. A. G. M. (2001). Senior executives' use of information technology. *Information and Software Technology, 43*(15), 959–971.

Premchaiswadi, W., & Porouhan, P. (2012). An empirical study of the key success factors to adopt e-learning in Thailand. In *Proceeding of the international conference on information society*, 25–28 June 2012, London, United Kingdom (pp. 333–338).

Punnoose, A. C. (2012). Determinants of intention to use e-learning based on the TAM. *Journal of Information Technology Education: Research*, *11*, 301–337.

Rafiee, M., & Abbasian-Naghneh, S. (2019). E-learning: Development of a model to assess the acceptance and readiness of technology among language learners. *Computer Assisted Language Learning*, 1–21. https://doi.org/10.1080/09588221. 2019.1640255

Rogers, E. M. (1995). *Diffusion of innovations* (4th ed.). Free Press.

Ronnie, H. S., Deneen, C. C., & Eugenia, M. W. Ng. (2011). Analysis of the TAM in examining students' behavioural intention to use an e-portfolio system. *Australasian Journal of Educational Technology*, *27*(4), 600–618.

Ryan, R. M., & Deci, E. L. (2000). Intrinsic and extrinsic motivations: Classic definitions and new directions. *Contemporary Educational Psychology*, *25*(1), 54–67. https://doi.org/10.1006/ceps.1999.1020

Selim, H. M. (2003). An empirical investigation of student acceptance of course websites. *Computers & Education*, *40*(4), 343–360.

Sharma, S. K., & Chandel, J. K. (2013). *Technology acceptance model for the use of learning through websites among students*.

Sujeet, K. S., & Jyoti, K. C. (2013). TAM for the use of learning through websites among students in Oman. *International Arab Journal of E-Technology*, *3*(1), 44–49.

Taylor, S., & Todd, P. (1995). Decomposition and crossover effects in the theory of planned behavior: A study of consumer adoption intentions. *International Journal of Research in Marketing*, *12*, 137–156.

Teo, T. (2012). Examining the intention to use technology among pre-service teachers: An integration of the technology acceptance model and theory of planned behavior. *Interactive Learning Environments*, *20*(1), 3–18.

Teo, T., & Jarupunphol, P. (2015). Dhammic TAM (DTAM): Extending the TAM using a condition of attachment in Buddhism. *Journal of Educational Computing Research*, *52*(1), 133–148.

Teo, T., Milutiinovic, V., Zhou, M., & Bankovic, D. (2017). Traditional vs. innovative uses of computers among mathematics pre-service teachers in Serbia. *Interactive Learning Environments*, *25*(7), 811–827.

Theng, Y. L. (2008). An empirical study of students' perceptions on e-learning systems. In *Proceeding of the 2nd international convention on rehabilitation engineering and assistive technology*, 13–15 May 2008, Bangkok, Thailand. Singapore: START Centre (pp. 245–249).

Van der Heijden, H. (2004). User acceptance of hedonic information systems. *MIS Quarterly*, *28*(4), 695–704.

Venkatesh, V., & Bala, H. (2008). Technology acceptance model 3 and a research agenda on interventions. *Decision Sciences*, *39*(2), 273–315.

Venkatesh, V., & Davis, F. (2000). A theoretical extension of the technology acceptance model: Four longitudinal field studies. *Management Science*, *46*(2), 186–204.

Venkatesh, V., & Speier, C. (2000). Creating an effective training environment for enhancing telework. *International Journal of Human-Computer Studies*, *52*(6), 991–1005.

Vogelsang, K., Steinhuser, M., & Hoppe, U. (2013). *A qualitative approach to examine technology acceptance.*

Walker, S. C., & Pearson, J. (2012). Intent to use technology: Facilitation effect of group presence. *International Journal of Business and Information Technology, 1*(1), 1–15.

Wongvilaisakul, W., & Lekcharoen, S. (2015). The acceptance of e-learning using SEM approach: A case of IT literacy development for PIM students. In *Proceedings of 12th international conference electrical engineering/electronics, computer, telecommunications and information technology (ECTI-CON)*, 2015, June (pp. 1–6).

Wu, J. H., & Wang, S. C. (2005). What drives mobile commerce? An empirical evaluation of the revised technology acceptance model. *Information & Management, 42*(5), 719–729.

Xue, S., & Churchill, D. (2019). A review of empirical studies of affordances and development of a framework for educational application of mobile social media. *Educational Technology Research & Development, 67*(5), 1231–1257.

Yoon, C., & Kim, S. (2007). Convenience and TAM in a ubiquitous computing environment: The case of wireless LAN. *Electronic Commerce Research and Applications, 6*(1), 102–112.

Yusoff, M. Y. (2009). Individual differences, PEOU, and PU in the e-library usage. *Journal of Computer and Information Science, 2*(1).

Zogheib, B., Rabaa'I, A., Zogheib, S., & Elsaheli, A. (2015). University student perceptions of technology use in mathematics learning. *Journal of Information Technology Education, 14*, 417–438.

Chapter 9

Metamorphosis of Retail Purchase Through Customer Segmentation in Pandemic Times

Upasana Diwan[a], D. D. Chaturvedi[b] and S. L. Gupta[c]

[a]Rukmini Devi Institute of Advanced Studies, India
[b]Sri Guru Gobind Singh College of Commerce, India
[c]Birla Institute of Technology, India

Abstract

This chapter aims to examine the role of consumer demographics over the chosen parameters of online shopping. Online shopping had emerged as an important platform for the consumers during the phase of pandemic spread in India which even included several phases of lockdowns. The state of pandemic commenced at a severe note leading to restrictive movement, social distancing, observing least contact with objects, and several other limitations. Due to this, many businesses had moved to online selling in order to target greater sales. This study was conducted in order to provide insights to various businesses, experts, and academic researchers in this domain to find out the role of demographical and behavioral differences of different consumer segments. It could serve as a robust study providing information about the current consumer behavior at the time of pandemic spread toward online shopping. This would help marketing experts explore the different opportunities and challenges involved in this new scenario formed due to COVID-19. Apart from adding value to the existing literature, this study leads a way to future research.

Keywords: Demographics; convenience; feedback management; credit availability; billing facility; COVID-19

Introduction

The advent of COVID-19 in India can be traced from the month of March in the year 2020 (Balaji et al., 2020). After SARS, this has been considered the most

Navigating the Digital Landscape, 149–166
doi:10.1108/978-1-83549-272-720241009

severe pandemic that had affected the global geographies (Niknamian & Zaminpira, 2020). COVID-19 has not only resulted in the depletion of health of homo-sapiens (Harapan et al., 2020), it had also caused major economic destructions (yStats GmbH & Co. KG report, 2020). Several changes were witnessed by the business environment across economies since the outbreak of this pandemic (Mabaloc, 2020). One of the common features seen was the massive digital consumption at different levels (Gao et al., 2020). This made the business owners and marketers locate the means to survive and they found online selling as one of the solutions amid the various social restrictions (Weill et al., 2020). In context of Indian economy with diverse population and the economy having witnessed the phase of digital age paradox (Lipiäinen & Karjaluoto, 2015), it became imperative for the sellers to explore the online platform. However, in order to formulate an effective sales strategy program, a concrete knowledge of the existing marketing segments as formed during pandemic was required. In India, consumers have been documented to still be addicted to offline shopping and this transformation of switching to the online shopping option was not uniform across various consumer segments (Orion Market Research report, 2020). It is due to this reason that the current study would be considered useful as through this research, an attempt has been made to examine the online purchase patterns of consumers during the pandemic by examining their demographic and behavioral details. Further, through the metamorphosis of the two, certain market segments were identified that could be further examined by the marketers in the light of specific product categories that are sold online (Levy et al., 2020).

COVID-19 brought immense problems in terms of traditional modes of shopping being discarded during lockdowns and even post-lockdown, there was a drop in the demand from offline shopping (Balaji et al., 2020). A major shift toward online shopping was witnessed during the pandemic situation (Sharma & Jhamb, 2020). Some imposed factors were lockdown restrictions, social distancing norms, and precautionary measures (Chakraborty et al., 2021). Some of the facilitating services which promoted online shopping were digital payments (PwC Report, 2020), security (RBI Bulletin, 2019), and mobile banking (Pan et al., 2020). Several online shopping sites are available offering variety of products and ensuring timely delivery (Gupta et al., 2013). During COVID times, these companies provided contactless delivery (Bhavya & Sambhav, 2020) of goods to their customers. These factors propelled the newly emerged trend of online shopping during the pandemic.

Many benefits came with online purchases which were not available with traditional purchase trend (Yasmin et al., 2015). Online shopping saved efforts in terms of traveling the stores (Izogo & Jayawarshena, 2018) making comparative analysis of the competing brands. Further, timely delivery at required destination is another benefit (Healthy Eating Research, Center for Science in the Public Interest, Johns Hopkins Bloomberg School of Public Health, The Food Trust report, 2020). Therefore, the customers documented several reasons for switching from offline to online shopping (Akroush & Al-Debei, 2015). This has generated the concern of the marketers regarding the continuation of this trend as it would mean a major turnaround in the marketing strategies (UNCTAD and Netcomm Suisse eCommerce Association report, 2020).

Review of Literature

Even Brown (1990) had presented a construct of convenience stating that this variable was not properly defined and operationalized by the marketing managers. He proposed convenience being multidimensional. He further proposed a conceptual framework for the examination of the convenience of services, hence, allowing strategic as well as tactical marketing opportunities to be considered. Convenience was identified as one of the principal motivations lying beneath customer inclinations for adopting online shopping (Jiang et al., 2013). When referring to online shopping, convenience was taken as a variable under study. Shankar (2021) conducted a study which indicated that access convenience, search convenience, benefit convenience, and post-benefit convenience held a considerable impact on the consumers' webrooming intention or purchasing online.

A study conducted by Nazir et al. (2012) in Pakistan over a sample of 120 customers revealed that most of the respondents were already shopping online and had a preference for online purchases over the offline media. Factors like psychological factors, social factors, emotional factors along with privacy factors affected the online shoppers' attitudes. The gaps were that it didn't represent respondents from India and the sample size was not representative. This didn't reflect the situation of a pandemic. Research study by Ecola et al. (2020) through the survey conducted in America revealed that the proportion of online shoppers in terms of increased frequency of online purchases had increased during the pandemic in comparison to the before COVID-19 situation. The results showed increased frequency of online purchases across different age groups. The gaps identified were that it was in foreign context and the major demographic factor to assess consumer behavior was age. It didn't include any customer segmentation. According to another report by Giosue (2020), due to the shutting down of various brick-and-mortar stores in America for customer and employee safety, either voluntarily or due to official restrictions, more people are forced to buy online. This study again doesn't reflect online buyers in India and doesn't include statistical testing tools and techniques application.

Hsieh et al. (2013) conducted a research study which showed that online behavior patterns were exhibited with regional differences, because the regional segments affected individual segments of different use patterns. It was found that rural consumers used other payment methods other than credit cards more often than those in urban areas. Further, consumers with higher-level income spent comparatively more money on online shopping and they frequently used various internet applications of payments. Product returns were found to act as a significant feedback for the entire organization. Nazr et al. (2018) highlighted the importance of customer feedback and extended the understanding of the under-researched concept of personal positive customer feedback. This research involved the comparison and contrast of front-line employees' and customers' perspectives. It provided a deeper understanding of the main elements and characteristics of personal positive customer feedback along with its various impacts and the perceived significance of the stipulated proposition for both the parties. Feedback management can be documented as another variable for online purchases. Klapalová (2019) conducted a study regarding the customer product returns in terms of feedback and knowledge management. This study highlighted the significance of knowledge management (even in a rather simple form) for resolving problematic situation and documented the necessary interconnections between the different areas of business processes management along with the need for managing knowledge.

Credit availability was another significant element of consumer online purchase behavior. Akram et al. (2018) studied how website quality affected the online impulse buying. It involved the study of the moderating effects of sales promotion and usage of credit facility through credit cards. He investigated the impact of website quality on online impulse buying behavior in China. It was found that the online impulse purchases were positively influenced by the use of credit card. Further, the use of credit card was found to enhance the relation between the website quality and the online impulse buying.

Another variable highlighted was billing facility with respect to online buying. Sivathanu (2019) conducted a study titled, "Adoption of digital payment systems in the era of demonetization in India: An empirical study." The results of this study suggested that the behavioral intention (BI) to use as well as innovation resistance (IR) affect the usage of digital payment systems. The relation between BI to use digital payment systems is moderated by the stickiness to cash payments.

Research Methodology

The research design is conclusive and descriptive to be more specific. A self-structure questionnaire to gather demographic and behavioral details of the respondents with respect to their online buying behavior during pandemic was constructed. The questionnaires were developed with questions regarding whether respondents are online buyers, how long they have been into online buying, and what is the occurrence of their buying patterns. A self-administered questionnaire was sent out using an online survey. A questionnaire link was sent out to the respondents via social media platforms and email. In addition, the questionnaire link shared with the respondents included a note stating that this study seeks responses from online buyers only and that respondents who were not online buyers were not required to record responses.

Sample consisted of 373 consumers who were sent the questionnaires online and thereafter, the collected data were tabulated for analysis. Convenience sampling was done for this study. The statements regarding the behavioral aspects were made on Likert's 5-point scale: (1) strongly disagree, (2) rather disagree, (3) neither agree nor disagree, (4) rather agree, (5) strongly agree. The research techniques used were contingency tables along with chi-square test to examine the following objectives. Further, tabulation was done to generate segments through the metamorphosis of demographic and behavioral dimensions.

Objectives

- To examine the relation between demographic variables and convenience factor for online purchase pattern.
- To examine the relation between demographic variables and credit availability factor for online purchase pattern.
- To examine the relation between demographic variables and feedback management factor for online purchase pattern.
- To examine the relation between demographic variables and billing facility factor for online purchase pattern.
- To segment the consumer market based upon the intersection of demographic and behavioral segmentation.

Hypotheses

$H_0 1a$. No significant relation between age and convenience factor for online purchase pattern.

$H_0 1b$. No significant relation between gender and convenience factor for online purchase pattern.

$H_0 1c$. No significant relation between marital status and convenience factor for online purchase pattern.

$H_0 1d$. No significant relation between income and convenience factor for online purchase pattern.

$H_0 2a$. No significant relation between age and credit availability factor for online purchase pattern.

$H_0 2b$. No significant relation between gender and credit availability factor for online purchase pattern.

$H_0 2c$. No significant relation between marital status and credit availability factor for online purchase pattern.

$H_0 2d$. No significant relation between income and credit availability factor for online purchase pattern.

$H_0 3a$. No significant relation between age and feedback management factor for online purchase pattern.

$H_0 3b$. No significant relation between gender and feedback management factor for online purchase pattern.

$H_0 3c$. No significant relation between marital status and feedback management factor for online purchase pattern.

$H_0 3d$. No significant relation between income and feedback management factor for online purchase pattern.

$H_0 4a$. No significant relation between age and billing facility factor for online purchase pattern.

$H_0 4b$. No significant relation between gender and billing facility factor for online purchase pattern.

$H_0 4c$. No significant relation between marital status and billing facility factor for online purchase pattern.

$H_0 4d$. No significant relation between income and billing facility factor for online purchase pattern.

Data Analysis and Interpretation

From Table 9.1, the cross-tabulation for various demographic variables – age, gender, marital status, and income with the "Convenience" factor has been

Table 9.1. Contingency Table for Convenience Score and Demographics.

Convenience Score	<14	14–20	>20	Chi-Square Test
Age				
18–30 years	5	32	47	378.512, p <0.001
30–40 years	40	69	46	
40–50 years	29	62	5	
>50 years	44	4	0	
Gender				
Male	42	94	84	112.508, p <0.001
Female	76	73	14	
Marital status				
Married	53	117	84	166.661, p <0.001
Unmarried	44	17	00	
Widow/widower	3	13	00	
Divorced	18	20	14	
Income				
Up-to Rs 50,000	16	2	00	438.088, p <0.001
Rs (50,000–100000)	48	6	00	
Rs (100,000–150000)	49	87	3	
>Rs 150,000	5	72	95	

presented. Convenience being one of the factors associated with online purchases was calculated as a score of respondent responses that were summated. Further, the total scores for this component were distributed equally and then after applying percentiles, there categories reflecting the scores as low, medium, and high were created. For each of the mentioned categories, the number of responses for every demographic variable was reported separately and then, cross-tabulated. Further, chi-square test was applied for hypotheses testing. From Table 9.1, it was clear that for the relationship between age and convenience, the chi-square statistic (378.512) was statistically significant as $p < 0.05$. Thus, H_01a was rejected as there existed a significant relationship between age and convenience factor for online purchase pattern. Further, chi-square statistic (112.508) was statistically significant at 5% level of significance with $p < 0.05$. Thus, H_01b was rejected as there existed a significant relationship between gender and convenience factor for online purchase pattern. Further, chi-square statistic (166.661) was statistically significant at 5% level of significance with $p < 0.05$. Thus, H_01c was rejected as there existed a significant relationship between marital status and convenience factor for online purchase pattern. The chi-square statistic (438.088) was statistically significant at 5% level of significance with $p < 0.05$. Thus, H_01d was rejected as there existed a significant relationship between income and convenience factor for online purchase pattern.

Referring to Table 9.2, the cross-tabulation for various demographic variables – age, gender, marital status, and income with the "Feedback management" factor has been presented. Feedback management being one of the factors associated with online purchases was calculated as a score of respondent responses that were summated. Further, the total scores for this component were distributed equally and then after applying percentiles, there categories reflecting the scores as low, medium, and high were created. For all of the given categories, the number of responses for each of the demographic variables were reported and then, cross-tabulated. Then, the chi-square test was applied for hypotheses testing. From Table 9.2, it was evident that for the relationship between age and feedback management, the chi-square statistic (325.447) was statistically significant as $p < 0.05$. Thus, H_02a was rejected as there existed a significant relationship between age and feedback management factor for online purchase pattern. Further, chi-square statistic (97.626) was statistically significant at 5% level of significance with $p < 0.05$. Thus, H_02b was rejected as there existed a significant relationship between gender and feedback management factor for online purchase pattern. Also, chi-square statistic (199.063) was statistically significant at 5% level of significance with $p < 0.05$. Thus, H_02c was rejected as there existed a significant relationship between marital status and feedback management factor for online purchase pattern. The chi-square statistic (453.384) was statistically significant at 5% level of significance with $p < 0.05$. Thus, H_02d was rejected as there existed a significant relationship between income and feedback management factor for online purchase pattern.

In Table 9.3, the cross-tabulation for various demographic variables – age, gender, marital status, and income with the "credit availability" factor has been documented. Credit availability being one of the factors associated with online

Table 9.2. Contingency Table for Feedback Management and Memographics.

Feedback Management

Score	<14	14–20	>20	Chi-Square Test
Age				
18–30 years	3	25	56	325.447, $p < 0.001$
30–40 years	29	72	54	
40–50 years	31	54	11	
>50 years	45	3	0	
Gender				
Male	45	70	105	97.626, $p < 0.001$
Female	63	84	16	
Marital status				
Married	47	104	103	199.063, $p < 0.001$
Unmarried	47	14	00	
Widow/widower	2	13	1	
Divorced	12	23	17	
Income				
Up-to Rs 50,000	15	3	00	453.384, $p < 0.001$
Rs (50,000–100,000)	51	3	00	
Rs (100,000–150,000)	37	94	8	
>Rs 150,000	5	54	113	

purchases was calculated as a score of respondent responses that were summated. Further, the total scores for this component were distributed with equal distribution and then after applying percentiles, these categories reflecting the scores as low, medium, and high were created. For all of the given categories, the number of responses for each of the demographic variables were reported and then, cross-tabulated. Then, the chi-square test was applied for hypotheses testing. From Table 9.3, it was evident that for the relationship between age and credit availability, the chi-square statistic (342.503) was statistically significant as $p < 0.05$. Thus, H_03a was rejected as there existed a significant relationship between age and credit availability factor for online purchase pattern. Further, chi-square statistic (116.212) was statistically significant at 5% level of significance with $p < 0.05$. Thus, H_03b was rejected as there existed a significant relationship between gender and credit availability factor for online purchase pattern. Also, chi-square statistic (192.103) was statistically significant at 5% level of significance with $p < 0.05$. Thus, H_03c was rejected as there existed a significant relationship between

Table 9.3. Contingency Table for Credit Availability and Demographics.

Credit Availability				
Score	**<14**	**14–20**	**>20**	**Chi-Square Test**
Age				
18–30 years	3	31	00	342.503, p <0.001
30–40 years	27	80	7	
40–50 years	30	59	48	
>50 years	44	4	50	
Gender				
Male	41	89	90	116.212, p <0.001
Female	63	85	15	
Marital status				
Married	49	116	89	192.103, p <0.001
Unmarried	45	14	2	
Widow/widower	3	12	1	
Divorced	7	32	13	
Income				
Up-to Rs 50,000	15	3	00	467.502, p <0.001
Rs (50,000–100,000)	53	1	00	
Rs (100,000–150,000)	32	102	5	
>Rs 150,000	4	68	100	

marital status and credit availability factor for online purchase pattern. The chi-square statistic (467.502) was statistically significant at 5% level of significance with p <0.05. Thus, H_03d was rejected as there existed a significant relationship between income and credit availability factor for online purchase pattern.

In Table 9.4, the cross-tabulation for various demographic variables – age, gender, marital status, and income with the "billing facility" factor has been documented. Credit availability being one of the factors associated with online purchases was calculated as a score of respondent responses that were summated. Further, the total scores for this component were distributed with equal distribution and then after applying percentiles, there categories reflecting the scores as low, medium, and high were created. For all of the given categories, the number of responses for each of the demographic variables were reported and then, cross-tabulated. Then, the chi-square test was applied for hypotheses testing. From Table 9.3, it was evident that for the relationship between age and billing facility, the chi-square statistic (365.121) was statistically significant as p <0.05. Thus, H_04a was rejected as there existed a significant relationship between age

Table 9.4. Contingency Table for Billing Facilities and Demographics.

Billing Facilities

Score	<14	14–20	>20	Chi-Square Test
Age				
18–30 years	6	25	53	365.121, p <0.001
30–40 years	30	74	51	
40–50 years	30	64	2	
>50 years	46	2	00	
Gender				
Male	36	94	90	134.112, p <0.001
Female	76	71	16	
Marital status				
Married	52	113	89	183.218, p <0.001
Unmarried	47	14	00	
Widow/widower	8	7	1	
Divorced	5	31	16	
Income				
Up-to Rs 50,000	16	2	00	461.676, p <0.001
Rs (50,000–100,000)	54	00	00	
Rs (100,000–150,000)	34	103	2	
>Rs 150,000	8	60	104	

and billing facility factor for online purchase pattern. Further, chi-square statistic (134.112) was statistically significant at 5% level of significance with p <0.05. Thus, H_04b was rejected as there existed a significant relationship between gender and billing facility factor for online purchase pattern. Further, chi-square statistic (183.218) was statistically significant at 5% level of significance with p <0.05. Thus, H_04c was rejected as there existed a significant relationship between marital status and billing facility factor for online purchase pattern. The chi-square statistic (461.676) was statistically significant at 5% level of significance with p <0.05. Thus, H_04d was rejected as there existed a significant relationship between income and billing facility factor for online purchase pattern.

Tables 9.5–9.8 show the various customer segments that have been created on the basis of the demographic and behavioral parameters. The scores for the given variables convenience, feedback management, credit availability, and billing facility were summed individually. Then, after their equi-distribution, on the

Table 9.5. Segmentation of Online Consumers Based on Convenience Factor During Pandemic.

Market Segments	Details
Uninitiated consumers (low score)	
Demographic profiles	>50 years, males/females, married/unmarried, 1 lakh–1.5 lakhs income
Behavioral profiles	The consumers in this segment belonged to an older age group comprising both married as well as unmarried respondents of both genders. They were not found to be very affected by the factor of convenience which online shopping could provide them and hence their purchase pattern was not driven in spite of the convenience factor being into picture. The possible reasons could be difficulty with adoption and lack of openness to adopt online media for shopping in comparison to the offline media/store visits as a part of their routine shopping.
Situational consumers (medium score)	
Demographic profiles	30–50 years, males, married, above 1 lakh income
Behavioral profiles	This segment consisted of individuals in the middle-age group who were majorly married males with above 1 lakh of monthly income. They responded on a moderate level with respect to the convenience factor of online shopping. Depending upon the situational requirement of buying a product, they still showed a higher score in their purchase pattern. Further, considering that respondents were married and had families, this type of products demanded was also greater and for several purposes. During pandemic, this category tried to venture into more online shopping also because of various restrictions imposed on retail stores/shops, social distancing, and other norms.
Comfort seekers (high score)	
Demographic profiles	18–30 years, males, married, >1.5 lakhs income
Behavioral profiles	This segment comprised comparatively younger generation who were mostly males and married with higher income. They showed higher purchase pattern as they were affected by the factor of convenience which online shopping provided. Also, earning higher income would be keeping them busy with work and they would prefer ordering things online to avail the option of comfort and convenience and also, due to compulsion during lockdown phases of pandemic. Further, the high score was supported by the higher income they had.

Table 9.6. Segmentation of Online Consumers Based on Feedback Management Factor During Pandemic.

Market Segments	Details
Unaffected buyers (low score)	
Demographic profiles	>40 years, males/females, married/unmarried, 50,000–1 lakh income
Behavioral profiles	This segment comprising married and unmarried respondents were above 40 years age and had comparatively lower income than other segments. They displayed low score on feedback management benefit provided from online shopping. They were not affected by how well their complaints were being addressed or the other party was being receptive. More or less, they were not found to be very interested in online shopping. Income constraint could be one of the reasons for the respondents not showing interest in spite of having online shopping as being customer-driven.
Potent buyers (medium score)	
Demographic profiles	30–40 years, males, married, 1 lakh–1.5 lakhs income
Behavioral profiles	This segment comprised middle-aged males who were married and earned reasonable income per month. They showed their move from offline to online buying during the pandemic on being influenced by the kind of customer feedback management that was provided. This switch was also pushed by the kind of widespread impetus which online sources got. This segment was identified as being potential to move to higher online purchases if the customer handling gets done appropriately by the online vendors.
Avid buyers (high score)	
Demographic profiles	18–40 years, males, married, above 1.5 lakhs income
Behavioral profiles	This segment belonged to young buyers who were majorly married males with higher income. They showed higher score for the customer feedback management which acted as a factor in affecting their purchase pattern. These buyers were frequent buyers of buying through online media. They were indulged into online shopping to a high degree and their economic capacity also supported such behavior. The factor of being addressed properly and valued as a customer was quite important for these customers. That's why they showed high purchase pattern of online shopping during the pandemic.

Table 9.7. Segmentation of Online Consumers Based on Credit Availability Factor During Pandemic.

Market Segments	Details
Sleeping shoppers (low score)	
Demographic profiles	>50 years, males/females, married/unmarried, 50,000–1 lakh income
Behavioral profiles	This category of customers constituted respondents both married or unmarried who were older than 50 years and were low on earnings on a comparative basis with the total sample. They displayed a low score on facility of credit provided to online shoppers. They didn't find this factor to move them into buying products online. The customers are not actively involved in online shopping in this segment.
Convertible buyers (medium score)	
Demographic profiles	30–40 years, males, married, 1 lakh–1.5 lakhs income
Behavioral profiles	It consisted of middle-aged married males who earned a monthly income between 1 lakh and 1.5 lakhs. These buyers showed a moderate buying pattern and could be seen as growing in terms of online purchases. This segment could be seen as a prospective one and working on the credit facility could act as an attraction for them to get more involved in online purchases.
Inconsequential buyers (high score)	
Demographic profiles	>40 years, males, married, above 1.5 lakhs income
Behavioral profiles	This segment consisted of males above 40 years who were married and earned more than 1.5 lakhs per month. They showed high online purchase pattern. They found credit facility as a great offer as while shopping they didn't have to bother too much about instant consequential payment and relied on the credit cycle payment.

application of percentiles, they were divided into three categories which were low, medium, and high. Dependent upon the higher frequency of the demographic variables for respective levels of scores for each component were taken for the process of market segmentation and then, the following segments were created. The metamorphosis of the segments created has been presented here.

Table 9.8. Segmentation of Online Consumers Based on Billing Facility Factor During Pandemic.

Market segments	Details
Dormant buyers (low score)	
Demographic profiles	>50 years, males/females, married/unmarried, 50,000–1 lakh income
Behavioral profiles	This segment consisted of males and females who were above 50 years and married/unmarried and had comparatively low income. They were not very enthusiastic of shopping online. Age could be factor in not letting them break their conventional pattern of shopping from brick-and-mortar stores and still believed in the same. Quickness and comfort related to billing wasn't a motivational factor for them to engage in online shopping.
Budding consumers (medium score)	
Demographic profiles	30–40 years, males, married, 1 lakh–1.5 lakhs income
Behavioral profiles	These were middle-aged married males with decent amount of income earned monthly. They seemed to have made a move to online shopping during the pandemic and were getting influenced by the kind of billing facilities available, especially in the scenario of pandemic spread. They had found it to be a good experience to get involved in online shopping due to ease and security of billing and transaction process. It simultaneously helped them overcome the time and distance barriers.
Satisfied shoppers (high score)	
Demographic profiles	18–30 years, males, married, above 1.5 lakhs income
Behavioral profiles	This segment consisted of young generation of married males earning a monthly income above 1.5 lakhs. They seemed to be highly involved in online shopping as they found the entire billing process very easy, accurate and secure. Good financial earnings also supported this online purchase pattern. This segment was found to assess online shopping as providing high service quality.

Conclusion

Now, it can be stated that all the null hypotheses formulated for this study got rejected as all the demographic variables held a statistically significant relationship with the components of online purchase pattern. The null hypotheses – H_01a, H_01b, H_01c, and H_01d were rejected as the relation between demographic variables (age, gender, marital status, income) and convenience was statistically significant at 5% level of significance. The null hypotheses – H_02a, H_02b, H_02c, and H_02d were rejected as the relation between demographic variables (age, gender, marital status, income) and feedback management was statistically significant at 5% level of significance. Further, the null hypotheses – H_03a, H_03b, H_03c, and H_03d were rejected as the relation between demographic variables (age, gender, marital status, income) and credit availability was statistically significant at 5% level of significance. Also, the null hypotheses – H_04a, H_04b, H_04c, and H_04d were rejected as the relation between demographic variables (age, gender, marital status, income) and billing facility was statistically significant at 5% level of significance. Thus, it can be documented that the study has resulted in proving significant relation between given demographic variables and chosen components of online shopping behavior during pandemic. Further, the study resulted in creating market segments based on the intersection of demographic variables with the factors defining online buying behavior. The segments created showed varied behaviors ranging from customers being unaffected by the components of convenience, feedback management, credit availability, and billing facility, whereas there were segments showing high purchases under the chosen motivational factors. The intermediate behavior category was seen as a potential segment who had experienced online shopping and could be influenced further to get engaged in online shopping in the future. Thus, it can be concluded that demographical and behavioral profiles are important to be examined by the marketers and experts to launch successful online marketing campaigns for their products and services. Further, the future scope of this study is wide open in terms of cross-sectional studies, innovations in online shopping, possibility of sustenance of newly adopted online shopping behavior of customers, and updations in segments formations in the future.

References

Akram, U., Peng, H., Khan, M. K., Tanveer, Y., Mehmood, K., & Ahmad, W. (2018). How website quality affects online impulse buying. *Asia Pacific Journal of Marketing and Logistics, 30*(1), 235–256. https://doi.org/10.1108/apjml-04-2017-0073

Akroush, M. N., & Al-Debei, M. M. (2015). An integrated model of factors affecting consumer attitudes towards online shopping. *Business Process Management Journal, 21*(6), 1353–1376. https://doi.org/10.1108/BPMJ-02-2015-0022

Balaji, M. K., Sankararaman, G., & Suresh, S. (2020). A study on impact of Covid-19 in India. *Test Engineering and Management, 83*(3), 16056–16062. https://www.academia.edu/43352226/A_Study_on_Impact_of_Covid_19_in_India

Bhavya, R., & Sambhav, S. (2020). Role of mobile communication with emerging technology in Covid-19. *International Journal of Advanced Trends in Computer Science and Engineering*, *9*(3), 3338–3344. https://www.academia.edu/43611308/ Role_of_Mobile_Communication_with_Emerging_Technology_in_COVID_19

Brown, L. G. (1990). Convenience in services marketing. *Journal of Services Marketing*, *4*(1), 53–59. https://doi.org/10.1108/EUM0000000002505

Chakraborty, T., Kumar, A., Upadhyay, P., & Dwivedi, Y. K. (2021). Link between social distancing, cognitive dissonance, and social networking site usage intensity: A country-level study during the COVID-19 outbreak. *Internet Research*, *31*(2), 419–456. https://doi.org/10.1108/intr-05-2020-0281

Ecola, L., Lu, H., & Rohr, C. (2020). *How is COVID-19 changing Americans' online shopping habits?* https://www.rand.org/pubs/research_reports/RRA308-6.html

Gao, X., Shi, X., Guo, H., & Liu, Y. (2020). To buy or not buy food online: The impact of the COVID-19 epidemic on the adoption of e-commerce in China. *PLoS One*, *15*(8). https://doi.org/10.1371/journal.pone.0237900

Giosuè, L. (2020, July 21). *Understanding the impact of COVID-19 on online shopping trends*. https://www.jpost.com/special-content/understanding-the-impact-of-covid-19-on-online-shopping-trends-635791

Gupta, A., Bansal, R., & Bansal, A. (2013). Online shopping: A shining future. *International Journal of Techno-Management Research*, *1*(1), 1–10. https://www. researchgate.net/publication/318224640_Online_Shopping_A_Shining_Future

Harapan, H., Itoh, N., Yufika, A., Winardi, W., Keam, S., Te, H., Megawati, D., Hayati, Z., Wagner, A. L., & Mudatsir, M. (2020). Coronavirus disease 2019 (COVID-19): A literature review. *Journal of Infection Public Health*, *13*(5), 667–673. https://doi.org/10.1016/j.jiph.2020.03.019

Healthy Eating Research, Center for Science in the Public Interest, Johns Hopkins Bloomberg School of Public Health, The Food Trust report. (2020, November). *Retail strategies to support healthy eating*. Healthy Eating Research. https:// healthyeatingresearch.org/research/retail-strategies-to-support-healthy-eating/

Hsieh, T., Yang, K., Yang, C., & Yang, C. (2013). Urban and rural differences. *Internet Research*, *23*(2), 204–228. https://doi.org/10.1108/10662241311313321

Izogo, E. E., & Jayawarshena, C. (2018). Online shopping experience in an emerging e-retailing market. *The Journal of Research in Indian Medicine*, *12*(2), 193–214. https://doi.org/10.1108/JRIM-02-2017-0015

Jiang, L. A., Yang, Z., & Jun, M. (2013). Measuring consumer perceptions of online shopping convenience. *Journal of Service Management*, *24*(2), 191–214. https://doi. org/10.1108/09564231311323962

Klapalová, A. (2019). Customer product returns – Feedback and knowledge management. *Measuring Business Excellence*, *23*(2), 149–164. https://doi.org/10.1108/ MBE-11-2018-0099

Levy, P., Morecroft, J., & Rashidirad, M. (2020). Developing a transformational digital strategy in an SME: The role of responsible management [version 1; peer review: 1 approved]. *Emerald Open Research*, *2*(52). https://doi.org/10.35241/ emeraldopenres.13842.1

Lipiäinen, H. S. M., & Karjaluoto, H. (2015). Industrial branding in the digital age. *Journal of Business & Industrial Marketing*, *30*(6). https://www.emerald.com/ insight/content/doi/10.1108/JBIM-04-2013-0089/full/html

Mabaloc, C. R. (2020). The covid-19 pandemic and social inequality. *Eubios Journal of Asian and International Bioethics, 30*(5), 234–237. https://www.academia.edu/43310559/_The_Covid_19_Pandemic_and_Social_Inequality_In_Eubios_Journal_of_Asian_and_International_Bioethics_Volume_30_Number_5_June_2020_234_237

Nazir, S., Tayyab, A., Sajid, A., Rashid, H., & Javed, I. (2012). How online shopping is affecting consumers buying behavior in Pakistan. *IJCSI International Journal of Computer Science.* https://www.ijcsi.org/papers/IJCSI-9-3-1-486-495.pdf

Nazr, L., Burton, J., & Grubor, T. (2018). Developing a deeper understanding of positive customer feedback. *Journal of Services Marketing, 32*(2), 142–160. https://doi.org/10.1108/JSM-07-2016-0263

Niknamian, S., & Zaminpira, S. (2020). The historical/evolutionary cause and possible treatment of pandemic COVID-19 (SARS-CoV-2, 2019-CORONA VIRUS): World-War III: The blackout of the modern world by neglected small infectious agent. *HSOA Journal of Alternative, Complimentary and Integrative Medicine, 6*(99), 2–21. https://www.academia.edu/42706623/The_Historical_Evolutionary_Cause_and_Possible_Treatment_of_Pandemic_COVID_19_SARS_CoV_2_2019_CORONA_VIRUS_World_War_III_The_Blackout_of_the_Modern_World_by_Neglected_Small_Infectious_Agent

Orion Market Research Report. (2020, May). *Impact of COVID 19 on the e-commerce market.* https://www.researchandmarkets.com/reports/5013567/impact-of-covid-19-on-the-e-commerce-market

Pan, Z., Lu, Y., Gupta, S., & Hu, Q. (2020). You change, I change: An empirical investigation of users' supported incremental technological change in mobile social media. *Internet Research, 31*(1), 208–233. https://doi.org/10.1108/intr-06-2019-0226

PwC Report. (2020, May). *Impact of covid-19 outbreak on digital payments.* https://www.pwc.in/consulting/financial-services/fintech/dp/impact-of-the-covid-19-outbreak-on-digital-payments.html

RBI Bulletin. (2019, August 4). *Drivers of digital payments: A cross country study.* https://www.rbi.org.in/scripts/BS_ViewBulletin.aspx?Id=18409

Shankar, A. (2021). How does convenience drive consumers' webrooming intention? *International Journal of Bank Marketing, 39*(2), 312–336. https://doi.org/10.1108/IJBM-03-2020-0143

Sharma, A., & Jhamb, D. (2020). Changing consumer behaviours towards online shopping – An impact of covid 19. *Academy of Marketing Studies Journal, 24*(3), 1–10. https://www.abacademies.org/articles/Changing-consumer-behaviours-towards-online-shopping-an-impact-of-covid-19-1528-2678-24-3-296.pdf

Sivathanu, B. (2019). Adoption of digital payment systems in the era of demonetization in India: An empirical study. *Journal of Science and Technology Policy Management, 10*(1), 143–171. https://doi.org/10.1108/JSTPM-07-2017-0033

UNCTAD and Netcomm Suisse eCommerce Association Report. (2020, October 8). *COVID-19 has changed online shopping forever, survey shows.* https://unctad.org/news/covid-19-has-changed-online-shopping-forever-survey-shows

Weill, J., Stigler, M., Deschênes, O., & Springborn, M. (2020). Social distancing responses to COVID-19 emergency declarations strongly differentiated by income. *Proceedings of the National Academy of Sciences of the United States of America, 117*(33), 19658–19660. https://doi.org/10.1073/pnas.2009412117

Yasmin, A., Tasneem, S., & Fatema, K. (2015). Effectiveness of digital marketing in the challenging age: An empirical study. *International Journal of Management Science and Business Administration*, *1*(5), 69–80. http://researchleap.com/wp-content/uploads/2015/04/6.-Effectiveness-of-Digital-Marketing-in-the-Challenging-Age-An-Empirical-Study1.pdf

yStats GmbH & Co. KG report. (2020, May). *COVID-19 impact on global e-commerce and online payments – 2020*. https://www.researchandmarkets.com/reports/5026196/covid-19-impact-on-global-e-commerce-and-online#relb0-5013567

Chapter 10

Impact of the Pandemic on Consumer Behavior – A Review

Ulfat Andrabi, Aaliya Ashraf and Priyanka Chhibber

Lovely Professional University, India

Abstract

Knowledge of consumer behavior is important to a corporation's accomplishment. Organizations may change for the better deal with the promotion mix, product administration, and buyer interaction by knowing how the buyer performs and what motivates him. Selecting the influencing elements for consumers is frequently exceedingly challenging to accurately detect because they are inside forces. The COVID-19 pandemic's wide-scale spread has significantly altered peoples' daily lives and purchasing patterns. The Indian government implemented several steps across the nation to limit the fatal disease to slow the spread of COVID-19. Following its initial breakout in China in early 2020, the novel coronavirus pandemic rapidly developed all over the globe, giving an unfavorable influence on the global financial system and industries. During the COVID-19 pandemic, the authors seek to uncover changes in consumer behavior when purchasing everyday items including food, medications, clothing, footwear, and technology. To understand how the current pandemic conditions compare to the aforementioned shock events, we carried out a comprehensive review of the literature with a focus on the presentation of panic buying and pack mentality behavioral patterns and changes to voluntary consumer spending as defined by Maslow's hierarchy of needs.

Keywords: Pandemic; COVID-19; consumer behavior; customers; consumer attitude; online market

Navigating the Digital Landscape, 167–180

Copyright © 2024 Ulfat Andrabi, Aaliya Ashraf and Priyanka Chhibber

Published under exclusive licence by Emerald Publishing Limited

doi:10.1108/978-1-83549-272-720241010

Introduction

International trade faces both possibilities and risks because of globalization. The degree of globalization, privatization, and liberalization affects global economic growth. In addition to this, economic growth is contingent on the best possible use of resources, money invested, labor force, and technology employed in production and population consumption levels. International trade is boosted by world peace and the different nations' cooperative attitude. On November 11, the World Health Organization (WHO) formally proclaimed coronavirus disease 2019 (COVID-19) to be a pandemic. A pandemic is a scenario in which a disease has spread from person to person across several nations. The people become afraid as a result. When the initial lockdown was announced, the market's rush instantly escalated. Even at their lowest point, store inventories of necessities were impressive. During the initial phases of the lockdown, numerous medicinal trade collections were knocked out of face surgical masks and hand disinfectants. It led to the black marketing of necessities and healthcare products.

To tackle the COVID-19 pandemic, demand for crucial medical equipment skyrocketed. To give one example, products like masks, gowns, gloves, and respirators, among others, were crucial in enabling healthcare professionals to address the pandemic. While the supply has been steadily rising to try to keep up with the strong demand for these products, countries are beginning to experience supply shortages and are being compelled to ration these products more and more. Countries turned to trade policy because of their rising concern over supply shortages for these necessary items. As they rushed to locate medical supplies to combat COVID-19, some countries lifted their limitations, while others reduced their exports, in imports, according to Evenett and Winters (2020). While some nations dropped their import trade restrictions to make it easier for people to get these commodities, others made it more difficult for domestic companies to sell these goods abroad.

An important change in online purchasing behavior has been brought about by lockout enforcement's adoption. It has also evolved into a new standard of conduct using real shopping as a substitute to stop the spread of the disease. The COVID-19 outbreak has had a significant impact on the economy, although e-commerce is still unaffected. The COVID-19 curve flattens because of the distance established by online purchasing, where viruses are less inclined to spread, and interaction rates are lower. However, there are also worries about how unpredictable online purchasing may be because more information might be revealed when making a purchase. Customers are concerned that submitting personal information like their address and ID number would disclose and misuse their data. Customers worry that online merchants may compile a record of their data and send them unwelcome marketing messages.

Background

In late December 2019, an unknown etiology pneumonia outbreak occurred in Wuhan, Hubei Province, China, and quickly spread nationwide. The Chinese

Centre for Disease Control and Prevention (CCDC) identified 2019-nCoV, now officially known as severe acute respiratory syndrome coronavirus (Gorbalenya et al., 2020), as the cause of the pandemic. This was the third outbreak of a zoonotic coronavirus in the first two decades of the 21st century, allowing for the human-to-human transmission and raising global health concerns. The pandemic grew exponentially at the start of 2020, and this could only be the tip of the iceberg due to delayed case reporting and a lack of testing kits (Li et al., 2020). Coronaviruses are a large group of viruses that are known to cause illnesses ranging from the common cold to more serious diseases such as serious critical respiratory syndrome (SARS) as well as the Middle East respiratory syndrome (MERS). In December 2019, a new coronavirus was discovered in Wuhan, Hubei Province, China. However, phyllo-epidemiologic analyses suggested that 2019-Nov did not originate in the Huanan market. The virus was brought in from elsewhere and spread in the crowded market (Yu et al., 2020). This virus is a new strain that has not previously been identified in people. The disease is now well-known as SARS-CoV-2 (severe acute respiratory syndrome coronavirus), along with the infection that leads to the known COVID-19. The Chinese government had taken immediate, transparent, and extraordinary measures to control the outbreak and had achieved preliminary success. The WHO is deeply concerned about the unprecedented rapid global spread and severity of the outbreak, as well as some countries' ignorance and inaction. As a result, in March 2020, the WHO declared the novel coronavirus outbreak a global pandemic. On January 30, 2020, India reported the first case of the disease. Since then, the number of reported cases has steadily and significantly increased. Given the nature of the disease, which is highly contagious, policy actions such as the imposition of social distancing, self-isolation at home, closure of institutions and public facilities, restrictions on mobility, and even lockdown of an entire country are being considered.

Objectives (Fig. 10.1)

- To study about international trade of essential goods during a pandemic.
- To study consumer behavior during crises situation in a pandemic.
- To study online shopping behavior during the pandemic.
- To study the impact of COVID-19 on the food supply chain.

Review of Literature

According to Rastogi (2010), online shopping has a very bright future in India. In India, people's attitudes toward online shopping are improving. Consumers can shop online from anywhere, at any time, and with simple and secure payment options. Consumers can conduct product and online store comparison shopping. Narayana Rao and Ratnamadhuri (2018) together determined that little variations in revenue points occur, indicating that distinct groupings choose or have

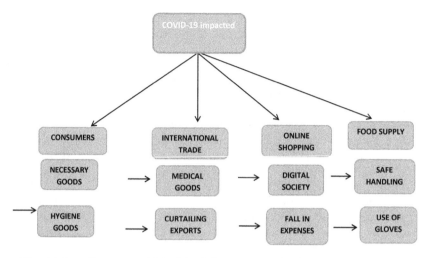

Fig. 10.1. Conceptual Model of the Impact of COVID-19 on Various Sectors. *Source:* Authors.

several judgments on the consumer obtaining behavior. It attracted my curiosity to find out which clusters' ideas contrasted the greatest. Each character has numerous positions in their day-to-day lives, whether professional or social. Each of these roles has an impact on consumer purchasing behavior. Each role has a separate societal status, and consumer behavior is severely influenced by this factor. Sales can be significantly increased if marketers understand the factors that most influence purchasing decisions. Huang et al. (2020) discovered that on January 2, 2020, 41 admitted hospital patients had laboratory-confirmed 2019-nCoV (COVID-19) infection. Most infected patients were men, and less than half had underlying diseases such as diabetes, hypertension, or cardiovascular disease. The median age was 470 years. Twenty-seven of the forty-one patients had been exposed to the Wuhan seafood market. All 41 patients had pneumonia and abnormal chest CT findings. Acute respiratory distress syndrome, acute cardiac injury, and secondary infection were among the complications. Agricultural construction, postharvest usage, administering, dissemination/retail/service, and expenditure are the five stages of the food supply chain. In the food supply chain, dual procedures are applied to make certain food conditions and shelter. The primary is created on principles and regulations that hire required specifications that are examined by state-owned agencies. Another option is to be sure of the intended guidelines recognized by market directives or worldwide associations (Bendekovic et al., 2015). Food employee health issues, personal hygiene, use of shielding apparatus such as headdresses and handbags, decontamination of surfaces and waged surroundings, safe management/groundwork/transfer of nutrition, and care of social distance are all examples of protection measures to confirm the continuousness food movement at each stage. Caring methods in the final steps of the food source chain-up are significant because more families might be involved in the same way as the chain-up develops (Rizou et al., 2020). Unlike foot and mouth disease, bird flu, *E. coli*, or Listeria, the COVID-19 pandemic has no direct impact on production because it is not transmitted through livestock or agricultural products (FAO, 2020). However, because of the pandemic, governments around the world have imposed significant restrictions on goods transportation (by land, sea, and air) as well as labor migration. According to reports, the use of buses for foodstuff dissemination has slumped to 60% in France, while the limitations put down from 30% earlier than the virus (Bakalis et al., 2020; FAO, 2020). Another factor that disrupted food chains during the COVID-19 outbreak was centralized food manufacturing. This paradigm aided food processors in increasing output while decreasing costs. However, there are some drawbacks to centralization, such as rigid and lengthy supply chain issues. Furthermore, using a small number of very large production facilities to meet demand may cause issues (Almena et al., 2019), such as the closure of the entire facility in the event of an outbreak, leaving high-capacity production lines with fewer alternatives. Ali (2020) With the increasing penetration of the internet, online shopping has become commonplace, with payments and deliveries made simple. Furthermore, because of COVID-19, online purchasing has become even more appealing, considering the limited circumstances. This study investigates the possible relationship of COVID-19 to purchaser purchasing behaviors of electronic durable items in Iraq, with a particular emphasis on expertise purchaser deviations from the related regulations. Wijaya et al. (2020) describes the impact of the COVID-19 outbreak on customer behavior in Indonesia in this newsletter. This article discusses the factors that shape panic shopping behavior in Indonesia as a result of COVID-19. The study used exploratory studies on a large number of people who experienced panic buying in areas where COVID-19 was banned and local regulations were in place (Pantano et al., 2020). The COVID-19 pandemic (which began in early 2020) is causing several disruptions in the short and medium term, to which businesses must adapt. Some outlets responded immediately to the emergency, displaying a wide range of intervention types. The author's goal is to summarize the challenges that retailers are facing as a result of the COVID-19 emergency. We do this from the perspective of both customers and executives, intending to provide guidelines and examples of how outlets can deal with this extraordinary situation. The findings of Debnath (2020) show that the independent variable (massive price increases of merchandise and delayed online services) has a significant impact on consumer purchasing behavior. According to the statistics, male respondents with monthly profits ranging from 0 to 30,000 and an age range ranging from 25 to 35 have a significant influence on customer purchasing behaviors. Sharma et al. (2021) Because of low-cost internet access during the COVID-19 pandemic length, online shopping has increased in Nepal. This is true: COVID-19 is reshaping patron shopping behavior by hook or by crook. According to the studies, respondents are also the high quality when it comes to online purchases. However, the customer believes that there are still many issues and problems associated with online purchases in Nepal, such as product credibility, first-rate guarantee, logo configuration, and so on.

International Trade of Essential Goods During a Pandemic

The ongoing COVID-19 pandemic has resulted in a significant increase in demand for critical medical equipment to combat it. For example, items such as masks, gowns, gloves, and respirators, among others, are critical in allowing healthcare workers to address the ongoing pandemic. While supply has gradually increased to try to meet the high demand for these goods, countries have experienced supply shortages and are being forced to ration these goods. Countries have resorted to trade policy in response to growing concerns about supply shortages of these essential goods. "As they scramble to find medical supplies to combat COVID-19, some countries are eliminating import restrictions while others are curtailing exports," Evenett and Winters (2020) write. Access to global markets has provided enormous benefits to countries that are open to international trade and have production patterns determined by comparative advantage. However, the pandemic in initial 2020 revealed conflicts and shortcomings in the strategy of worldwide market policy. Nations that depend severely on the consequences of significant well-being try goods, such as private defensive apparatus, discovered themselves at a distinct inconvenience when the virus affected a sudden boost in need for these commodities across the globe. Universal trade is essential in supplying people with gain access to important health-check manufactured goods. Their manufacture is focused in a few nations, and the mainstream of people import them. The increase in requirement for these commodities, mixed with the slow-down increase in trade, was followed by international deficiencies.

Leibovici and Santacreu (2021) reflected in their study on International Trade Policy During a Pandemic *that s*hows numerous nations use up trade strategies to improve these deficiencies. By March 2020, 58 nations had executed trade limitations, and 50 had liberalized the consequences of these goods. Though these guidelines were generally provisional, they were still in place in numerous nations at the end of 2020, nine months into the virus.

Consumer Purchasing Behavior During Crises Situation in a Pandemic

According to Amado et al. (2018), social networks have a significant influence on cardiopulmonary bypass (CPB). Additionally, as per Nistorescu and Puiu (2009), CPB tends to alter throughout challenging, traumatic flashes of a disaster due to a transformation in observed stages of threat, presuming that emergencies are precisely associated with hazards. This possibility was not automatically substantial or genuine; instead, it was the awareness of the danger that created individuals terrified throughout calamities (Altheide, 2002). Most of this perception begins from evidence acknowledged buyers' calamities. So far as the data sources persisted and concentrated on the causes of the calamity, apparent danger may be manipulated. The greater the psychological impact that the crisis may have on consumers, the more information they processed about an uncertain future, harsher conditions, rising unemployment, decreasing wages, or an increase in infected people or deaths. Additionally, social media programs were developing progressively more widely held political platforms for intelligence pursuing and developed as an essential module in the distribution and exploration of data. Gottfried and Shearer (2016) realized that 62% of US grown people got their news broadcast from social media, still even though social media can accelerate the speedy increase of fake news (i.e., news with intentionally false information). The prevailing distribution of fake news might damage individuals and communities, and thus may be implicated in hazard awareness and its spiritual influence.

The space as we understand it has been radically transformed by the COVID-19 pandemic. Individuals are acting, grocery shopping, and, in many ways, imagining, in a different way. Supply chains have been put to trial. Stores are closing their entrances. Worldwide clients are impending commodities and companies with a warm perception. The illness has radically augmented long-term fundamental movements and restricted the manufacturing of buyer goods in a concern of weeks. As per the research, new practices designed now leave once this calamity, permanently modifying our ideals, grocery shopping designs, and everyday life. Purchasers are particularly worried about the Coronavirus impact, from equally a monetary and health perspective. Different individuals react to different circumstances, and they have various thoughts, performances, and grocery-shopping inclinations. As they attempt to adapt to a new routine, individuals across the globe are frightened. As people consider what this predicament indicates for them, but more crucially, what it suggests for their, families, and society as a whole, dread is running high.

There are numerous options for consumers to respond to the issue. Because they are tense and stressed, several people purchase basic and hygiene products. On the contrary side, some clients continue to behave normally and are indifferent about the epidemic despite government and medical advisories. Consumer packaging companies will need to understand how their clients are reacting to develop customized and unique business strategies for each. Marketing that applies to all situations no longer works. The coronavirus outbreak is changing the reasons behind it and the products that people buy.

Client demands have improved to place the extremely fundamental demands in the beginning, which has improved the requirement for sanitation, maintenance, and fundamentals while diminishing it for nonessential classifications. The considerations affecting brand name outcomes are increasing intensity as the "buy local" movement does as well. The online exchange has extended to more than individuals buying online. After the epidemic, this shape is almost certainly getting to continue. In these cases, our requirement for basics takes priority. That the consumers in our study put their well-being before that of their friends and family should come as no revelation. Financial stability, personal safety, the security of the food supply, and access to medical care were among the other top priorities. Individual safety, food chain safety, and access to healthcare.

Online Shopping Behavior During a Pandemic

An assessment of 3,700 clients in nine emerging and advanced reductions discovered that the COVID-19 plague has constantly transformed available grocery shopping habits. More than half of those analyzed thought they currently store online more frequently and depend more on the internet for news, health-related data, and digital performance as a result of the pandemic. According to the poll, shoppers in developing markets have shifted to internet shopping the most. The COVID-19 epidemic has sped up the transition to a more digital society. As the global economy starts to recover, the reforms we make now will have an ongoing impact, according to UNCTAD head Mukhisa Kituyi. He stated that as the alterations from the pandemic come back to retrieval, the quickening of internet ordering worldwide highpoints the requirement of certifying that all countries can take benefit of the offered by digitalization. The Brazilian Network Information Center (NIC.br) and Inveon participated in the UNCTAD and Netcomm Suisse eCommerce Association survey, which revealed a 6%–10% point rise in online sales across most product categories. Electronic gadgets, horticultural, medications, teaching, furniture/everyday goods, and makeup/private care are the industries with the largest gains.

However, the typical monthly internet spending per customer has dropped substantially. Consumers in developing markets prioritize necessities more so than those in developed economies, who have both put off making larger purchases. The most significant decline was seen in the tourism and travel sectors, where online buyers' average spending fell by 75%.

With more people already engaging in e-commerce, Switzerland and Germany saw the weakest growth in internet purchases during COVID-19, while China and Turkey saw the largest increases. As per the study, females and those having tertiary edification resorted to more virtual procurements as compared to other demographic groups. Matched to youth, individuals between the ages of 25 and 44 reported a greater increase. In the case of Brazil, women and the weaker sections of society experienced the biggest growth. Due to the increased demand for online retail, several social networking sites added more commerce capabilities, allowing customers of partnering retail outlets to browse and buy things without ever exiting the platform. These platforms are frequently tightly connected with eCommerce systems, allowing eCommerce operators to promote their products with ease across many channels.

COVID-19 Impact on the Food Supply Chain

Agricultural production, handling after harvesting, dealing out, circulation/marketing/overhaul, and end users are the five processes of the Colloquially Farm to Fork. In this process, two techniques are utilized to check foodstuff class as well as protection. The main one is grounded on procedures and commandments that use obligatory criteria reviewed by government interventions. The other choice is to bank on deliberate ideals recognized by marketplace rulings or worldwide establishments. Food employee health issues, personal hygiene, use of individual defensive apparatus like hoods and gloves, purification of exteriors and occupied surroundings, nontoxic management/making/distribution of foodstuff, and keeping of societal aloofness are all examples of protection methods to safeguard the permanency of foodstuff movement at every juncture. Safety procedures in the ultimate junctures of the foodstuff logistics are grave as added folks may be exaggerated as the chain progresses. Since the majority of farm operations are dependent on the time of year and the seasonal changes, these operations need to comply with a routine that is both precise and flexible to ensure that rapid measures can be taken whenever they are necessary. As each of the steps and procedures in a value chain are interconnected and dependent on one another, even a momentary hiccup or defer in one of them can set off a huge impact, which results in a major reduction in production and harvest. There have been numerous reports of farmers being forced to destroy their crops. The effect of epidemic difficulties on agronomic systems is heavily influenced due to the quantity and composition of agronomic input changes according to the produce and the economy as mentioned in fig IV (Poudal et al., 2020). In high-income yielding economies, labor-saving techniques are usually used for agronomic produce, whereas production is primarily labor-intensive in low-income economies. As a consequence of this, the distribution chain should continue to operate normally while placing special focus on the important facets of the practical problem. The supply chain can have an impact on food processing facilities that need several skilled workers, in addition to having an impact on producers, wholesalers, and end-users of the product. It was mainly in animal flesh food manufacturers during the epidemic that numerous plants witnessed production declines, expulsions, or provisional shuts down due to which efficiency of workmen who were diagnosed with coronavirus and were hesitant to report to work for panic that they may become ill while they were on duty due to their condition. This was the case in almost every production plant. Late in April, it was projected that the potential for producing pork had declined by approximately 25% as a consequence of these considerations.

Research Methodology

This research relied on secondary data gathered from Scopus and the Web of Science from various journals, books, and articles to synthesize consumer behavior during a pandemic.

The study focuses on identifying the need for digitalization in trade and commerce during pandemics so that contactless sales and purchases can be developed. It will also help in the development of a conceptual framework based on the literature review. Our research also identifies the various benefits and drawbacks of e-marketing.

Advantages and Disadvantages of Online Marketing

Advantages

- *Online marketing is cost-effective*: Web marketing's low price is among its vital advantages. Organizations can boost themselves on the internet without spending a great deal of wealth and time. According to a HubSpot study, it is 61% less expensive than traditional offline marketing. The removal of expenses for travel, printing, etc., led to this huge cost decrease.

- *Internet marketing is globally accessible*: In contrast to traditional offline promotional techniques, online marketing is not limited by geographic location. This opens up the possibility of establishing global marketing initiatives in a timely and cost-effective manner. Even the smallest of businesses have the potential to draw in clients throughout the globe if they establish an eCommerce marketing website. As a result, businesses have the potential to broaden their visibility and extend across the globe with a little bit of transformation.

- *Improved regional reach*: Regional visibility is optimized by e-marketing, which is extremely vital if your organization relies on customers located in the region. More customers will be drawn to your business if you use local SEO and advertisements that are hyper-focused on your geographic region. When compared to more conventional forms of offline marketing, investing time and value in this initiative would not require nearly the same level of commitment.

- *Brand labeling*: The process of building a brand includes making a multitude of activities to believe customers that a brand is dependable and credible in all situations. This has been made much more convenient through the utility of e-marketing because it allows you to engage with customers and provide them with an overview of your brand through the application of customized promotional activities. Favorable effects are created because of properly addressing the importance of your brand and its distinctive selling points.

- *Online marketing aids businesses in showcasing their expertise*: The biggest challenge for businesses that provide professional services is to exhibit that they are proficient. There are indefinite occasions in traditional marketing to set up and display competence. Although, this could also be done in different ways with e-marketing. You can share pertinent content to several marketing programs to disperse your signal and prove that you are a specialist in your area. This will indulge the customers toward you want to reach, which in turn will extend your growth.

- *You can contact potential customers where they are using online marketing*: people frequently use innumerable internet sources when seeking a specific product or service. It is decisive that you understand where they are looking for goods in your region because of this. You may generate a considerable and distinct online existence with online marketing. Your website, review sites, search engines, social media, video marketing websites, meetings, and other networks are all possibilities.

Disadvantages

- *Time commitment*: The most significant drawback of online advertising is that it takes up a lot of time. The achievements and failures of your brand's multiple advertisement approaches will become visible to you with time. After you have directed your technique, you can accelerate things by using the most efficient ways. This means that before launching into online marketing, you ought to have a well-thought-out policy complete with scientific methods.

- *Privacy and security concerns*: As one enters the world of digital marketing, safety and privacy become of the utmost importance. The safety of customer data is necessary for corporate companies. Clients won't do business with a brand or a corporate if they don't trust in its ability to keep their personal information safe.
- *Inadequate access*: Regardless of the possibility that digital marketing encourages brand names to have an impact on a worldwide platform, it is not feasible to interact with each location or individual on the globe using the internet. Because rural areas frequently have inadequate web access or a lack of network connections, those who are illiterate or elderly and are unaware of the internet cannot be reached by digital marketing. Additionally, customers who do not utilize the internet cannot be reached by online marketing.
- *Technological dependence*: For the successful survival of online marketing, newly introduced technological advancements and gadgets like smartphones and high-speed internet are necessary. To meet this purpose, a good sum of money is spent on them. Despite this, it is impossible to communicate with the consumers of these technologies.
- *Technical difficulties*: Due to old technological designs like old-generation search engines, poor loading page quality, website downtime, and other similar issues can have a drastic impact on your website's online traffic. Customers indulge at the hands of your opponents, who are strictly innovative and offer an extensive, streamlined online experience.
- *Globally oriented competition*: With the help of online marketing, every company can communicate with customers throughout the globe. Despite this, you would have to deal with people from all over the globe. You'll require to come up with and use strategies to counter numerous rivals who are also aiming for the same audience. Because to attract the interest of your customers, you must stand out from the competition.

Suggestions and Recommendations

The pandemic caused some issues that significantly impacted global trade. Additionally, it influenced how customers behave. During the pandemic, shopping trends underwent a significant adjustment. The food supply network also collapsed. All areas share the fact that no industry was prepared to handle such an unforeseen circumstance. Therefore, it is important to consider the following suggestions to ensure constant preparation to deal with future uncertainty.

- To facilitate efficient government policy reactions and international mutual understanding to establish trade, it is vital to have a firm-disclosed, transparent, and accessible online information foundation. It will be important for nations to honor their commitments and inform the World Trade Organization of any trade-related measures they undertake in reaction to COVID-19 (WTO).

- One of the most pressing priorities is keeping accessible and operational the essential distribution networks for the necessities during the recession, like medical aid, packaged foods, and information and communication technology (ICT) products and services.
- The current epidemic has a great number of unavoidable repercussions, and it is even more essential to refrain from taking any activities that will boom prices for both businesses and individual customers. The imperative of evading export controls on basic needs such as medical supplies and essentially food supplies. More than 60 countries have restrained the exports of basic necessary items and rising agronomic and food products.
- Governments require to impose supplementary constraints on businesses and reestimate the record of commodities for which national production is needed. The policies for procurement may also be reviewed.
- Establishing a content strategy that reflects changing consumer demands, whether it's ensuring customers that your service will be provided in the future, updating them on company news, or simply educating them about something new that may be helpful.
- Younger generations actively want businesses to assist in combat the pandemic, not merely appreciate it when they do so. Businesses must recognize and consider the needs of these generations because they make up the bulk of the workforce.
- During economic crises, customers ignore the concept of the brand while marketing. They provide awareness and guidance. Corporations need to look for profitable strategies while also providing customers with the most satisfying experience.
- Customer retention has been a crucial aspect of the pandemic, with marketers realizing the value of generating revenue from existing clientele as the pandemic's impacts make it less likely for many businesses to expand into other regions at this time.

Conclusion

It is resolved that consumers did not take suitable safety measures in the market. During the early stages of the lockdown time, they failed to maintain social distancing in the market. Consumers were cautious in the marketplace when the government strictly enforced lockdowns and placed restrictions on people's freedom of movement. The government's and enforcement departments' efforts to maintain law and order resulted in the development of consumer discipline. Lockdown affected 96.66% of respondents purchasing behavior. 28 out of 30 respondents agree with the anxiety and panic of a pandemic situation. One of the most crucial sectors, along with health, during a pandemic is ensuring the flow of food and farm supplies. Avoiding food insecurity and minimizing its damaging effects on the world economy. Even though there haven't been any substantial issues with food supply systems to now, the future is still unpredictable. Each nation must therefore acknowledge the seriousness of the problem and modify its policies following the pandemic's progress. Additionally, the supply chain needs to be capable of adapting to difficulties in the food production process.

References

Ali, I. (2020). The covid-19 pandemic: Making sense of rumor and fear: Op-ed. *Medical Anthropology, 39*(5), 376–379.

Almena, A., Fryer, P. J., Bakalis, S., & Lopez-Quiroga, E. (2019). Centralized and distributed food manufacture: A modeling platform for technological, environmental and economic assessment at different production scales. *Sustainable Production and Consumption, 19*, 181–193.

Altheide, D. L. (2002). Children and the discourse of fear. *Symbolic Interaction, 25*(2), 229–250.

Amado, A., Cortez, P., Rita, P., & Moro, S. (2018). Research trends on Big Data in Marketing: A text mining and topic modeling based literature analysis. *European Research on Management and Business Economics, 24*(1), 1–7.

Bakalis, S., Valdramidis, V. P., Argyropoulos, D., Ahrne, L., Chen, J., Cullen, P. J., Cummins, E., Datta, A. K., Emmanouilidis, C., Foster, T., Fryer, P. J., Gouseti, O., Hospido, A., Knoerzer, K., LeBail, A., Marangoni, A. G., Rao, P., Schlüter, O. K., Taoukis, P., Xanthakis, E., & Van Impe, J. F. M. (2020). Perspectives from CO+ RE: How COVID-19 changed our food systems and food security paradigms. *Current Research in Food Science, 3*, 166.

Bendeković, J., Naletina, D., & Nola, I. (2015). Food safety and food quality in the supply chain. *Trade Perspectives, 2015*, 151.

Debnath, S. (2020). Impact of covid-19 on consumer purchase behaviour in retail sector-study based in Kolkata area. Available at SSRN 3634598.

Evenett, S. J., & Winters, L. A. (2020). Preparing for a second wave of COVID-19: A trade bargain to secure supplies of medical goods. *Global Trade Alert, 27*.

FAO (Food and Agriculture Organization of the United Nations). (2020). Policy responses to keep input markets flowing in times of COVID-19. [Online]. http://www.fao.org/3/ca8979en/CA8979EN.pdf. Accessed on May 8, 2020.

Gorbalenya, A. E., Baker, S. C., Baric, R. S., de Groot, R. J., Drosten, C., Gulyaeva, A. A., ... Ziebuhr, J. (2020). Severe acute respiratory syndrome-related coronavirus: The species and its viruses–a statement of the coronavirus study group. *bioRxiv*.

Gottfried, J., & Shearer, E. (2016). *News use across social media platforms 2016*. Pew Research Center.

Huang, C., Wang, Y., Li, X., Ren, L., Zhao, J., Hu, Y., Zhang, L., Fan, G., Xu, J., Gu, X., Cheng, Z., Yu, T., Xia, J., Wei, Y., Wu, W., Xie, X., Yin, W., Li, H., Liu, M., & Cao, B. (2020). Clinical features of patients infected with 2019 novel coronavirus in Wuhan, China. *The Lancet, 395*(10223), 497–506.

Leibovici, F., & Santacreu, A. M. (2020). *International trade policy during a pandemic*. FRB St. Louis Working Paper (2020-10).

Li, C., Yang, Y., & Ren, L. (2020). Genetic evolution analysis of 2019 novel coronavirus and coronavirus from other species. *Infection, Genetics and Evolution, 82*, 104285.

Narayana Rao, T., & Ratnamadhuri, K. (2018). Digital marketing communication and consumer buying decision process: An empirical study in the Indian passenger bike market. *International Journal of Management, Technology And Engineering*, *8*(XII), 3092–3107.

Nistorescu, T., & Puiu, S. (2009). *Marketing strategies used in crisis-study case*. MPRA Paper 17743, University Library of Munich.

Pantano, E., Pizzi, G., Scarpi, D., & Dennis, C. (2020). Competing during a pandemic? Retailers' ups and downs during the COVID-19 outbreak. *Journal of Business research*, *116*, 209–213.

Poudel, P. B., Poudel, M. R., Gautam, A., Phuyal, S., Tiwari, C. K., Bashyal, N., & Bashyal, S. (2020). COVID-19 and its global impact on food and agriculture. *Journal of Biology and Today's World*, *9*(5), 221–225.

Rastogi, A. K. (2010). A study of Indian online consumers and their buying behavior. *International Research Journal*, *1*(10), 80–82.

Rizou, M., Galanakis, I. M., Aldawoud, T. M., & Galanakis, C. M. (2020). Safety of foods, food supply chain and environment within the COVID-19 pandemic. *Trends in Food Science and Technology*, *102*, 293–299.

Sharma, K., Koirala, A., Nicolopoulos, K., Chiu, C., Wood, N., & Britton, P. N. (2021). Vaccines for COVID-19: Where do we stand in 2021? *Paediatric respiratory reviews*, *39*, 22–31.

Wijaya, T. T., Zhou, Y., Purnama, A., & Hermita, N. (2020). Indonesian students learning attitude towards online learning during the coronavirus pandemic. *Psychology, Evaluation, and Technology in Educational Research*, *3*(1), 17–25.

Yu, N., Li, W., Kang, Q., Xiong, Z., Wang, S., Lin, X., Liu, Y., Xiao, J., Liu, H., Deng, D., Chen, S., Zeng, W., Feng, L., & Wu, J. (2020). Clinical features and obstetric and neonatal outcomes of pregnant patients with COVID-19 in Wuhan, China: A retrospective, single-centre, descriptive study. *The Lancet Infectious Diseases*, *20*(5), 559–564.

Chapter 11

Consumers in the Pandemic: Contented or Discontented

Kriti Arya[a] *and Richa Chauhan*[b]

[a]KR Mangalam University, India
[b]Jaypee Business School, Jaypee Institute of Information Technology, India

Abstract

This chapter investigates pandemic impact in a variety of industries, including food, travel, education and pharmaceuticals, considering elements such as isolation, emotions and social influences, which can lead to panic buying. The goal of this research is to ascertain how COVID-19 influences the buying decisions of customers. Additionally, the study aims to identify consumer consumption trends for a spectrum of products and services, including fast-moving consumer goods (FMCGs), entertainment, pharmaceuticals, travel and tourism. A comprehensive review of different research papers is done to conclude. The papers considered are from 2020 to 2022. Different keywords are used to search the relevant papers such as 'pandemic', 'COVID-19', 'behaviour', 'impulsive', etc. TCCM framework has been applied while reviewing the articles. During the isolation, consumer behaviour moved to panic buying and stockpiling, favouring organic basics, and encouraging e-commerce, as well as economic nationalism favouring made-in-India products. This study helps in knowing the reasons for change in consumers' behaviour for different products and services due to unforeseeable situations like COVID-19 and can find possible ways to deal with them. Business owners learn about changing consumer purchasing behaviours and how to modify products. The government can change policies to improve medical tourism and social protection.

Keywords: Consumer buying behaviour; panic buying; COVID-19; e-commerce; FMCG; tourism; pharmaceuticals

Navigating the Digital Landscape, 181–216
Copyright © 2024 Kriti Arya and Richa Chauhan
Published under exclusive licence by Emerald Publishing Limited
doi:10.1108/978-1-83549-272-720241011

Introduction

In March 2020, India faced the rapid global spread of COVID-19, which lead to a pandemic. Market access was more difficult in red and orange zones due to limitations, a shortage of transportation and lockdown confusion, compared to green zones, which had better access (Cariappa et al., 2021). Despite regional effects, the study highlighted COVID-19's impact on Indian consumers, emphasising the necessity for effective countermeasures. Consumer attitudes are influenced by sociocultural and economic elements, and personal perspectives on finance, control and goals determine issue management, with crisis severity playing a critical role (Hasan et al., 2021).

Job losses caused by the lockdown resulted in significant income reductions, influencing consumer food purchasing and consuming behaviours (Cariappa et al., 2021). Consistent consumer experience is critical; supply chain disruptions resulted in brand evaluation owing to a lack of options (Rashi et al., 2021). Consumer behaviour shifts have an impact on entertainment, travel, media, small enterprises, education and other industries (Harshal & Simran, 2020).

For businesses, traders, producers of domestic and imported goods and legislators to make consumer-focused decisions, these circumstances provided insightful information (Hasan et al., 2021). The global epidemic also presented many business organisations with a never-to-be-missed chance to expand their customer base and save operating expenses (Kaur et al., 2022).

Post-pandemic, responder age, demographics and work sector influence money, influencing purchasing patterns. Consumption fell as a result of restraint (Valaskova et al., 2021). Following are the factors through which we can see the changing attitude of consumers.

Effects of Lockdown on Consumers' Purchasing Decisions

Due to the changed mindset caused by rigorous lockdowns that instilled fear and isolation, the pandemic encouraged increased purchasing of necessary and hygiene products (Srivastava & Bhanot, 2022). There was a decrease in food intake among all food categories, with almost 25% of households reporting a reduction in their intake of fruits, pulses and cereals (Travasso et al., 2023). Although people with ration cards were less likely to reduce their consumption of all food items, they still did not stop consuming any food (Husain et al., 2022; Travasso et al., 2023). Due to scarcity, high pricing and COVID-19 worries, the lockdown affected non-vegetarians' meat intake, changing consumption habits (Mondéjar-Jiménez et al., 2022; Rahman et al., 2021). This in turn led to a sense of insecurity and fear in the consumers which further resulted in panic and impulsive buying during lockdown.

An analysis showed that receiving cash transfers during lockdown did not affect the diet diversity of the consumers (Travasso et al., 2023). Food scarcity, market constraints and higher costs created uncertainty and hampered food access. Lack of information exacerbated customer difficulties (Sukhwani et al., 2020). To avoid such eventualities, governments should maintain rural social protection efforts that transmit benefits to poor households while also providing dietary diversity and security (Travasso et al., 2023).

During the pandemic lockdown, displaced migrants faced ongoing difficulties and were unable to consume necessary goods (Allard et al., 2022). COVID-19 had a direct impact on rural employment and income, as well as food consumption. The varied effects increased reliance on subsidised essentials (Suresh et al., 2022). Food scarcity resulted in less eating out, more home cooking, more snacking, meal prepping, online buying and bulk purchasing (Menon et al., 2022). The restrictions on going out during lockdown also encouraged the flourishment of online food delivery apps (Pal et al., 2022).

While the lockdown was damaging, it had a good effect on the diets of diabetics. More fruits and vegetables consumed; less alcohol and animal protein consumed (Lashkarbolouk et al., 2022).

Lockdowns increased dependency on the internet for entertainment, resulting in negative consequences such as anxiety and sleep issues as a result of misuse (Kumar, Garg, et al., 2022). Social distancing and fear of infection led to banning the movie's release in theatres which resulted in a rise in the adoption of OTT (over-the-top) viewership (Pant & Sahay, 2022). During the lockdown period, an increased number of individuals became cognizant of phishing/hacking attacks with increased usage of the internet (Shrilatha et al., 2022). Humour through social media served as a coping technique during the shutdown (Lenggogeni et al., 2022).

The global outbreak of this epidemic and the subsequent imposition of lockdown measures have disrupted the field of education also (Jha et al., 2023). It was found that in comparison to traditional in-person teaching and learning, online education has a reduced environmental impact. The students faced behavioural and technological hindrances in adopting the online system of education (Kumar, Garg, et al., 2022).

In February and March, 26 travellers in India had bad attitudes towards locals due to suspicions and noncompliance with health rules (Bauer, 2022). The importance of considering lockdown confinement and the desire for travel made it essential to examine tourism demand during periods of restricted travel (Irimias & Zoltán Mitev, 2023).

Panic and Impulsive Buying Behaviour of the Consumers

Positive emotions drive impulsive purchasing behaviour, making it critical to regulate their impact, particularly in sales campaigns (Chauhan et al., 2021). However, because of the COVID-19 situation and people's fear, both fashion involvement and marketing efforts were found to have little bearing on impulsive purchasing (Anas et al., 2022; Chauhan et al., 2021). At that time, people were mainly concerned with meeting their basic needs. Panic buying was no longer influenced by societal risks (Shahnawaz et al., 2022). The pandemic caused public humiliation as a result of the purchasing irrationally of COVID-19 purchasers who resort to subpar survival strategies (Jawad et al., 2022). Lockdown and health concerns restricted crucial purchases, causing panic and impulsive purchasing (Anas et al., 2022; Patil et al., 2022). Shoppers believe that making purchases during a pandemic involves a social risk because reference group norms might also encourage or reassure customers about their purchases (Jawad et al., 2022). The shift in working conditions from proximity to distance in society caused this difference in their behaviour during and after the pandemic's outbreak from before the pandemic's outbreak (Helisz et al., 2021).

Concerns about community effect, competition owing to scarcity and diverse beliefs and social risk perceptions all contribute to negative views towards panic buying (Jawad et al., 2022). Atypical purchases prompted by COVID-19 isolation prep, with a desire to isolate such transactions. Following panic buying, markets reverted to normal, illustrating their temporary character (Laato et al., 2020).

Healthy and Hygiene Choices of the Consumers

Under the conditions of the pandemic, high-income group people were more concerned with their health. Thus, they spent on health and hygiene goods (Kaur et al., 2022; Satish et al., 2021). Sales of health and hygiene products surged following the outbreak. Social isolation lowered shop trips, causing people to be more health-conscious for their protection and safety (Al Amin et al., 2022).

The pandemic altered purchase behaviour by influencing factors such as household affluence and demographics. Because of the decrease in income, people made more cautious purchasing decisions (Kaur et al., 2022). A greater desire for nutritious food to strengthen immunity and safeguard against COVID-19 (Sehgal et al., 2021). The epidemic resulted in more time spent at home, more home-cooked meals and less dining out, negatively reducing the intake of nutritious foods such as fruits and vegetables (Jaeger et al., 2021).

Throughout the lockdown period, individuals tended to have a lower intake of fresh food, especially fruits, vegetables and meat (Janssen et al., 2021). Some people adopted healthier home eating habits throughout the epidemic, while others indulged in unhealthy snacks owing to remote work and isolation (Gordon-Wilson, 2022). Food choice was significantly influenced by repeated food exposure (Janssen et al., 2021). Consumer preferences for ecological agricultural goods are shaped by aspects such as safety, nutrition, freshness, price, and other considerations, which represent rational consumption patterns (Chen & Shang, 2022).

Food Consumption Pattern

Positive experiences, as supported by behaviour change theories, induce long-term behaviour change; unpleasant experiences have the reverse impact (Janssen et al., 2021; Kumar & Abdin, 2021). COVID-19 caused temporary dietary changes: less fresh food in Denmark and Germany, more shelf-life products and more snacks in Canadian households (Janssen et al., 2021).

Positive dietary improvements resulted from the epidemic when people responded to it. It was revealed that socio-demographic factors are linked to the probability of positive dietary changes (Jaeger et al., 2021). Changes in eating behaviours during the pandemic were caused by constraints, changing grocery shopping frequency, COVID-19 risk assessment, income loss and socio-demographic determinants (Janssen et al., 2021).

Since the emergence of the COVID-19 epidemic, attitudes towards sourcing meals have remained largely unchanged (Pan & Rizov, 2022) Modern consumer experiences were mostly related to safety and health issues (Sehgal et al., 2021) subject to financial affordability. However, throughout the COVID-19 epidemic, marketing and advertising efforts continued to be crucial (Sayyida et al., 2021). Social media platforms gained as an important medium for interacting with customers about their habits around food access (Pan & Rizov, 2022; Rout et al., 2022). Fear of the virus is a key factor in determining how customers would use technology during the pandemic (Al Amin et al., 2022). During pandemics, customers demand frictionless options, expanding the retail-wholesale food price difference due to supply concerns and retailer prices (Cariappa et al., 2021). The pandemic changed consumption habits, resulting in unified eating behaviour during lockdown, minimising previous variations (Janssen et al., 2021). The pandemic altered consumption patterns, influencing purchasing and self-control, particularly about alcohol and fatty snacks (Chaturvedi et al., 2021; Gordon-Wilson, 2022). The epidemic changed consumption patterns, lessening the impact of prior contextual variations and encouraging changes in other consumption behaviours as people adapted to the crisis (Gordon-Wilson, 2022). A relationship between changes in food consumption and changes in shopping frequency, income loss from the pandemic, perception of COVID-19 risks, closure of actual workplaces, coffee shops, and eateries, having children in the home, gender and decreased shopping frequency was discovered (Janssen et al., 2021). 'Always-at-home' workers reduced food waste, whereas intermittent remote work increased stress in food-related operations. Smart food delivery increased awareness, changed purchasing behaviours and reduced waste indirectly. People must be educated from an early age to reduce food waste in the long run (Amicarelli et al., 2022). Households boosted their food purchases throughout the pandemic, indicating stockpiling behaviour (Anas et al., 2022; Bandyopadhyaya & Bandyopadhyaya, 2021; Satish et al., 2021). Households are paying more per purchase during the pandemic because of greater volume, higher pricing, different store preferences, home delivery and an emphasis on quality and brands, indicating a shift towards necessary purchases (Bandyopadhyaya & Bandyopadhyaya, 2021).

FMCG Goods

Customers in India, like their global counterparts, were concerned about COVID-19 but remained optimistic. Despite social distance, more money was spent on necessities through blended-mode purchasing (offline and online), with increased sales of personal and home cleaning products (Chauhan & Shah, 2020; Kumar & Abdin, 2021). Hygiene products were added to the list of what we believe to be necessities because of the COVID-19 pandemic (Papagiannidis et al., 2023; Satish et al., 2021), while sectors like clothes moved to the discretionary category. As more people look for ways to boost their immune systems, there is a surge in demand for health supplements like Ayurvedic medicines and products in the post-COVID era (Chauhan & Shah, 2020). However, since the lockout was enforced, the rising growth of fast-moving consumer products has slowed noticeably, and companies are grappling with disruptions in the supply chain and manufacturing (fast-moving consumer goods (FMCGs)) (Anas et al., 2022; Chauhan et al., 2021).

E-Commerce

India's demographics and changing consumer behaviour as a result of COVID-19 create an ideal atmosphere for big e-commerce growth, which will help the country's economy (Nougarahiya et al., 2021).

E-commerce is growing in India as individuals adapt to digital payments, thanks to flexible payment alternatives, rising smartphone usage and expanding internet access (Nougarahiya et al., 2021; Satish et al., 2021). The digitalisation has brought a revolution in the field of e-commerce (Schulze, 2021). Discounts, improved shipping, warehouse management and the ease of obtaining varied products are driving e-commerce growth in India (Nougarahiya et al., 2021). The COVID-19 crisis has altered how consumers shop (Nougarahiya et al., 2021; Salem & Nor, 2020). Attitude, satisfaction, utility and self-efficacy all influence e-wallet usage intention. During the epidemic, e-wallets were frequently utilised as a health precaution (Daragmeh et al., 2021).

Customers, even seniors who were unfamiliar with mobile food shopping, welcomed the change from strict routines. COVID-19 lockdowns boosted the frequency of online grocery buying (Nougarahiya et al., 2021). The difficulties of remote employment are exacerbated by the high call volume in e-commerce. The shutdown boosted sales on platforms such as Grofers, Big-Basket and Amazon Prime (Harshal & Simran, 2020). Recent advancements in e-commerce encourage companies to concentrate their efforts on effectively satisfying existing or potential customer needs (Popa et al., 2022).

Retail Channels

Because of demand issues and the proximity of Kirana outlets, organised retail's increasing share during the lockout dropped. The lockdown resulted in increased one-kilometre excursions and widespread walking, increasing the attractiveness of online retail across socioeconomic categories (Patil et al., 2022).

Online and offline retail channels typically work better together than against one another (Moon et al., 2021; Roy & Datta, 2022). In the modern retail era, several buyers have migrated from conventional physical retail channels to useful and safe internet channels (Moon et al., 2021; Sayyida et al., 2021). Before the crisis, consumers would occasionally use offline or online shopping options, as per their needs (Moon et al., 2021); however, the expectation today is that consumers would actively use internet purchasing choices quickly (Sayyida et al., 2021; Thakur & Kiran, 2021). The unanticipated COVID-19 outbreak necessitated intact shopping, changing the retail economy. Traditional retail channels are declining as online sales are increasing, altering the competitive landscape (Moon et al., 2021; Sayyida et al., 2021). People who disregarded social norms tended to shop through offline channels. When COVID-19 conditions are extreme and individuals believe they are vulnerable offline retail declines (Moon et al., 2021). Additionally, when consumers are sufficiently informed about COVID-19, they actively take precautions for their safety (Moon et al., 2021; Sehgal et al., 2021), which encourages more online buying. Consumers who are discouraged by others tend to resort to internet buying, although offline channels offer tactile sensations and speciality merchandise. Offline shops must diversify their store usage to thrive. Government assistance may have an impact on the balance of online and offline shopping (Moon et al., 2021; Safara, 2020).

Product shortages in retail can have an emotional impact on customers and lead to hasty purchases motivated by rivalry for limited-edition items (Jawad et al., 2022). This may also happen as a result of their anxiety (Omar et al., 2021). The impact of honesty on internet shopping ethics is minor. When compared to perceived health risks, online retail ethics have less influence, causing customers to prioritise well-being when shopping online (Fihartini et al., 2021).

Entertainment

India's Prime Minister Narendra Modi declared the first shutdown in March 2020, affecting the entertainment industry. Box office income was halted due to theatre closures and film delays, impacting crew and daily pay workers. During the lockdown, OTT platforms grew in popularity. Following the reopening of theatres with safety measures, interest in cinema viewing increased (Harshal & Simran, 2020).

The lockdown increased social media activity but had little effect on buying interest or brand image for creative economy businesses. Word of mouth has a considerable impact on both, particularly when brand image serves as a means of communication (Aditi et al., 2023).

Travel and Tourism

Flight restrictions have harmed airlines, but Indian Railways has transported essentials, turned train coaches into quarantine facilities and resumed online reservations with health protocols, while government and private vehicles have been suspended, and taxi safety precautions are in the works (Harshal & Simran, 2020).

During the pandemic, heritage tourism improves well-being by minimising loneliness and anxiety and boosting happiness through inclusive cultural activities and heritage preservation (He et al., 2023). The pandemic affected religious tourism, requiring health officials at religious sites and pilgrim countries to make urgent judgements. Overcrowding and physical contact issues emerged, affecting disease propagation (Bauer, 2022).

Medical Tourism

The practice of seeking medical treatment outside of one's home country is known as medical tourism. Many people use medical tourism facilitators to help plan their trips (Cormany & Baloglu, 2011; Hira & Kaur, 2023). However, this sector has been greatly impacted by the COVID-19 outbreak (Hira & Kaur, 2023). Return intentions to health tourism destinations are influenced by brand equity and association, which are tempered by trust, dependability, qualities and experience (Rahman et al., 2022).

Cross-border travel restrictions and lower aircraft capacity owing to social distance hampered medical tourism, resulting in increased airfare prices (Sharma et al., 2021). According to Ministry of Tourism data, foreign medical visits to India fell by 73% in 2020 (182,000 from 697,000 in 2019) (Yadav, 2022).

However, it was found that medical tourists, who were typically not sensitive to changes in prices, were not expected to be discouraged by potential price hikes resulting from the COVID-19 pandemic (Abbaspour et al., 2021). According to the survey, the recovery of medical tourism after the pandemic will take 1–3 years. After the lockdowns were lifted, the Indian industry started addressing major cases (Sharma et al., 2021).

In medical tourism, perceived cost, destination image and service quality all influence satisfaction. Trust, value, food and culture are all important (Rungklin et al., 2023). The future of healthcare tourism is dependent on economics, good infrastructure, trust, wellness and service quality (Abdul-Rahman et al., 2023).

COVID-19 has caused a global increase in telehealth; Indian medical tourism may spread. Legalised telemedicine, National Digital Health Mission integration; Ayurveda holds promise for the rise of medical tourism in India (Sangwan, 2021). The crisis hastened the online shift, emphasising customer safety, health, cleanliness, the environment and financial awareness (Garcez et al., 2021). The efficient administration of Indian medical tourism is critical for the growth of the economy, healthcare and tourism. Recovery and promotion require multidimensional planning involving stakeholders (Dar & Kashyap, 2022).

The global health network, which includes military intelligence and medical intelligence, must monitor, share data and assist vulnerable populations against biological threats (Baker et al., 2023).

Newspaper Delivery

Shutdowns raised vendor and delivery concerns, resulting in fewer publications. Customers have migrated to digital news, which has had an impact on print media and advertising. Consumer behaviours were shaped by the popularity of online news apps such as The Times of India and The Hindu (Harshal & Simran, 2020).

Eateries and Restaurants

Initially, restaurants were closed, and home delivery was prohibited. Later, due to virus concerns, limited openings and cautious online food ordering were implemented (Harshal & Simran, 2020; Sehgal et al., 2021). Due to the nationwide lockdown, every restaurant, bar and club was closed, which had a significant impact on the dine-out industry. Customers' loyalty to closed restaurants was a sign that individuals were willing to buy 'take-out' to sustain the sector (Helisz et al., 2021).

Education

Lockdown necessitated technological advancements for distance work and learning. Online classes were not available at low-income institutions due to a lack of resources. Certifications were launched by e-learning platforms, with contributions from Google, Coursera, Unacademy, WHO and AICTE (Harshal & Simran, 2020). Earlier students faced problems in adopting the e-learning system (Kumar, Garg, et al., 2022), but eventually, they discovered that e-learning is effective and can replace the traditional way of learning (Surpam et al., 2022). Thus, e-learning provides approved courses to help with exam preparation. There is a clear movement in education consumer behaviour from offline to online (Harshal & Simran, 2020).

Pharmaceuticals

The pandemic increased demand for vitamins and immune boosters, and penicillin prices skyrocketed. Pharma purchases have altered, but the post-pandemic need remains (Harshal & Simran, 2020).

Agriculture and Food Supply

The most important problem faced by the government during the lockdown was making sure that customers in rural and urban areas could access vital foods like grains, fruits and vegetables. It was crucial that the supply chain runs smoothly and includes suitable safety precautions for all parties. Another issue was the significant labour shortage in rural areas. Consumer preferences for agricultural products remained constant, but farming practices underwent a significant shift as a result of many vendors being denied access to towns where they could sell their goods, which resulted in losses for farmers (Harshal & Simran, 2020).

Economic Nationalism

COVID-19 sparked economic nationalism: buying Indian brands and supporting the local economy after the lockdown (Verma & Naveen, 2021). Countries prioritise home production; India promotes indigenous commodities, influencing consumer behaviour (Kumar & Abdin, 2021; Verma & Naveen, 2021). Indian consumer preference for native goods over foreign items demonstrates economic nationalism and ethnocentrism that is unaffected by pre/post-pandemic fluctuations (Verma & Naveen, 2021).

Other Factors

Social factors influence activity feelings; post-pandemic purchases are linked to loved ones. Online purchasing is associated with a sense of ease (Al Amin et al., 2022).

Literature Review

For the review of literature, the TCCM (Theory Context Characteristics and Methodology) framework is used. A total of 83 kinds of literature have been included which consist of research papers, review articles, online magazine/ journal articles, dissertations and conference papers.

Table 11.1 (below) shows the literature review in TCCM framework.

Table 11.1. Literature Review (TCCM Framework).

Author	Theory	Context	Characteristics	Methodology
Abbaspour et al. (2021)		Post-COVID crisis, Tourism industry, Iran	Medical tourists, normally unaffected by price variations, are unlikely to be deterred by prospective cost increases due to the COVID-19 outbreak.	Exploratory (naturalistic enquiry approach)
Abdul-Rahman et al. (2023)		Post-COVID crisis, Healthcare sector, Egypt	Medical tourism was affected by low costs, a solid medical infrastructure, trust, and well-being, but service quality had little influence.	Convenience sampling, Quantitative study, Analysis through R Studio and PLS-SEM
Aditi et al. (2023)		Micro-economic products/creative economy products, Go-jek service users, Indonesia	Word-of-mouth had a much greater influence on brand perception than social media.	Descriptive and Inferential statistics, Analysis using SMART PLS (factor analysis and path analysis)
Akter et al. (2021)	Theory of planned behaviour	Amidst lockdown and COVID-19, Online shopping, Bangladesh	Investigate how the pandemic epidemic has affected consumer behaviour in a developing country.	Quantitative study, Convenient sampling, and Analysis using PLS-SEM

Al Amin et al. (2022)	Technology Acceptance Model and Theory of Planned Behaviour	Amidst COVID-19, Mobile applications (Online grocery shopping Apps), in Bangladesh	Following the outbreak, sales of hygiene products increased, with an emphasis on personal cleanliness.	Quantitative study, Analysis using SMART-PLS 3 SEM
Allard et al. (2022)		Amidst lockdown, Labour migrants, India	During the lockdown caused by the pandemic, migrants who were displaced faced persistent challenges and were not able to access essential goods.	Quantitative study, Convenience sampling, Difference-in-means analysis, Stratified sampling,
Amicarelli et al. (2022)		Post lockdown, Food waste management, Italy	Pandemic homebound people lowered food waste awareness and adopted efficient delivery procedures, which aided mindfulness.	Quantitative study, Explorative analysis, Cumulative logit model
Anas et al. (2022)		Amidst COVID-19, Multiple products, India	Because of the COVID-19 outbreak and the general public's anxiety, impulse buying was found to be unaffected by fashion involvement and sales promotion.	Quantitative study, Convenience sampling, SPSS 22 (SEM, factor analysis)

(Continued)

Table 11.1. (*Continued*)

Author	Theory	Context	Characteristics	Methodology
Andrenelli, A., Gonzalez, J. L., Sorescu, S.		Healthcare sector, COVID-19	The research investigates the role of commerce in worldwide COVID-19 vaccine supply chains, focussing on purchase, distribution, and temperature-controlled shipping.	Review article
Baker et al. (2023)		Lockdown, Military/ Defence sector, USA	By monitoring biothreats, sharing data, and assisting communities, a global health network with military-medical intelligence can help prevent crises.	Qualitative
Bandyopadhyaya et al. (2021)		Lockdown, FMCG sector, India	Increased post-pandemic household spending is linked to volume, inflation, delivery, brand attention and an emphasis on basics.	Quantitative (survey), Longitudinal study, Analysis using Apriori algorithm

Author (Year)	Context	Objective/Finding	Method
Bauer (2022)	COVID-19, Tourism Industry, India	To provide an overview of tourism research conducted in 2020, which explored various aspects related to the pandemic's impact on travel.	Literature review
Cariappa et al. (2021)	Lockdown, Agriculture commodity sector, India	Consumers seek contactless solutions in the face of limits, resulting in retail-wholesale pricing disparities.	Additive outlier (AO) model	Quantitative study, Longitudinal quasi-experimental technique (Interrupted Time Series Analysis (ITSA))
Chaturvedi et al. (2021)	COVID-19, Organic food industry, India	Consumers' consumption habits, such as changes in their shopping behaviours and decreased self-control, were significantly linked.	Descriptive statistics, non-parametric test, Analysis using SPSS 24 (KMO and Bartlett's test, Kruskal Wallis)
Chauhan et al. (2021)	COVID-19, Fashion Industry, India	Positive emotions encourage impulsive purchasing, and happiness has been linked to fashion engagement, pleasure shopping and promotions.	Stimulus Organism Response (S-O-R) Theory	Quantitative, Analysis using PLS-SEM 3 software (importance-performance map analysis (IMPA))

(Continued)

Table 11.1. (*Continued*)

Author	Theory	Context	Characteristics	Methodology
Chauhan and Shah (2020)		COVID-19, Media Consumption, India	In the face of COVID worries, resilient customers turn to hybrid shopping for necessities, boosting hygiene product sales.	Convenience sampling, Quantitative study, and Analysis using SPSS
Chen and Shang (2022)		Post-pandemic, Ecological Agricultural products, Thailand	The selection of ecological agriculture products shows rational consumption motivated by safety, nutrition, freshness and cost.	Quantitative study, Binary Logit Model, Dual Logit Regression Model
Cormany and Baloglu (2011)		The tourism sector, in Africa	To assist in planning their travel, many people turn to medical tourism facilitators.	Exploratory research, Correspondence analysis
Dar et al. (2022)		COVID-19, Tourism sector, India	Examining the growth of telemedicine in a developing country, considering medical tourism policies, planning and outcomes.	Quantitative study

Author (Year)	Theory/Model	Context	Findings	Methodology
Daragmeh et al. (2021)	Health Belief Model (HBM), Technology Continuous Theory (TCT)	E-payment services, Post pandemic adoption	E-wallet acceptance as a pandemic prevention measure is influenced by user attitude, enjoyment, utility perception and confidence.	Quantitative study, Analysis using SPSS, PLS-SEM, Causal-predictive model
Dutt (2021)		E-commerce, India	To identify and gain insights into the primary factors that online customers.	Quantitative study
Fihartini et al. (2021)		COVID-19, E-commerce, FMCG industry, Indonesia	With health being the primary concern for internet customers, honesty remains crucial in online purchase ethics.	Quantitative study, Analysis by SPSS
Garcez et al. (2021)	Explanatory Model	Lockdown, Tourism Sector	Consumer behaviour changed as a result of the crisis, favouring internet platforms, safety, health and environmental consciousness, as well as financial worries.	Quantitative study

(Continued)

Table 11.1. *(Continued)*

Author	Theory	Context	Characteristics	Methodology
Gordon-Wilson (2022)	Protection Motivation Theory, Temporal Construal Theory, Self-Determination Theory	COVID-19, FMCG industry, UK	Consumer practices are linked to self-control studies, with changes in shopping, unhealthy snack eating and alcohol usage highlighted.	Quantitative (Netnography), Exploratory strategy
Harshal and Simran (2020)		COVID-19, Multiple sectors	The COVID-19 survey demonstrates consumer shifts in the following areas: technology use, proactive purchasing, health focus, stockpiling and critical needs.	Literature review
Hasan et al. (2021)		COVID-19, Retail, Bangladesh	The study aims to discover how demographic factors influence changes in crisis perception, purchasing patterns and consumer economic conditions.	Convenience sampling Quantitative study, Inferential statistics, Common Method Bias Test

He et al. (2023)	Post-COVID-19, Tourism sector, China	Through cultural activities in intimate settings, pandemic heritage tourism alleviates mental anguish, lowers loneliness and increases happiness.	A quantitative study, MAXQDA 2020
Helisz et al. (2021)	COVID-19, FMCG industry	The pandemic changed people's behaviour as they moved from proximity to remote work, resulting in divergent behaviours during and after the epidemic.	Quantitative study
Hira and Kaur (2023)	COVID-19, Tourism sector	Examine medical tourism providers' perspectives, factors and the impact of COVID-19.	Quantitative study, judgement and snowball sampling, use of Atlas.ti software.
Husain et al. (2022)	Pre and post-lockdown, Public Distribution System (PDS), India	Ration card holders were unwilling to reduce and abstain from food consumption.	Quantitative study, Exploratory analysis

(Continued)

Table 11.1. *(Continued)*

Author	Theory	Context	Characteristics	Methodology
Irimias and Zoltán Mitev (2023)	Intrusion Theory	Lockdown, Tourism sector	Examining visitor demand amid travel limitations is critical, given the impact of closures and people's desire to travel.	Empirical research
Jaeger et al. (2021)		COVID-19, FMCG industry, USA	Homebound tendencies are associated with more home-cooked meals and less dining out, which has an impact on healthy food intake.	Quantitative study and analysis using XLSTAT software
Janssen et al. (2021)	Social Cognitive Theory	Pre and Post-COVID-19, FMCG industry, Denmark	Because of the shared lockdown circumstances, the pandemic linked consumption, reducing pre-existing macro- and micro-contextual inequalities.	Quantitative, Multinomial logistic regression models using STATA version 15.1
Jawad et al. (2022)	Theory of Planned Behaviour, Theory of Deliberate Behaviour, Privateness Calculus Theory, Protection Motivation Theory	COVID-19, Multiple Sectors, Europe	In low-inventory stores, the pandemic causes impulsive purchases, competition and social risk perception.	Quantitative, Snowball sampling, Analysis using SPSS

Jha et al. (2023)	COVID-19, Education sector, E-education, India	The worldwide Coronavirus pandemic outbreak and the ensuing implementation of lockdown measures harmed schooling as well.	Quantitative approach
Kaur et al. (2022)	Education and IT sector, India	The pandemic altered purchasing decisions; household wealth and age were important factors. Lower salaries prompted prudence.	Quantitative approach
Kumar et al. (2022)	COVID-19, Education sector, India	Online education faces behavioural and technological hurdles. Anxiety and sleep problems are caused by the widespread usage of the internet.	Web-based cross-sectional study, Quantitative, SPSS 21.0
Kumar et al. (2022)	Lockdown, Education sector, E-education, India	The study investigates Indian educators' perspectives on student online learning issues during COVID-19, with a focus on sustainability.	Quantitative, Purposive sampling technique, Descriptive and inferential statistics

(Continued)

Table 11.1. *(Continued)*

Author	Theory	Context	Characteristics	Methodology
Kumar and Abdin (2021)		COVID-19, Urban and rural sector, India	India prioritises home manufacturing to lessen foreign dependency; behaviour influences change.	A quantitative study, SPSS 25
Laato et al. (2020)	Stimulus-Organism-Response (S-O-R) framework	COVID-19, Education sector and employees, Finland	COVID-19 caused initial expenditure concerns, which were quickly followed by market normalisation and panic purchasing.	Quantitative study, Analysis using PLS-SEM
Lashkarbolouk et al. (2022)		COVID-19, Medical sector	Lockdowns harmed individuals, although they enhanced food options for diabetics. Less booze and animal protein, more fruits and vegetables.	Systematic review and Meta-analysis (PRISMA), Assessment using the Newcastle-Ottawa Quality Scale
Lenggogeni et al. (2022)	Coping Theory	Early COVID-19, Pre and Amidst lockdown, Tourism sector, Indonesia	It broadens the application of psychology in managing crises and disasters within the tourism industry by using humour as a coping mechanism.	Quantitative, Thematic analysis

Study	Theory	Context	Findings	Methodology
Li et al. (2020)	Theory of Planned Behaviour	Initial COVID-19, FMCG sector, China	Preliminary observations into early COVID-19 pandemic purchasing behaviour alterations are provided.	Quantitative, Snowball sampling, Principal Component Analysis (PCA)
Mondéjar-Jiménez et al. (2022)		COVID-19, Meat industry	The lockdown disrupted meat supply, causing dramatic changes in non-vegetarian eating habits.	Literature review, Bibliometric analysis
Moon et al. (2021)	Protection Motivation Theory, Theory of Planned Behaviour	Amidst COVID-19, E-commerce, Korea	Consumers migrated between online and offline purchasing during COVID-19 based on their shifting demands and situations.	Quantitative, quota sampling, ordered logit model
Nougarahiya et al. (2021)		E-commerce industry, India	With new payments, smartphones, discounts, logistics and COVID-19, Indian e-commerce is thriving, appealing to even older generations.	Literature review
Omar et al. (2021)	Behavioural Inhibition System Theory, Reactance Theory, and Expectancy Theory	Lockdown, Retail sector, Malaysia	According to research findings, non-deceptive practices have little impact on consumers' ethical behaviour when making online purchases.	Quantitative, snowball sampling

(Continued)

Table 11.1. (*Continued*)

Author	Theory	Context	Characteristics	Methodology
Pal et al. (2022)	Uses and Gratification Theory (UGT)	Hospitality industry, India	During this time, the limits on outside activities fuelled the emergence of online meal delivery apps.	Quantitative Analysis using PLS-SEM, SPSS 17, Exploratory analysis
Pan and Rizov (2022)	Lancaster's random utility theory	Pre and amidst pandemic, E-commerce, FMCG industry, India	Post-COVID, attitudes towards food sources have remained mostly unaltered, while social media engagement in food practices has increased.	Qualitative and Quantitative analysis, snowball sampling, use of latent class model
Pant and Sahay (2022)	Swot analysis	Media/Entertainment Industry, India	Because of social isolation and virus fears, OTT (over-the-top) streaming has grown in popularity, limiting theatre releases.	Case study
Papagiannidis et al. (2023)	Protection Motivations Theory	Lockdown, UK, Retail	Consumer behaviour particularly about stockpiling is studied.	Quantitative research, analysis using PLS-SEM, Multi-group analysis

Patil et al. (2022)	Pre and amidst lockdown, essential commodities, India	The pandemic prompted a fall in organised retail, encouraging Kirana, online shopping and panic buying.	Quantitative research
Popa et al. (2022)	Post-COVID, E-commerce, Romania	Recent e-commerce innovations urge businesses to focus their efforts on successfully meeting current or projected client wants.	Statistical reports drawn up by reputable companies at an international (Eurostat) and national level
Rahman et al. (2021)	Lockdown, COVID-19, Meat industry, India	The COVID-19 lockdown caused non-vegetarians to change their meat consumption patterns owing to a variety of circumstances.	Quantitative research
Rahman et al. (2022)	Health tourism	Traveller return to health tourism is impacted by brand equity, trust and personal characteristics.	Empirical study, covariance-based SEM
Rashi et al. (2021)	Post-COVID-19, Advertising	A great customer experience keeps or builds brand loyalty; interruptions change choices.	Literature review, Psychometric Tests, detailed social media data analysis through Big Data Approach.

(Continued)

Table 11.1. (*Continued*)

Author	Theory	Context	Characteristics	Methodology
Rout et al. (2022)	Protection Motivation Theory and Technology Acceptance Model	Second wave of COVID-19, E-commerce, Retail, India	Social media platforms have become an important means of engaging with customers about their habits and practices related to food access.	Quantitative research, Analysis using SMART-PLS 3, Positivist approach, Cross-sectional, study, use of Single-factor method
Roy and Datta (2022)		E-commerce, Retail sector	COVID-19 effects on online and offline shopping were evaluated, and affecting factors were identified.	Literature review using term-based search approach
Rungklin et al. (2023)		COVID-19, Tourism sector, Thailand	Cost, destination, service quality, value and trust all contribute to medical tourism satisfaction. Satisfaction is influenced by cultural knowledge.	Quantitative and Qualitative research, Random sampling, Purposive sampling, SEM Analysis
Safara (2020)		Amidst COVID-19, E-commerce	With government support, offline stores diversify space utilisation, changing the online-offline retail balance.	Statistical approach, Machine learning approach.

Author (Year)	Theory	Context	Findings	Method
Salem and Nor (2020)	Technology Acceptance Model, Theory of planned behaviour	COVID-19, E-commerce, Saudi Arabia	E-commerce has changed the way of buying from stores to online method.	Snowball sampling, Quantitative study, analysis using SMART PLS-SEM, Structural model assessment
Sangwan (2021)		COVID-19, Healthcare sector, Tourism sector, India	Ayurveda and wellness in India could prosper in post-COVID medical tourism, but preparedness is required.	Review Article
Satish et al. (2021)	Planned purchase behaviour theory, psychological reactance theory, Stimulus-organism-response theory	Lockdown, pre, amidst and post-COVID-19, India	The pandemic drove people to hoard more food than usual.	SPSS 26, simple random sampling
Sayyida et al. (2021)		COVID-19, Retail, United States, England, Germany, France, Canada and Latin America	To assess the influence of the COVID-19 pandemic on consumer behaviour in the retail sector by analysing shopping trends.	Quantitative research
Schulze (2021)	Theory of Reasoned Action, Abraham Maslow's theory of the hierarchy of needs	COVID-19, Retail, UK	There is a change in the behaviour of customers in both physical and online stores, considering the impact of digitalisation and the COVID-19 pandemic.	Quantitative research

(Continued)

Table 11.1. (*Continued*)

Author	Theory	Context	Characteristics	Methodology
Sehgal et al. (2021)		COVID-19, FMCG industry, India	Determined the safety measures adopted by both consumers and retailers to cope with the sudden shift in shopping practices.	Quantitative research
Shahnawaz et al. (2022)	Health belief model, Social identity theory	COVID-19, Retail, India	Investigated the risk factors at both individual and group levels that assist in promoting preventive health measures and frenzied shopping during the COVID-19 outbreak in India.	Quantitative research, Analysis using SPSS 22, Convenience sampling
Shen et al. (2022)	Utility maximisation theory	Pre, amidst and post-COVID-19, FMCG industry, USA	COVID-19's effects on grocery shopping methods, including attitudes and decisions, are being studied.	Quantitative research, Binary logit models
Shrilatha et al. (2022)		Lockdown, India, entertainment/internet	To assess the media usage during the lockdown by Indian residents.	Conference proceedings, Quantitative research, Simple Random and Convenient Sampling Technique

Sriram et al. (2021)	Theory of Planned Behaviour	Digital marketing, Retail, India	To know the impact of Indian customers' attitudes towards online shopping, particularly in the realm of digital marketing.	Quantitative study, Analysis using PLS-SEM and Smart PLS 3
Srivastava and Bhanot (2022)		COVID-19, Essentials and hygiene products, India	To investigate the buying habits and mental attitudes of Indian consumers, with a specific focus on their online purchasing behaviour, during a period of lockdown.	Judgement sampling, Quantitative study
Sukhwani et al. (2020)		Lockdown, Food supply, India	Evaluating the impact of panic buying and stockpiling, as well as the dissemination of false information, on the local level and how they contributed to the development of food insecurity, through government initiatives.	Quantitative study

(Continued)

Table 11.1. (*Continued*)

Author	Theory	Context	Characteristics	Methodology
Suresh et al. (2022)		Lockdown, Self-help groups, FMCG sector, India	To find that there was a shift in food consumption patterns, which included an increase in consumption of subsidised staple foods.	An exploratory study, systematic random sampling, and Analysis using SPSS 23
Surpam et al. (2022)		COVID-19, Education sector, India	Finding that traditional learning can be effectively replaced by new ways of learning (e-learning).	Quantitative study
Thakur and Kiran (2021)		FMCG industry, India	Growth in the FMCG sector has slowed due to supply chain and production challenges.	Descriptive and Inferential statistics, Quantitative study
Travasso et al. (2023)		Pre and amidst lockdown, FMCG sector, India	Ration cardholders consumed consistently across all categories, while 25% of households lowered their consumption of fruits, pulses and grains.	Quantitative study, Analysis using SPSS 25

Valaskova et al. (2021)	COVID-19, Retail, Slovakia	Post-pandemic, age, demographics and employment all have an impact on money, affecting spending habits. Consumption is reduced by caution.	A categorical analysis (Pearson's chi-square test) and correspondence analysis (simple and multivariate), Fisher's exact test, contingency coefficient (Cramer's V)
Vázquez-Martínez et al. (2021)	First wave peak of COVID-19, Multi products	A COVID-like crisis distorted product purchases, and consumer behaviour changed as a result of shifting incentives.	Qualitative and Quantitative study
Verma and Naveen (2021)	COVID-19, Indigenous product, India	Following the lockout, buyers boosted the Indian economy by purchasing local products, demonstrating economic nationalism. Pre-COVID behaviours remained intact.	Quantitative research and analysis using PLS-SEM
Yadav (2022)	COVID-19, Tourism sector, India	According to data from the Ministry of Tourism website, fewer foreign tourists are now coming to India for medical treatment.	Review article

TCCM (Theory Context Characteristics and Methodology) framework.
Source: Developed by Author.

Research Gap

As presented in the literature review section, many studies have been done related to the behaviour of consumers towards a particular product/service. Also, papers dedicated to the study of consumer attitudes during lockdown have been found. However, in this study, the behaviour of the consumers has been studied for different goods and services during a pandemic, taking into consideration the changes during the lockdown as well.

Objectives of Study

- To examine how COVID-19 has changed consumer buying behaviour during the pandemic.
- To investigate the changes in attitude of buyers due to the lockdown.
- To study post-COVID changes in the buying behaviour of consumers.
- To find the factors affecting the consumers' behaviour towards various goods and services.

Research Methodology

The study is based on a thorough analysis of research papers that are focused on the consumers 'buying attitudes' during and post-pandemic. The papers considered are from 2020 to 2022. The keywords used to search the relevant papers were 'pandemic', 'COVID-19', 'corona', 'coronavirus', 'post-COVID-19', 'consumers', 'consumption', 'consumption pattern', 'behaviour', 'attitude', 'buyers', 'buying', 'impulsive' and 'panic'. The study includes research papers, review papers, articles, chapters and dissertations. It also studies buying behaviour in various sectors. A deep study and analysis are done, which forms the basis of this chapter.

Discussion and Conclusion

The pandemic of COVID-19 caused profound changes in consumer behaviour. Sanitisers and other hygiene goods gained popularity, while pharmaceutical sales climbed due to increasing health consciousness. Economic nationalism increased the sales of Indian items, and e-commerce and e-payment techniques developed. For entertainment, OTT platforms have replaced traditional theatres, and e-learning has increased while educational institutions have shuttered. Due to limited travel options, online ticketing has become necessary. These developments affected a variety of industries, reflecting shifting shopping, education and entertainment patterns. The pandemic worked as a catalyst for rapid shifts in consumer attitudes and behaviours in a variety of areas.

Limitations and Recommendations

Some very important suggestions include the following:

(1) to promote trust, ensuring a sufficient (more than what is typically available) supply of necessities; (2) enforce laws to stop predatory pricing; (3) requiring retail customers and owners to adhere to social distancing and mask rules; (4) enabling neighbourhood Kirana businesses for making payments and purchase goods and services via internet; (5) influencing regulated retail establishments to raise the quality of their products; (6) research can potentially be used to create emergency freight demand models for cities and (7) critical to create a thorough emergency goods demand model for potential disruption scenarios.

The authors recommend measures for client retention, weight loss and taking COVID-19 risks into account. Ethnocentric promotions and adaptive spaces can assist offline stores. Long-term consequences include increased digital transactions and hygiene product use. For efficient retail strategy and customer service, more research is required. The scope of the study is confined to examining research publications and excluding specific regional studies. Future research could concentrate on specific customer groups throughout various Indian states. Some limitations may also include:

- A study on the behaviour of consumers on fashion, apparel, beauty and cosmetic products has not been covered.
- Study on the behaviour of energy and fuel consumption has not been covered.
- Consumer behaviour in a particular area/region has not been studied.

References

Abbaspour, F., Soltani, S., & Tham, A. (2021). Medical tourism for COVID-19 post-crisis recovery? *Anatolia, 32*(1), 140–143.

Abdul-Rahman, M. N., Hassan, T. H., Abdou, A. H., Abdelmoaty, M. A., Saleh, M. I., & Salem, A. E. (2023). Responding to tourists' intentions to revisit medical destinations in the post-COVID-19 era through the promotion of their clinical trust and well-being. *Sustainability, 15*(3), 2399.

Aditi, B., Silaban, P., & Edward, Y. (2023). The effect of social media and word of mouth on buying interest and brand image in creative economic business. *International Journal of Data and Network Science, 7*(1), 225–234.

Akter, S., Ashrafi, T., & Waligo, V. (2021). Changes in consumer purchasing behavior due to COVID-19 pandemic. *Changes, 77*.

Al Amin, M., Arefin, M. S., Hossain, I., Islam, M. R., Sultana, N., & Hossain, M. N. (2022). Evaluating the determinants of customers' mobile grocery shopping application (MGSA) adoption during COVID-19 pandemic. *Journal of Global Marketing, 35*(3), 228–247.

Allard, J., Jagnani, M., Neggers, Y., Pande, R., Schaner, S., & Moore, C. T. (2022). Indian female migrants face greater barriers to post− Covid recovery than males: Evidence from a panel study. *EClinicalMedicine, 53*, 101631.

Amicarelli, V., Lagioia, G., Sampietro, S., & Bux, C. (2022). Has the COVID-19 pandemic changed food waste perception and behavior? Evidence from Italian consumers. *Socio-Economic Planning Sciences, 82*, 101095.

Anas, M., Khan, M. N., Rahman, O., & Uddin, S. F. (2022). Why consumers behaved impulsively during COVID-19 pandemic? *South Asian Journal of Marketing, 2022.*

Baker, M. S., Canyon, D. V., Kevany, S., & Baker, J. (2023). Improving pandemic response with military tools: Using enhanced intelligence, surveillance, and reconnaissance. *Disaster Medicine and Public Health Preparedness, 17*, e254.

Bandyopadhyaya, V., & Bandyopadhyaya, R. (2021). Understanding the impact of COVID-19 pandemic outbreak on grocery stocking behaviour in India: A pattern mining approach. *Global Business Review*, 0972150921988955.

Bauer, I. L. (2022). COVID-19: How can travel medicine benefit from tourism's focus on people during a pandemic? *Tropical Diseases, Travel Medicine and Vaccines, 8*, 26. https://doi.org/10.1186/s40794-022-00182-6

Cariappa, A. A., Acharya, K. K., Adhav, C. A., Sendhil, R., & Ramasundaram, P. (2021). COVID-19 induced lockdown effects on agricultural commodity prices and consumer behaviour in India–Implications for food loss and waste management. *Socio-Economic Planning Sciences*, 101160.

Chaturvedi, A., Rashid Chand, M., & Rahman, M. (2021). Impact of the COVID-19 on consumer behavior towards organic food in India. In *Predictive and preventive measures for Covid-19 pandemic* (pp. 127–148). Springer.

Chauhan, S., Banerjee, R., & Dagar, V. (2021). Analysis of impulse buying behaviour of consumer during COVID-19: An empirical study. *Millennial Asia*, 09763996211041215.

Chauhan, V., & Shah, M. H. (2020). An empirical analysis into sentiments, media consumption habits, and consumer behaviour during the coronavirus (COVID-19) outbreak. *Purakala* with ISSN, 971, 2143.

Chen, X., & Shang, J. (2022). Analysis of urban residents' consumption behavior and influencing factors of ecological agricultural products in the post-pandemic era of COVID-19. *Applied Bionics and Biomechanics, 2022.*

Cormany, D., & Baloglu, S. (2011). Medical travel facilitator websites: An exploratory study of web page contents and services offered to the prospective medical tourist. *Tourism Management, 32*(4), 709–716.

Daragmeh, A., Sági, J., & Zéman, Z. (2021). Continuous intention to use e-wallet in the context of the covid-19 pandemic: Integrating the health belief model (hbm) and technology continuous theory (tct). *Journal of Open Innovation: Technology, Market, and Complexity, 7*(2), 132.

Dar, H., & Kashyap, K. (2022). Indian medical tourism: COVID-19 situation, planning and reviving approaches. In A. Hassan, A. Sharma, J. Kennell, & P. Mohanty (Eds.), *Tourism and hospitality in Asia: Crisis, resilience and recovery*. Springer. https://doi.org/10.1007/978-981-19-5763-5_7

Dutt, N. (2021). Factors affecting consumers buying behaviour towards online shopping. *Review of International Geographical Education Online, 11*(7).

Fihartini, Y., Helmi, R. A., Hassan, M., & Oesman, Y. M. (2021). Perceived health risk, online retail ethics, and consumer behavior within online shopping during the COVID-19 pandemic. *Innovative Marketing, 17*(3), 17–29.

Garcez, A., Franco, J., & Correia, R. A. F. (2021, June 23). Tourism and COVID-19: Impacts and implications on the tourist consumer behavior. 2021 16th Iberian conference on information systems and technologies (CISTI). In *Presented at the 2021 16th Iberian conference on information systems and technologies (CISTI), Chaves, Portugal.* https://doi.org/10.23919/cisti52073.2021.9476405

Gordon-Wilson, S. (2022). Consumption practices during the COVID-19 crisis. *International Journal of Consumer Studies, 46*(2), 575–588.

Harshal, V., & Simran, M. (2020). Impact of COVID-19 pandemic situation on consumer buying behaviour in Indian market-a review. *International Journal for Research in Applied Science and Engineering Technology*, 2584–2589.

Hasan, S., Islam, M. A., & Bodrud-Doza, M. (2021). Crisis perception and consumption pattern during COVID-19: Do demographic factors make differences? *Heliyon, 7*(5), e07141.

Helisz, P., Gwiozdzik, W., Kaczmarczyk, N., & Calyniuk, B. (2021). Consumer behaviour during COVID-19 pandemic. *Roczniki Państwowego Zakładu Higieny, 72*(4), 403–408.

He, X., Zang, T., Sun, B., & Ikebe, K. (2023). Tourists' motives for visiting historic conservation areas in the post-pandemic era: A case study of Kuanzhai Alley in Chengdu, China. *Sustainability, 15*(4), 3130.

Hira, J. K., & Kaur, R. (2023). Supply side stakeholders' viewpoints about medical tourism in India and the effects of COVID 19. *Journal of Patient Safety and Risk Management.* https://doi.org/10.1177/25160435231161125

Husain, Z., Ghosh, S., & Dutta, M. (2022). Changes in dietary practices of mother and child during the COVID-19 lockdown: Results from a household survey in Bihar, India. *Food Policy, 112*, 102372.

Irimias, A., & Zoltán Mitev, A. (2023). Tourists as caged birds: Elaborating travel thoughts and craving when feeling captive. *Journal of Travel Research, 62*(1), 91–104.

Jaeger, S. R., Vidal, L., Ares, G., Chheang, S. L., & Spinelli, S. (2021). Healthier eating: Covid-19 disruption as a catalyst for positive change. *Food Quality and Preference, 92*, 104220.

Janssen, M., Chang, B. P., Hristov, H., Pravst, I., Profeta, A., & Millard, J. (2021). Changes in food consumption during the COVID-19 pandemic: Analysis of consumer survey data from the first lockdown period in Denmark, Germany, and Slovenia. *Frontiers in Nutrition, 60*.

Jawad, M., Rizwan, S., Ahmed, S., Bin Khalid, H., & Naz, M. (2022). Discovering panic purchasing behavior during the COVID-19 pandemic from the perspective of underdeveloped countries. *Cogent Business & Management, 9*(1), 2141947.

Jha, A., Bhatele, K. R., Sharma, C., & Tripathi, A. (2023). Online education and its repercussions on engineering students during covid-19: A survey. *Journal of Engineering Education Transformations, 36*(3).

Kaur, M., Sinha, R., Chaudhary, V., Sikandar, M. A., Jain, V., Gambhir, V., & Dhiman, V. (2022). Impact of COVID-19 pandemic on the livelihood of employees in different sectors. *Materials Today: Proceedings, 51*, 764–769.

Kumar, R., & Abdin, M. S. (2021). Impact of epidemics and pandemics on consumption pattern: evidence from Covid-19 pandemic in rural-urban India. *Asian Journal of Economics and Banking.*

Kumar, G., Dash, P., Jnaneswar, A., Suresan, V., Jha, K., & Ghosal, S. (2022). Impact of internet addiction during COVID-19 on anxiety and sleep quality among college students of Bhubaneswar city. *Journal of Education and Health Promotion*, *11*(1), 156.

Kumar, P., Garg, R. K., Kumar, P., & Panwar, M. (2022). Teachers' perceptions of student barriers to sustainable engagement in online education. *International Journal of Knowledge and Learning*, *15*(4), 373–408.

Laato, S., Islam, A. N., Farooq, A., & Dhir, A. (2020). Unusual purchasing behavior during the early stages of the COVID-19 pandemic: The stimulus-organism-response approach. *Journal of Retailing and Consumer Services*, *57*, 102224.

Lashkarbolouk, N., Mazandarani, M., Pourghazi, F., Eslami, M., Mohammadian Khonsari, N., Nouri Ghonbalani, Z., ... Qorbani, M. (2022). How did lockdown and social distancing policies change the eating habits of diabetic patients during the COVID-19 pandemic? A systematic review. *Frontiers in Psychology*, *5769*.

Lenggogeni, S., Ashton, A. S., & Scott, N. (2022). Humour: Coping with travel bans during the COVID-19 pandemic. *International Journal of Culture, Tourism and Hospitality Research*, *16*(1), 222–237.

Li, J., Hallsworth, A. G., & Coca-Stefaniak, J. A. (2020). Changing grocery shopping behaviours among Chinese consumers at the outset of the COVID-19 outbreak. *Tijdschriftvooreconomischeensocialegeografie*, *111*(3), 574–583.

Mondéjar-Jiménez, J. A., Sánchez-Cubo, F., & Mondéjar-Jiménez, J. (2022). Consumer behaviour towards Pork meat products: A literature review and data analysis. *Foods*, *11*(3), 307.

Moon, J., Choe, Y., & Song, H. (2021). Determinants of consumers' online/offline shopping behaviours during the COVID-19 pandemic. *International Journal of Environmental Research and Public Health*, *18*(4), 1593.

Nougarahiya, S., Shetty, G., & Mandloi, D. (2021). A review of e–commerce in India: The past, present, and the future. *Research Review International Journal of Multidisciplinary*, *6*(03), 12–22.

Omar, N. A., Nazri, M. A., Ali, M. H., & Alam, S. S. (2021). The panic buying behavior of consumers during the COVID-19 pandemic: Examining the influences of uncertainty, perceptions of severity, perceptions of scarcity, and anxiety. *Journal of Retailing and Consumer Services*, *62*, 102600.

Pal, D., Funilkul, S., Eamsinvattana, W., & Siyal, S. (2022). Using online food delivery applications during the COVID-19 lockdown period: What drives University students' satisfaction and loyalty? *Journal of Foodservice Business Research*, *25*(5), 561–605.

Pan, Y., & Rizov, M. (2022). Consumer behaviour in sourcing meals during COVID-19: Implications for business and marketing. *Sustainability*, *14*(21), 13837.

Pant, K., & Sahay, A. (2022). PVR limited at a crossroads. *Emerald Emerging Markets Case Studies*, *12*(4), 1–28.

Papagiannidis, S., Alamanos, E., Bourlakis, M., & Dennis, C. (2023). The pandemic consumer response: a stockpiling perspective and shopping channel preferences. *British Journal of Management*, *34*(2), 664–691.

Patil, G. R., Dhore, R., Bhavathrathan, B. K., Pawar, D. S., Sahu, P., & Mulani, A. (2022). Consumer responses towards essential purchases during COVID-19 pan-India lockdown. *Research in Transportation Business & Management*, *43*, 100768.

Popa, A., Spatariu, E. C., & Gheorghiu, G. (2022). Changes and trends in consumers' behaviour and online purchasing: A post-COVID-19 analysis. *Ovidius University Annals, Series Economic Sciences, 22*(1).

Rahman, M. S., Bag, S., Hassan, H., Hossain, M. A., & Singh, R. K. (2022). Destination brand equity and tourist's revisit intention towards health tourism: An empirical study. *Benchmarking: An International Journal Benchmarking, 29*(4), 1306–1331. https://doi.org/10.1108/BIJ-03-2021-0173

Rahman, C. F., Khan, S., Kumar, R., Chand, S., Bardhan, D., & Dhama, K. (2021). Impact of COVID-19 pandemic and lock-down on the meat consumption pattern in India: A preliminary analysis. *Journal of Experimental Biology and Agricultural Sciences, 9*, 172–182.

Rashi, P., Bist, A. S., Asmawati, A., Budiarto, M., & Prihastiwi, W. Y. (2021). Influence of post covid change in consumer behaviour of millennials on advertising techniques and practices. *Aptisi Transactions on Technopreneurship (ATT), 3*(2), 201–208.

Rout, K., Sahoo, P. R., Bhuyan, A., Tripathy, A., & Smrutirekha. (2022). Online grocery shopping behavior during COVID-19 pandemic: An interdisciplinary explanation. *Cogent Business & Management, 9*(1), 2084969.

Roy, P., & Datta, D. (2022). Impact of COVID-19 on consumer buying behavior towards online and offline shopping. *Journal of Emerging Technologies and Innovative Research (JETIR)*. https://papers.ssrn.com/sol3/papers.cfm?abstract_id=4144203

Rungklin, D., Trichan, K., & Rinthaisong, I. (2023). Satisfaction, revisit and electronic word of mouth intention among medical tourists in Southern Thailand during COVID 19 situation. *Kasetsart Journal of Social Sciences, 44*(1), 105–114.

Safara, F. (2020). A computational model to predict consumer behaviour during COVID-19 pandemic. *Computational Economics*, 1–14.

Salem, M. A., & Nor, K. M. (2020). The effect of COVID-19 on consumer behaviour in Saudi Arabia: Switching from brick and mortar stores to E-Commerce. *International Journal of Scientific & Technology Research, 9*(07), 15–28.

Sangwan, A. (2021, May 10). *Significance of medical tourism post COVID pandemic – BW*. https://bwhealthcareworld.businessworld.in/article/Significance-Of-Medical-Tourism-Post-COVID-Pandemic/10-05-2021-389125/

Satish, K., Venkatesh, A., & Manivannan, A. S. R. (2021). COVID-19 is driving fear and greed in consumer behaviour and purchase pattern. *South Asian Journal of Marketing, 2*, 113–129.

Sayyida, S., Hartini, S., Gunawan, S., & Husin, S. N. (2021). The impact of the COVID-19 pandemic on retail consumer behavior. *Aptisi Transactions on Management (ATM), 5*(1), 79–88.

Schulze, J. (2021). *Online and offline shopping in the UK: The impact of COVID-19 on consumer buying behaviour and the digitalization process*. Doctoral dissertation, Bournemouth University.

Sehgal, R., Khanna, P., Malviya, M., & Dubey, A. M. (2021). Shopping safety practices mutate consumer buying behaviour during COVID-19 pandemic. *Vision*, 09722629211010990.

Shahnawaz, M. G., Gupta, K., Kharshiing, K. D., Kashyap, D., Khursheed, M., Khan, N. H., & Rehman, U. (2022). Individual and group level risk factors in preventive health and panic buying behaviors during COVID-19 pandemic in India. *Current Psychology*, 1–17.

Sharma, G. D., Thomas, A., & Paul, J. (2021). Reviving tourism industry post-COVID-19: A resilience-based framework. *Tourism management perspectives, 37*, 100786.

Shen, H., Namdarpour, F., & Lin, J. (2022). Investigation of online grocery shopping and delivery preference before, during, and after COVID-19. *Transportation Research Interdisciplinary Perspectives, 14*, 100580.

Shrilatha, S., Aruna, K., & Christinal, H. (2022). *The role of social media apps and its cyber attacks in India.* Paper presented at the CEUR workshop proceedings, 3244, 59–65.

Sriram, K. V., Arora, M., Varshney, K., & Kamath, G. B. (2021). Online purchase intention: A study on consumer behaviour in Indian digital environment. *ABAC Journal, 41*(4), 67–87.

Srivastava, R. K., & Bhanot, S. (2022). Study on the impact of COVID-19 on the purchase and mental behaviour of Indian consumers during lockdown. *International Social Science Journal, 72*(244), 437–459.

Sukhwani, V., Deshkar, S., & Shaw, R. (2020). Covid-19 lockdown, food systems and urban–rural partnership: Case of Nagpur, India. *International Journal of Environmental Research and Public Health, 17*(16), 5710.

Suresh, V., Fishman, R., von Lieres, J. S., & Rao, B. R. (2022). Impact of the COVID-19 lockdown on the economic situation and food security of rural households in India. *Journal of Agribusiness in Developing and Emerging Economies, 12*, 491–509.

Surpam, S., Anjankar, S., Dhok, A., & Kumbhare, J. M. (2022). E-learning: A boon in pandemic. *ECS Transactions, 107*(1), 18395.

Thakur, V., & Kiran, P. (2021). Impact of the covid-19 pandemic outbreak on panic buying behavior in the FMCG sector. *Ushus Journal of Business Management, 20*(2), 71–90.

Travasso, S. M., Joseph, S., Swaminathan, S., John, A. T., Makkar, S., Webb, P., ... Thomas, T. (2023). Impact of the COVID-19 lockdown on household diet diversity in rural Bihar, India: A longitudinal survey. *Nutrition Journal, 22*(1), 1–12.

Valaskova, K., Durana, P., & Adamko, P. (2021). Changes in consumers' purchase patterns as a consequence of the COVID-19 pandemic. *Mathematics, 9*(15), 1788.

Vázquez-Martínez, U. J., Morales-Mediano, J., & Leal-Rodríguez, A. L. (2021). The impact of the COVID-19 crisis on consumer purchasing motivation and behavior. *European Research on Management and Business Economics, 27*(3), 100166.

Verma, M., & Naveen, B. R. (2021). COVID-19 impact on buying behaviour. *Vikalpa, 46*(1), 27–40.

Yadav, B. M. (2022, February 17). *Medical tourism struggles to recuperate from Covid pandemic losses.* https://www.thehindubusinessline.com/news/variety/medical-tourism-struggles-to-recuperate-from-covid-pandemic-losses/article65056369.ece

Chapter 12

COVID-19 Impact on Consumer Preferences Toward Convenience Store Versus Hypermarkets

Ajay Singh[a] and Rahul Gupta[b]

[a]ABES Business School, India
[b]Amity Business School, India

Abstract

The COVID-19 pandemic had severely impacted global commerce, leading to market closure and travel restrictions. Due to the extreme limitations on shopping and market possibilities, consumers' buying habits have changed significantly and they are still changing what they buy and how they purchase for everyday necessities. They are trying to shop locally, carefully, and economically. Consumers are buying their stuff from wherever goods are available. Purchasing nonessential items is restricted. Restaurants, tourism, apparel, and furniture are the industries that have been impacted the most. The objective behind this study is to find out the post-COVID-19 effects on consumer buying of essentials from a convenience store over hypermarkets and how consumer behavior will revive postpandemic toward retail shopping. In the study, responses were collected through structured questionnaire to explore the consumer buying behavior for their daily essentials both at convenience stores and hypermarkets. The study reveals that consumers prefer to buy essential commodities/goods of daily needs from convenience store compared to hypermarket due to the risk of being exposed to COVID-19 pandemic and this behavior will change future trend of retail shopping experience. The major limitation of the study is sampling frame. Future studies can replicate this study in different context with different target population. Pertaining to the current ongoing situations of the pandemic, a very high percentage of the respondents would still choose nearby convenience stores over hypermarkets. This study estimates the behavioral change in retail consumers in future; therefore, it suggests retailers adopt innovative marketing strategy in future.

Navigating the Digital Landscape, 217–230
Copyright © 2024 Ajay Singh and Rahul Gupta
Published under exclusive licence by Emerald Publishing Limited
doi:10.1108/978-1-83549-272-720241012

Keywords: COVID-19; convenience stores; hypermarkets; retail stores; consumer behavior; grocery store

Introduction

People across the globe have been impacted by the COVID-19 pandemic. Significant disruption has been caused by the pandemic and lockdown for individuals, communities, brands, and enterprises. People's daily lives around the world have changed in unexpected way. However, it's crucial to remember that global consumers were already evolving quickly even as businesses sought solutions. This process is moving much faster than anyone could have predicted. Because of the crisis, consumer optimization has declined in India. Customers remained concerned about their personal and family health and safety as restrictions began to be lifted. Online shopping for necessities and in-home entertainment has increased for nearly everything. They have gradually adopted digital and less-physical contact activities at home, employing online payment methods and streaming television shows, and the majority of them want to keep doing these things after COVID-19 also.

Consumer buying habits have changed due to lockdown during pandemic, and they are spending more on hygiene and health-related products, leading to shortage of product availability, also opting for home deliveries rather than visiting stores physically. The current situation is also impacting category and brand preferences, shopping behavior, along with spending patterns. In this unfavorable situation due to pandemic, 40% consumers are stockpiling food and household goods, resulting in an 80% increase in consumer store visits to supermarkets and grocery stores. With 70% consumers preferring cooked meals at home, there is drop of 90% in restaurant visits. 16% of people say it's difficult to find grocery and food supplies. 39% peoples had difficulty finding hand wash and sanitizers.

The Indian retail is divided into two parts, organized and unorganized retail. As mentioned in IBEF report (IBEF, 2020), unorganized retail sector consists of around 13.8 million traditional shops, whereas the organized retail sector constitutes market which is less than 10%. Organized retail consists of all physical stores as well as online websites for shopping. Despite the growth of the B2C business model in India, the majority of Indian consumers continue to place their trust in local stores because they want to feel and physically touch the products before purchasing and also do discount bargaining over the counter. Vacant shelves in store during the pandemic have resulted in a variety of issues for customers (Lufkin, 2020). This COVID-19 epidemic has compelled consumers to change their habits of buying goods.

Convenience stores are well suited to pandemic conditions in some ways. They sell a wide range of necessities as well as other items. They work long hours, often staying open 24 hours a day, and are generally well located. Shoppers can come in, get what they need, and quickly return to the safety of their homes or cars. These small businesses also offer services such as accepting utility payments or online purchases. This is essential for unbanked populations and adds value for cautious consumers looking to limit their exposure to the outside world.

As the COVID-19 pandemic continues, convenience stores have remained resilient. According to a NACS survey, total inside sales of an industry have increased by 1.5% to a record of $255.6 billion in year 2020, even though a 13.9% decline in transactions was noted. Shopping cart has increased 18.4% with respect to the year 2019; the average shopping cart size reached $7.34 in 2020 relative to $6.20 in 2019.

"Due to high demand, convenience stores that stock these items are likely to have seen quick turnover and strong margins." Said by Charlie McIlvaine, CEO, Coen Markets Inc. Furthermore, due to pandemic restrictions, in-store gross profit dollar sales mix in 2019 of the Foodservice in convenience stores fell from 38.9% to 34.5%. COVID-19 pandemic had an impact on convenience stores, as it did on most other aspects of life (NACS, 2023). When travel was restricted at that time consumers do not leave their houses, convenience stores found themselves in an unusual situation, thinking to generate revenue through new techniques ensuring safety of consumers.

"Convenience stores have performed good over last few year due to a general retracement of safety and health protocols as well as advancement in technology," Al Bari said. "Convenience stores have added new convenient techniques to influence customers and giving better streamlined services." IBIS World revealed that revenue increased by 10% in 2021 after downfall of 6% in 2020 due to pandemic. It almost seems like a dream: bright lights filling the streets, joyful shoppers without masks in the market, and ecstatic store owners. It is unlikely that the world's behaviors have ever changed as drastically as they did in March 2020. Birthday parties and celebrations became a pipe dream as the COVID-19 pandemic pushed entire countries into lockdowns, and shopping, commuting to work, going to the movies, or meeting friends for coffee all became impossible. With a clear change in favor of online channels and resultant decrease in point of sales, employee size and the company's profitability, retail has experienced increasing crises and stagnation during the past 10 years restaurants, travel, apparel, and furniture are the industries badly impacted. It has affected drastically on almost every sector, like agriculture, FMCG, automobile, apparel, tourism, food markets, and even stores as small as general commodity stores have faced a lot of downfalls during these tough times. Hardly would have been an industry that would not see a surge fall in its operations and earnings throughout this global pandemic.

According to three primary criteria, the influence of COVID-19 on the sectors analyzed through trends that would have varying dynamics.

(1) Expected level of the restrictions on movements in the future months
(2) Goods type sold
(3) Alterations in spending patterns and the availability of funds

People have an instilled fear among themselves regarding this fatal virus that has taken huge number of lives throughout the world. People from all around the world saw and have undergone a shift from the physical world to the virtual world. It would be apt to say that the world went online became the usual norm to work, through online modes on online web portals, websites, and applications through their laptop devices, mobile devices, tablets, personal computers, etc.

Observing the panic and chaos that this deadly virus caused throughout the spherical globe, it became evident and need of the hour to know about the obvious negative effects that this global pandemic had over the consumers in the market and to see whether they had undergone a shift or change in their usual buying behavior.

COVID-19 has a major impact on the national economies, leading to possibility of change in market dynamics. In the study on "D2C Opportunities and Market Trends in the Covid-19," Abe (2020) found trends such as people doing theft at grocery store corridors, canceling the major events across the globe, and giving "non-essential" orders, businesses are temporarily shut down to prevent the spreading of corona virus. People spending from their income on nonessential items are very low during the pandemic (such as cosmetics, apparels, clothing, shoes, jewellery, games, and electronics). 56% of customers shop at nearby stores or purchase more locally manufactured goods, with 79%–84% of them planning to keep doing so in the future, respectively. The reasons for this can range from a desire for genuine and artisan goods to deliberately supporting local businesses or domestic goods. Similar to this, most consumers are likely to continue decreasing food waste and adopting more ethical, ecological, or environmentally friendly purchases.

Since the start of our research, e-commerce and the use of omni channel services have grown dramatically, and this trend is showing no indications of slowing down. The most recent research indicates that following the outbreak, e-commerce sales from new or less frequent users will rise by 169%. The overwhelming majority of customers who have increased the usage of digital and omni channel services, such as home delivery, pickup curb side, or purchasing via social media, anticipate doing so in the future. The major gap identified in retail shopping behavior of consumer is that the trend in retail shopping is changing across the globe due to pandemic and no major studies have suggested futuristic pattern of consumer spending in retail market postpandemic followed by appropriate innovative marketing strategies to be adopted by retailers.

Current study aims to examine the change in buying pattern of the consumers caused by COVID-19. People throughout the world have been in panic mode and this in turned has affected the consumer market. The virus has left no stone unturned in causing damage to the world emotionally, socially, physically, economically, as well as psychologically.

Objectives of the Study

- To understand the preferences of the consumers for shopping of essential commodities from a convenience store over a hypermarket.

- To find out the very phenomena of fear of consumers for stepping out to crowded places to buy essential goods in the COVID-19 era.
- To evaluate and examine the preference of people for discounts as one of the factors for buying essential goods and commodities.

Literature Review

In her 2009 article, Zamazalová analyses both internal and external elements that affect customer behavior. The macroenvironment of marketing that affects the development and implementation of marketing events focusing on target customers is stated as one of the external elements. The pace of environmental change is unrelenting. Social variables, which are further classified into cultural and demographic elements, technical factors and technological considerations, political factors, legal factors, economic factors as well as natural factors are all external factors that affect consumer behavior. Douchova et al. (1993) explained the most crucial factors impacting consumer behavior that are objective conditions of consumer behavior (objective economic situation as well as individual economic environment) along with personality of consumer, his social environment, and situational change.

The environment is evolving quickly. Social elements (further separated into demographic and cultural variables), political and legal factors, technical and technological aspects (legislative framework), and natural factors are the categories into which external influences influencing consumer behavior are categorized.

The most crucial factors impacting the behavior of consumer, as stated by Douchova et al. (1993), are as follows, first objective conditions of consumer behavior (related to individual economic environment along with his economic situation), personality of personality, social environment, and consumers situation.

COVID-19 and Consumer Behavior

This volatile situation due to pandemic has a major impact on regular consumer's lives. COVID-19 has had influenced business operations along with the changed consumer behavior. Laato et al. (2020) revealed, that the government of various countries enforced lockdown by closing school, restrictions on shop opening, closing food restaurants and all types of public services, potentially spreading fears about what might happen in the future. As a result, customers' buying habits can be estimated to change in future run. Sheth (2020) identifies four major concerns that govern or influence consumer habits. They are social concerns (for example, workplace changes and connections with friends and neighbors), emergence of new technology and its implementation (both delivery and online shopping), and the influence of new guidelines on consumption habits (regulation due to COVID-19).

According to Kirk and Rifkin (2020), past event shows that a crisis period is generally considered as a catalyst for major societal transformations, therefore recommend paying attention to behavior of consumer at each of the three stages: responding, replicating, behavior of do-it-yourself, and adaption in the long term.

The article found a shift in consumer behavior that was brought on by the COVID-19 epidemic, which theoretically can be explained as an external factor that belongs to category of natural factors; though the author considers it as a complementary factors that affected consumer behavior including economic factors, legislative factors as well as political factors that are represented by various constraints and future uncertainty about the economy.

Patil and Patil (2020) in their research focused on the ups and downs in the behavior of consumers in the COVID-19 situation and its overall effect over the market. The study also stated the fact that the consumers were not serious and preventive at the early stages but with the gradual recommendations of the government, they started to take preventive measures. The research also talks about how sellers were indulged into black marketing of essential goods like bread, milk, eggs, pharmaceutical products, and similar products. The study laid emphasis on the fact that around 30% of respondents rushed for buying essential goods within the very first week of the lockdown being imposed nationwide. It also stated that about 93.33% of respondents accepted alternative brands during lockdown phase. Another study attempted to know and enquire about the behavioral pattern of consumers for some of the essential items like hygiene, grocer, and pharma. The study concluded on the very fact that in case of nationwide lockdown, factors like digital support, smooth delivery, packaging, and labeling of services and products play a crucial role in affecting the behavior of consumers for buying the essential commodities (Yadav & Kumar, 2021). The study was done by C Vijai. P Nivetha examined the behavior of consumers and their buying behaviors during the COVID-19 pandemic phase with special reference to Chennai city which is the capital of Tamil Nadu. The study found out that the consumers were spending more money on health as well as hygiene and other health products. The study also inculcated the information gained through secondary data via sources like report, websites, and newspapers. A study was done in order to know the consumer buying behavior while making a buying decision to opt out the retailers and choose the most suitable among them for buying various essential goods and commodities, without which the survival seems almost impossible.

The COVID-19 pandemic put enormous strain on grocery retailers (Obermair et al., 2021). Grocery retail stores that provide essential goods to consumer were experiencing a new challenge of home delivery due to surge in demands of daily essential due to which they are facing issues such as inventory shortages, managing supply chain management, complexities in delivering products, and ensuring a safe and healthy environment (Roggeveen & Sethuraman, 2020). Restrictions imposed by government and fear of pandemic have changed consumer buying behavior, resulting in the migration of consumers from traditional formats to online businesses. Due to over stocking and other survival techniques adopted by retailers as well as consumers, the rapid change has occurred leading to the growth of e-commerce.

Markets were impacted by COVID-19 pandemic in a different way, each of which responded differently based on implemented measures. Although Sweden is already having the most mature market of e-commerce market in Nordic region with respect to the number of frequent e-shoppers, the pandemic ignited the speed of digital transformation. 96% of Swedish people aged between 15 and 79 are doing online shopping, as comparison with 88% in Denmark followed by 94% in Norway as well as 95% in Finland (Chan, 2021). Post Nord (2021) told in a report that online sales has increased by 40% in year 2020 to US$13 billion. Due to pandemic, most of the customers are frequently shopping online, and the ratio of Swedish e-commerce has risen to 6% in total retail sales. The ease of availability of online information, along with the current COVID-19 situation, direct contact with grocery retailers is reduced, forcing them to rethink their retail strategies (Sayidda et al., 2021a, 2021b). To stay alive with the COVID-19 crisis and its after effect, traditional retail outlets must change with the new reality by formulating revived sales strategies (Anik et al., 2021). Consumers have been familiarized with new ways of shopping and will continue postpandemic as well, so grocery outlets must put an online shopping choice similar to physical shopping so that they can encourage impulse buying. Additionally the food and grocery industry is also characterized by a volatile market since customer demands are changing and increased acceptance of online distribution model (Wollenburg et al., 2018). Hence companies need dynamic techniques to incorporate, reconfigure, expand, and provide resources in order to adjust with market change (Teece et al., 1997). Roggeveen and Sethuraman (2020) suggested in their research that retailers must be provided right guidance to meet with the challenges posed by COVID-19 pandemic, as consumer behavior is changing both in the long as well as short run, which is another justification revealed in the study. Chari et al. (2022) also suggested that industry-specific research must be conducted to understand complexities are existing in specific sectors.

Based on the literature reviewed on various studies conducted on consumer buying behavior at retail outlets in current pandemic situation becomes essential to understand Indian consumers and buying preferences to convenience store and hypermarket which will prolong even after pandemic.

Research Methodology

It is primary research where a structured questionnaire was prepared containing all key attributes related to retail buying behavior of consumers for daily/essential needs across the globe. All identified psychographic attributes related to retail consumer shopping behavior toward convenience store or hypermarket used in questionnaire was explored from past studies along with expert guidance. Few demographic attributes related to age, gender, income, and occupation were also used in the study. Thereafter, a Google form was created with questions related to demography, multiple choice questions, Likert scale questions was prepared and circulated online to Indian Consumers of National Capital Region as it contains cosmopolitan population which is true representation of people across India. Random sampling technique was adopted in the study. Questionnaire was sent to more than 150 respondents of Delhi region of Indian retail consumers; however, only 110 responses were received, out of which 102 responses were found to be useful. Further descriptive analysis was performed on these 102 responses. In descriptive analysis, firstly graphical representation of respondent's demography related to occupation was performed followed by graphical representation of respondents rating toward fear of going outside, frequency description of consumers choice of store visits toward hypermarket versus convenience store, followed by graphical representation of respondents' choice of buying essential commodities along with the factors for outside visits for retail buying during pandemic.

Data Analysis

Descriptive analysis was conducted to understand frequency distribution of different respondents on the collected data as.

In Fig. 12.1, 80% of the respondents belonged to the category of students. A total of 14% of the respondents belonged to the category of employed people. A total of 5% of the respondents belonged to the category of unemployed people. Whereas 1% of the respondents belong to the category of retired people.

Fig. 12.2 inferred that around 29.4% of the people gave a pointer scale of 3 out of 0–5, of fear of going outside during the COVID-19 phase so rating of stands as the most voted for rating on a scale of 0–5 (moving upwards, i.e., 0 least fear and 5 being the upper limit or most fear).

Around 11.8% of the respondents gave a rating of 0 from a scale of 0–5, which in other words means that around 11.8% of the respondents feel least fear in going outside in the current situation. Another 11.8% of the respondents gave a rating of

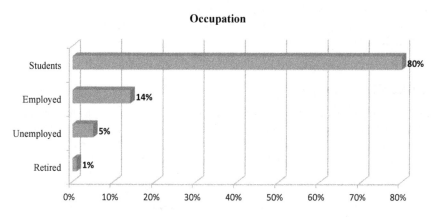

Fig. 12.1.   Occupation of Respondents.

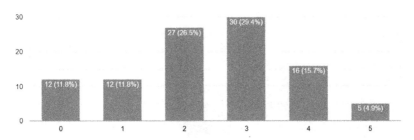

On a scale of 0-5 , rate your fear of going outside during the covid-19 phase.

102 responses

Fig. 12.2.   Respondents Rating Toward Fear of Going Outside.

1 from a scale of 0–5, which in other words mean that 11.8% of the respondents are very minutely fearful of stepping outside in the pandemic era. Around 26.5% of the respondents gave the rating of 2 on a scale of 0–5, of stepping outside in the pandemic era. Around 15.7% of the respondents gave the rating of 4 on a scale of 0–5, of fear in stepping outside in the currently.

Fig. 12.3 infers the fact that out of 102 respondents to whom the questionnaire was sent a total of 93 respondents opted for going to nearby convenience stores to buy essential commodities which accounts for around a total of 91.2% and thus stands as considerable figure.

On the other hand, a total of 15 respondents out of 102 sample of people, which stands as around 14.7% opted for going to hypermarkets for buying the essential goods during the lockdown phase which was observed due to the widespread of the corona virus.

From Fig. 12.4, around 69.9% of the total respondents were actually ready to buy the essential commodities even at a higher price from a nearby convenience

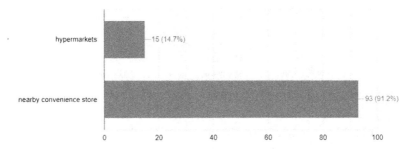

During the lockdown phase due to covid -19 in the year 2020, wherein special timings were allotted for daily operations, where did you visit to buy essential commodities?

102 responses

Fig. 12.3.   Hypermarket versus Convenience Store Visit.

Were you ready to buy essential commodities at an even higher price from a nearby convenience store rather than going to a hypermarket?

102 responses

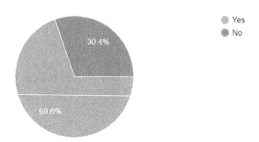

Fig. 12.4.   Respondents Choice of Buying Essential Commodities.

store rather than going to a hypermarket for buying those essential commodities. This directly portrays the very fact a very large portion of the respondents were ready to buy the essential commodities at even a higher rate rather than going to a hypermarket. This means that even the high prices of the commodities in the nearby stores could not act as an invading factor for them to shop from the nearby stores.

From Fig. 12.5, the violet color denotes strongly agree, green color denotes agree, yellow color denotes neutral, red color denotes disagree, and blue color denotes as strongly agree.

The factor of "discounts available at the hypermarket" got the most weight age as a factor that the respondents would consider the most while going outside to buy essential goods.

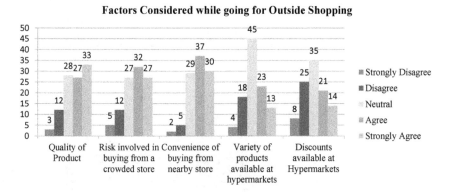

Fig. 12.5.   Factors for Outside Visits for Retail Buying During Pandemic.

Table 12.1. Tabulation of Factors Considered for Outside Buying.

	Quality of Products	Risk Involved in Buying From a Crowded Store	Convenience of Buying From Nearby Store	Variety of Products Available at Hypermarkets	Discounts Available at Hypermarket
Strongly disagree	3	5	2	4	8
Disagree	12	12	5	18	25
Neutral	28	27	29	45	35
Agree	27	32	37	23	21
Strongly agree	33	27	30	13	14

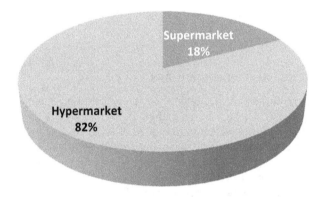

Fig. 12.6.   Choice of Retail Shopping.

Table 12.1 gives us the numeric figures of the respondents who opted for the various factors to take into consideration, while going outside in order to buy essential goods.

Fig. 12.6 indicates around 82.4% of the total respondents would go to the nearby convenience stores, pertaining to the current ongoing situations of the pandemic. Whereas a total of 17.6% from 102 respondents chose going to hypermarkets for buying essential goods.

Findings

After a detailed research and study, collecting of primary data through questionnaires, assembling the data, assorting of that data, and proper evaluation through the help of graphical representation as well as statistical methods, we have arrived at the following findings. Around 29.4% of the respondents gave a rating of 3 out of a scale of 0–5 in terms of fear of going outside in the pandemic era with 0 being the least fear and 5 being the most fear.

4.9% of the people gave a rating of 5, on a scale of 0–5 of fear of going outside in the pandemic era. Out of 102 respondents to whom the questionnaire was sent a total of 93 respondents opted for going to nearby convenience stores to buy essential commodities which accounts for around a total of 91.2%, during the lockdown phase. Total of 15 respondents out of 102 sample of people, which stands as around only 14.7%. They opted for going to hypermarkets for buying the essential goods during the lockdown phase. 69.9% of the total respondents were ready to buy the essential commodities even at a higher price from a nearby convenience store rather than going to a hypermarket for buying essential commodities. 82.4% of the total respondents would go to the nearby convenience stores, pertaining to the current ongoing situations of the pandemic. 53% of the respondents are willing to consider the convenience of buying from a nearby store over the risk involved in buying from a crowded store. The relationship between the "discounts available at hypermarkets and the variety of products available at hypermarkets" is very high which shows that it has a strong relationship among themselves.

Conclusion and Recommendations

Henceforth by gathering, breaking down, and concentrating the information, we inferred that people do have a fear in going out during the COVID-19 era. A very big and significant portion of the total sample of population opted for going to a nearby convenience store rather than going to a hypermarket during the lockdown period, wherein special timings were allotted for buying the goods of essential nature. Around 91.2% of the total population opted for going to the nearby stores over visiting a hypermarket. Furthermore, 69.9% of the total respondents were actually ready to buy the commodities even at a higher price from a nearby convenience store rather than going to a hypermarket for buying essential commodities, which clearly portrays the fact that even higher prices could not act as a barrier for them and they still chose nearby convenience store over the hypermarkets.

The finding of the study reveals that due to COVID-19 pandemic consumers have become very careful about health and safety along with their convenience. Consumers prefer to buy essential goods from convenience store rather than hypermarket as they are avoiding going out at crowded places due to pandemic. Observing this behavioral shift in consumer buying preferences toward retail stores which may continue postpandemic, the study suggest that new innovative marketing strategies need to be adopted by stores.

Future Research Direction

This study is restricted to limited sample size of Indian Consumers and data were collected in limited time frame. Future studies can further expand it across different region/countries of the world with greater sample size and variety of retail consumers of different countries which can be more helpful in understanding the global scenario of how retail buying behavior of consumers are changing toward convenience store and hypermarkets. As postpandemic consumers will be more careful about health and safety standards, also how convenience store and hypermarket retailers should innovate their marketing strategies by adopting more digital and contactless shopping experience to retail consumers across the globe.

References

Abe, S. (2020). *Market trends and D2C opportunities in the COVID-19 landscape*. The AdRoll Blog. https://www.adroll.com/blog/marketing/market-trends-and-d2c-opportunities-in-thecovid-19-landscape

Anik, M. A. H., Gindi, E. R., & Habib, M. A. (2021, September). *Examining the impacts of COVID-19 on retail industry and e-shopping*. Transportation Association of Canada Conference & Exhibition.

Chan, L. (2021). *Covid prospects; Sweden*. https://research.hktdc.com/en/article/OTEzNTU3ODAx

Chari, A., Niedenzu, D., Despeisse, M., Machado, C. G., Azevedo, J. D., Boavida-Dias, R., & Johansson, B. (2022). *Dynamic capabilities for circular manufacturing supply chains—Exploring the role of industry 4.0 and resilience*. Business Strategy and the Environment.

Douchová, J., Komárková, R., Mejtská, D., Rymeš, M., & Vysekalová, J. (1993). *Základy psychologie trhu*. H & H. https://www.rebelsrulers.com/consumer-behavior-in-post-crisis-market-scenarios

IBEF. (2020, April 18). https://www.ibef.org/industry/retail-india

Kirk, C. P., & Rifkin, L. S. (2020). I'll trade you diamonds for toilet paper: Consumer reacting, coping and adapting behaviors in the COVID-19 pandemic. *Journal of Business Research, 117*.

Laato, S., Islam, N. A. K. M., Farooq, A., & Dhir, A. (2020). Unusual purchasing behavior during the early stages of the COVID-19 pandemic: The stimulus-organism-response approach. *Journal of Retailing and Consumer Services, 57*(102224), 1–12.

Lufkin, B. (2020). Coronavirus: The psychology of panic buying. *The BBC*.

NACS. (2023, January 18). https://www.nacsmagazine.com/issues/november-2020/look-heroes

Obermair, E., Holzapfel, A., Kuhn, H., & Sternbeck, M. G. (2021). *Challenges and measures in disruptive times: Lessons learned for grocery retail operations from the COVID-19 pandemic*.

Patil, B., & Patil, N. (2020). *Mukt Shabd Journal, IX*(V).

Roggeveen, A. L., & Sethuraman, R. (2020). How the COVID-19 pandemic may change the world of retailing. *Journal of Retailing, 96*(2), 169–171.

Sayyida, S., Gunawan, S., & Husin, S. (2021). View of the impact of the Covid-19 pandemic on retail consumer behavior. *Aptisi Transactions on Management (ATM)*, 5(1), 79–88. https://doi.org/10.33050/atm. v5i1.1497

Sayyida, S., Hartini, S., Gunawan, S., & Husin, S. N. (2021). The impact of the COVID-19 pandemic on retail consumer behavior. *Aptisi Transactions on Management (ATM)*, 5(1), 79–88.

Sheth Jagdish, N. (2020). *The Howard-Sheth theory of buyer behavior*. Wiley & Sons.

Teece, D. J., Pisano, G., & Shuen, A. (1997). Dynamic capabilities and strategic management. *Strategic Management Journal*, 18(7), 509–533.

Vijai, C., & Nivetha, P. International conference on COVID-19 studies, 2020 – papers. ssrn.com.

Wollenburg, J., Hübner, A., Kuhn, H., & Trautrims, A. (2018). From bricks-and-mortar to bricks-and-clicks: Logistics networks in omni-channel grocery retailing. *International Journal of Physical Distribution & Logistics Management*, 48(4), 415–438.

Yadav, A., & Kumar, P. (2021). *International Journal of Management*. researchgate. ne.

Zamazalová, M. (2009). *Marketing obchodní firmy. Marketing obchodní firmy*. Grada Publishing.

Printed in the USA
CPSIA information can be obtained
at www.ICGtesting.com
JSHW011507290524
63996JS00004B/110

9 781835 492734